My first wish
is that you
may really
enjoy this book·
and my next wish
is that you may
remember where
you borrowed
· it ·

GEORGE CHARLES WOLF

THE PHILOSOPHY OF GOD

THE
PHILOSOPHY
of GOD

HENRI RENARD, S.J.

PROFESSOR OF PHILOSOPHY
CREIGHTON UNIVERSITY

THE BRUCE PUBLISHING COMPANY
MILWAUKEE

Imprimi potest: Joseph P. Zuercher, S.J.
Nihil obstat: John A. Schulien, Censor librorum
Imprimatur: ✠ Moses E. Kiley, Archiepiscopus Milwaukiensis

November 22, 1950

(3/57)

TO

FATHER WILLIAM L. ROSSNER, S.J.

"Amicus est amico amicus." (S. Th., II–II, 23, 1.)

FOREWORD

*"Esse est actualitas omnium actuum,
et propter hoc est perfectio omnium perfectionum."*[1]

The philosophy of St. Thomas is the only philosophy that is truly existential, for it is the philosophy of "to be" (*esse*).[2] The major endeavor of Thomistic existentialism centers in an effort to explain that which it calls the reality of realities, the perfection of perfections, the "to be." Its constant quest is to discover, in so far as the human intellect is able to discover, the intelligibility of this highest of all acts. It is significant, then, that in this philosophy the search for such a profound understanding of reality must terminate in a demonstration of the existence of a being, God, who is His "To Be," who is Intelligibility Itself and, therefore, the source of all existing reality and of all intelligibility. Consequently, in the thought of Aquinas, a natural theology, a science of God, results from a philosophical reflection which seeks to understand the absolute *why* of the existence of any sensible reality which we experience.[3]

This philosophical position expresses the most fundamental and the most far-reaching intellectual attitude in the existentialism of

---

[1] " 'To be' is the actuality of all acts, and for this reason it is the perfection of all perfections." (*De Potentia*, VII, 2, ad 9ᵐ.)

[2] We prefer to render *esse* by "to be" rather than by "existence." The reason is that existence is conceived as an abstract form, while "to be" used substantively is a concrete noun which expresses reality. That is why St. Thomas seldom makes use of the word *existentia*, whereas the infinitive noun *esse* is undoubtedly the key word of his existentialism. (Cf. Renard, "Essence and Existence," *Proceedings of the American Catholic Philosophical Association*, 1946, pp. 53–66.) In recent years, the expression "the act of existing" has found favor among some interpreters of St. Thomas. It seems indeed an excellent rendition of the *"actus essendi"* of St. Thomas.

[3] M. Gilson points out that the fundamental difference between the position of St. Thomas and that of all essentialists lies precisely in facing or not facing the problem of existence. (Gilson, *L'être et l'essence, passim* [Paris: Vrin, 1948].)

St. Thomas, an attitude which enters, at least implicitly, into every philosophical problem, and without which no solution is intelligible. God, the Subsisting "To Be," is the only rational explanation for a world of beings whose existence is limited and is constantly changing. For, as was explained in *The Philosophy of Being,* God is not only the efficient, but also the exemplary, as well as the final cause of the world. In other philosophies, on the contrary, too often do we find that a theory of reality is evolved without adverting to God. Indeed, God is so separated, so far removed, we may even say so unnecessary, to a world of essences that those philosophies which try to establish such a being need a new, a distinct science: not a natural theology, which is the highest fulfillment of metaphysics, but a *Leibnitzian theodicy* which is thought to be a justification of God. God, therefore, is something superadded to, and not really very essential in the metaphysical structure of the universe. In Thomistic existentialism, on the contrary, God needs no justification, for nothing is intelligible, nothing *is,* except as immediately from Him who is the "To Be."

That is why, at the beginning of metaphysics when we established the first and most comprehensive philosophical law, that act and potency encompass all beings, it was pointed out that a pure act is the supreme term of that division. Then, as this law was evolved and applied to the various problems of the philosophy of being — motion, multiplicity, limitation, the analogy of being, causality, finality — we were forced, as it were, to rise almost immediately to the Pure Act, the Subsisting "To Be," without which there could be no satisfactory solution to these various problems.

That is why, in the first pages of *The Philosophy of Man,* we insisted that the problem of life is an existential problem, and that its solution is unintelligible unless we rise to God, who alone is Life, because He alone is Existence. That is why we attacked the problem of knowledge, which is an intentional union of subject with object, by showing that perfect knowledge is attributed to God, because He is His own "To Be." For just as "to be" is the act and perfection of the one existing, so the "to understand" is the act and perfection of the one understanding. It follows, then, that God is "To Understand" because He is "To Be."

". . . For 'to be' is the most perfect of all reality . . . it is the act of all, even of the forms."[4] "The 'to be' is that which is most intimate to any being, that which is most profound, since it is the formal principle of reality."[5] The reason is that "all perfections belong to the perfection of existence. Accordingly, things are perfect inasmuch as they have 'to be.' "[6] It is true that "that which *participates* 'to be' does not necessarily participate every mode of existence. God, however, who *is* 'To Be,' includes life and wisdom, since no perfection of existence can be lacking in Him *who is Subsisting 'To Be.'* "[7]

Natural Theology is the philosophy of the Subsisting "To Be." It is the philosophy of *Existence*.

THE PHILOSOPHY OF GOD is a college textbook in natural theology. It represents an effort to offer to the student the philosophical thought of St. Thomas on the question of God as expressed in the *Summa Theologica*. This little book, then, may be considered a running commentary on the most important articles in the treatise on God. Hence, the author lays no claim to originality, for he has merely endeavored to introduce the student to the thought of Thomas of Aquin.

The author is aware that a book which is a mere commentary may be thought incomplete for use as a modern textbook. He is aware that there have been many developments in the philosophical treatise on God since the thirteenth century. To give only an example, everyone knows that there are other proofs — excellent proofs, no doubt — for the existence of God besides the Five Ways of St. Thomas. Yet at the risk of writing a work which would seem incomplete, the author has deliberately refrained from adding any positive development of doctrine to the thought of the *Summa*.[8]

---

[4] *S. Th.*, I, 4, 1, ad 3[m]. [6] *S. Th.*, I, 4, 2, c.

[5] *S. Th.*, I, 8, 1, c. [7] *S. Th.*, I, 4, 2, ad 3[m].

[8] Two notable exceptions to this are (1) the brief exposition of some modern errors regarding our knowledge of God's existence (*infra*, pp. 4–18) and (2) the treatise on the free futurables (*infra*, pp. 130–131).

His reason for doing so is that the book is intended to do precisely this: to present the natural theology of Aquinas. He feared lest any other development of doctrine might obscure the unity and beauty of the thought of the Angelic Doctor.[9]

The author sincerely hopes that this book may help the American student, not only to acquaint himself with the doctrine of a master, but to penetrate its depth, to understand its vast implications, and to live its truth. Education results largely from constant contact with great minds. If, by means of THE PHILOSOPHY OF GOD, the student will have been inspired to read and to meditate upon the profound writings of the Angelic Doctor, the book will have fulfilled its purpose.

I can never sufficiently thank those who have made this book possible. I should like most of all to express my profound gratitude to the Rev. William L. Rossner, S.J., to the Rev. Patrick G. Kelly, S.J., and to Miss Peggy Nan Maxey, who have helped considerably in the composition and redaction of this little book.

H. R.

---

[9] The student is warned that the many texts from St. Thomas which occur throughout this work are not quoted merely in order to indicate that the doctrine proposed is that of the Angelic Doctor; nor are they intended as an appeal to authority. Rather, it is because of the clarity, precision, and force of their argumentation that such texts are presented. They are therefore to be examined and analyzed in their own right, for they undoubtedly present the most satisfactory solution that could be brought to bear on the various problems proposed.

CONTENTS

INTRODUCTION

"Among All Human Wisdoms This Is the Highest."[1]

The Philosophy of God Is a Wisdom: "Those men are called wise who direct things themselves and govern them well. . . . Now the rule of all things must be taken from their end, for then is a thing well disposed when it is directed to the end, since the end of everything is its good. . . . Hence in a special manner the title of wise man is reserved to him who considers the supreme end."[2]

Now the supreme end is the good of the intellect, namely the true, and that is God. Hence the contemplation of God is the supreme good of man.[3] It is, therefore, the work of the wise man to study God. Consequently, the philosophy of God, or as it is generally called, natural theology, which deals with the study of God, is the highest human scientific endeavor. It is a wisdom.

The Object of Natural Theology: Natural theology treats of God. God, then, is the *material object* of this sublime science. A material object, however, does not determine, does not specify a science. To do so a *formal object* is needed, for a formal object is the aspect, the manner in which the material object presents itself. Now the manner in which the material object of this science, God, presents itself to be studied by man is not God as He is in Himself,[4] but God as the cause of all other beings. God, therefore, in so far as He is the cause of all other beings, is the formal object of natural theology.

---

[1] *S. Th.*, I, 1, 6.

[2] *C.G.*, I, c. 1.

[3] Cf. Henri Renard, S.J., *The Philosophy of Man* (Milwaukee: Bruce, 1948), p. 228.

[4] There cannot be a philosophical science of God as He is in Himself. (Cf. Renard, *op. cit.*, p. 151.) Such a study requires supernatural revelation and is termed sacred theology.

Our Knowledge of God: Because we do not know God as He is in Himself, it does not follow that God cannot be known positively by human reason.[5] He can be known most assuredly, but only through His effects and, therefore, only in an analogous manner. Consequently, there can be no connatural[6] knowledge of God but only an analogous understanding of Him who is the cause of all other beings.

Natural Theology Is the Metaphysics of God: The above consideration leads us to affirm that natural theology is not a distinct science; it is nothing else but metaphysics. It is, we may say, the last and the most sublime chapter of the philosophy of being. The reason is that metaphysics studies being as being, being in its ultimate causes. Natural theology, therefore, which considers God the ultimate cause of being, is nothing else but a part of metaphysics: it is the metaphysics of God.[7]

This is what St. Thomas explains in a profound page of the *Contra Gentiles.* "Metaphysics is ordered to the knowledge of God as to its last end; for this reason, it is called *scientia divina,* a divine science."[8] Commenting upon this text, M. Gilson aptly remarks that it is indeed the *prima philosophia* itself which becomes theology as it orders itself to the knowledge of God.[9]

The Division of This Treatise: The first and most important
1. part of this treatise will be a demonstration of the existence of God, that is, the existence of a first cause of the world. The
2. second part will study the essence of God. In this section, we shall consider what we may know of God's essence by reflecting upon the fact that creatures are a faint manifestation of the divine
3. perfection. The third part will examine the divine operations.

---

[5] Positively, that is, as to what He is, and not merely what He is not.

[6] Connatural knowledge means knowledge proportioned to the nature of the known. Man has connatural knowledge of corporeal essences.

[7] "Metaphysics is called the divine science, that is, theology (science of God)." (*In Met., Proemium, in fine.*)

[8] *C.G.,* III, c. 25.

[9] Cf. Gilson, *L'être et l'essence* (Paris: Vrin, 1948), p. 86.

CHAPTER I

THE EXISTENCE OF GOD

Division: Three philosophical positions, three intellectual attitudes toward a proof of the existence of God can be adopted. The first belongs to those philosophers who declare that there is no need for such a proof, since God's existence is too evident to be demonstrated. The second attitude of mind is found today among many who claim that God — if such a being exists — necessarily transcends all human knowledge. Accordingly, no proof of the existence of God, no true science of God, no natural theology, is possible. Finally, in opposition to these two doctrines, we propose to establish, by means of a metaphysical demonstration, the truth of God's existence. Because of the importance of our position, we shall devote two full questions to its exposition. This chapter, therefore, will contain four questions dealing with: (1) the necessity of proving the existence of God; (2) the demonstrability of the existence of God; (3) the metaphysical foundation for the Five Ways of St. Thomas; (4) the demonstration of the existence of God.[1]

---

[1] In a course of systematic philosophy such as this, we do not pretend to give an adequate presentation of the various developments of the philosophical positions just mentioned above. To do so would necessitate a serious and detailed study of the works of many authors. At this stage such research cannot be expected of the students. In order, however, to delineate more exactly the position of St. Thomas, by contrast, we need give only a concise exposition of the fundamental error of these various philosophies. Consequently, after briefly stating these errors, we shall present a fuller development of the proofs of St. Thomas.

Question I

DO WE NEED TO PROVE THE EXISTENCE OF GOD?

Division: In the history of human thought, there have been various schools of philosophers who taught that God's existence is evident, that it needs no demonstration. For the sake of clarity, we may classify these thinkers according to two philosophical positions.

1. Many mistook an effect of God's operation for God Himself. To give an example, they thought that our knowledge of truth was a knowledge of God; they argued that a feeling of God's presence, a religious, a mystical experience, gives us the highest, indeed the only possible certitude of God's existence. They argued, therefore, to an immediate quasi-intuitive knowledge of God. In such an idealistic frame of mind, these thinkers naturally rejected as childish and worthless the value of a demonstration which might presuppose an objective theory of knowledge.

2. Others, impressed by the perfection of the concept of the divine essence, thought that from an analysis of that concept we could immediately establish God's existence. Accordingly, they declared that there is no need whatever to argue from the fact of an existing limited being or of a changing world to the existence of the Supreme Cause that is God.

ARTICLE I: Is the Existence of God Known Immediately?

Among the philosophers who mistake an effect of God's operation for God Himself, we may mention the Ontologists of all time and the Modernists. To these, for the sake of convenience, we add the Traditionalists. Let us now briefly expose their fundamental tenets regarding the problems of the existence of God.

1. Ontologists: Perhaps the first writer of note to propose an articulate expression of ontologism is Nicolas Malebranche (1638–1715). Malebranche, as we saw in *The Philosophy of Being,* was an occasionalist.[2] He did not, therefore, admit the activity of bodies upon the sense faculties of man. Knowledge is immediately from God. God Himself causes the knowledge of man directly and not through creatures. God, therefore, is immanently present to our intellect as the immediate source of knowledge. Hence, Malebranche concludes, "Only God is known by Himself." Other things are seen in God. This, however, is not to see God in His essence, as He is, but only in so far as "the divine essence is relative to creatures and participated by them. In this way we see all things in God."[3]

A century later Gioberti (1801–1852) defines and develops the mild ontologism of Malebranche. Having identified the ontological order with the order of knowledge, Gioberti concludes that the first ontological reality, God, is the first known object. "God," he declares, "the first truth in the existential order is the first truth in the order of knowledge."[4] He speaks of a first intuition which, although imperfect, is an intuition of God.[5]

A more subtle version of ontologism is proposed in some of Rosmini's (1797–1855) writings. For him our intuition of being (*l'essere ideale*), the ideal "to be," although not the idea of God,

---

[2] Cf. *The Philosophy of Being* (Milwaukee: Bruce, 1948), p. 133.

[3] Malebranche, *De la Recherche de la Vérité,* Book III, part 2, c. 6, 7.

[4] "Dio, cioè l'essere, non è solamente la prima verità . . . nell'ordine delle esistenze, ma la prima verità nell'ordine della cognizioni." *Teoria della mente umana,* p. 43; cf. *Introduzione allo studio della filosofia,* Vol. II, c. 4. (Quoted by R. Arnou, S.J., *Theologia Naturalis,* p. 43.)

[5] St. Thomas proposes a difficulty which is not unlike the error of Malebranche and of Gioberti. He argues that there is in us a natural knowledge of God's existence which is implanted in all men. To this he answers that we have a vague and confused knowledge of God in this way, that we have a natural, a necessary desire for the absolute good, and that the absolute good is God, but that such a desire does not really suppose that we know that the good is God. This is evidenced by the fact that so many men seek happiness in things that take them away from God. Hence this natural desire for the good is really not a knowledge of the existence of God. (Cf. *S. Th.* I, 2, 1, ad 1[m].)

is nevertheless something divine. This divine something which is found in all creatures really pertains to God, and therefore is attributable to God; indeed, it must be said, it is the "To Be" of God.[6]

Criticism: It will be seen at once by those who have understood the objective theory of knowledge of St. Thomas[7] that the errors of Malebranche, as well as of all Ontologists, are due to a subjective postulate. According to these philosophers, it is not the existing object which causes sense knowledge from which, ultimately, the human intellect obtains the data necessary to rise to an affirmation of the existence of God. Rather, the concept results from God's direct action upon the soul; or more precisely, the knowledge itself is in some vague manner the very essence of God, not understood fully as He is, but nevertheless perceived in Himself merely as cause, and in no way as an effect of God's action. Obviously such a beginning in philosophical thought can only terminate in pantheism.

Let us then recall a fundamental thesis of St. Thomas which is the psychological foundation for his treatise on God. It is this: *the proper object of the human intellect is the material essences.* From the knowledge of these existing essences which are not existence but have a "to be," we are able to rise to a demonstration of an immaterial infinite cause. Only mediately and indirectly, therefore, can the human intellect know naturally immaterial substances, particularly God. It arrives at such understanding by means of a reflection based on our knowledge of material objects.[8]

2. The Religious Experience of the Modernists: These idealist philosophers, strongly influenced by the subjectivism of Kant, refuse any value to an argument based on a philosophical theory

---

[6] Cf. Descoqs, *Praelectiones Theologiae Naturalis,* I, p. 534. It is interesting to note that some forty propositions taken from the works of Rosmini were condemned by the Holy Office, December 14, 1887 (Denziger, No. 1891–1930). Of these, thirteen bear directly upon the question of our knowledge of God.

[7] Cf. Renard, *The Philosophy of Man,* pp. 69–152.

[8] *Ibid.,* p. 151.

which affirms that an existing corporeal object is the initial cause of our knowledge of God. "We cannot demonstrate God," they say; "we experience, we live God. . . . There is question here of a moral certitude based upon a direct experience of a moral reality."[9]

This experience or intuition of God is a religious emotion which does not manifest any revealed truth but gives us a consciousness, an "awareness" of God's existence. Nor is this divine reality anything distinct from our own awareness of it. God, therefore, is so immanent to us that He is somehow identical with our consciousness: thus Tyrell and others of the same school of thought.

Criticism: Here again it will suffice to point out that this error is founded upon a false theory of knowledge. Because these authors deny the objectivity of knowledge and the transcendental value of the principle of causality, they are reduced to postulate a vague subjective religious emotion as their sole evidence for God's existence. This unfounded affirmation, as appears from their writings, leads them to a mild form of pantheism.

Let us add, however, that while rejecting the errors of the Modernists as well as those of the Ontologists, we do not mean to deny that God may act directly upon the soul and that He actually does so. Not only our continuation in existence, not only the motion of grace in the supernatural order, but even the mystical experience of many mystics and saints are proof enough of this divine contact with the soul. The error of the Modernists is that they reject any objective demonstration of the existence of God. Accordingly, we are limited to a rare personal experience for this knowledge. The false philosophical postulate of these idealists — which we deny — is that the divine existence can in any manner be the *proper object* of *our intellect,* that it can ever constitute our act of understanding. For it is obvious that this divine something which is said to be perceived cannot be equally attributed to God and to creatures without definite implication of pantheism.

The doctrine of the Modernists has had a considerable influence on the thought of English and American writers such as Bradley,

---

[9] E. LeRoy, *Le Problème de Dieu*, p. 127.

William James, and Josiah Royce. It is one of the causes of the sweet, sentimental pantheism which is met with so frequently today in American thought and writings.[10]

N.B. Traditionalists: To these various schools, for the sake of convenience, we add the Traditionalists. This we do, not precisely because they — the Traditionalists — mistook the effect for God, its cause, but because their conclusions regarding our knowledge of the existence of God are without sufficient foundation. The Traditionalists instituted a reaction against the deistic and irreligious tendencies of the past century. They were a group of French Catholic writers who, under the leadership of Lamennais (1782–1854), explained that man in his present condition, invested as he is with a fallen nature, is incapable by himself and without a teacher of attaining truth with security and certitude. He needs a teacher, a revelation, a Church with its revealed doctrine, its tradition, to communicate to him knowledge and truth. Without these, man could never acquire the most fundamental knowledge; without these he could never know and, far less, prove the existence of God.

Criticism: These authors — they are called the Traditionalists and Fideists — base their teachings on a grave philosophical error. They hold that human knowledge consists in a mere passive reception. Accordingly, the intellect of man is passive and incapable of a real action; it must have a teacher, a doctrine handed down by tradition.[11] How far such a passive attitude is from the vital dynamism of Thomas, a dynamism which proclaims and establishes that the intellect of man in its most perfect action is able to reach

---

[10] We may also recall briefly the rather absurd and, today, almost-forgotten error of Thomas Reid (1710–1795), a Scot who thought that our criterion of truth was not the objective evidence of an existing reality, but what he called "common sense." The same error, couched in less rational words, was proposed by Jacobi (1743–1819), a German philosopher, whose criterion for discovering truth is not even common sense but a blind instinct. It seems sufficient to point out against such irrationalities that man is a rational animal whose highest faculty, a spiritual intellect, is capable of knowing the real because of the evidence manifested by the object of knowledge.

[11] It is significant that the doctrine of the Traditionalists was condemned by the Church in the Vatican Council.

objective reality and to know the true! *The intellect in act is the thing understood in act.*[12]

ARTICLE II: Does the Analysis of Our Concept of God Give Sufficient Evidence for an Inference That God Exists?

The Problem: We shall examine the theories of three philosophers, St. Anselm, Descartes, and Leibnitz. These men thought that from an analysis of our concept of God we can infer immediately that God *must* exist and, therefore, that He *does* exist. It will appear that these thinkers are less extravagant in their assertions, more restrained and modest in their claims, than Gioberti and Rosmini and, in general, than the Ontologists as well as the Modernists. These latter would have God as the object of our intellect and as known immediately by means of an intuition or a quasi-intuition. On the contrary, St. Anselm and all those who accept his position explain that it is not in an intuition of the existing God, but by means of an analysis of the concept, God, that we are able to attain the certitude of His existence.

The Ontological Argument:[13] St. Anselm himself persuasively explains that the name of God signifies so perfect a being that nothing, no other being, can be thought of as more perfect. But, to be sure, a being which exists only in the mind as a thought is less perfect than if it actually existed in the world of reality. Therefore, as soon as we understand what the concept of God means, that is, a concept of the most perfect being, we are able to conclude that He exists. We may say, then, that the proposition, God exists, is self-evident.

Centuries later, the same argumentation under different form was proposed by Descartes and Leibnitz.[14] Descartes founded his reasoning on an idealistic principle that whatever is clearly and

---

[12] Cf. *The Philosophy of Man,* p. 134.

[13] The argument of St. Anselm is frequently called the ontological argument. It should be noted that it is quite different from the argument of the Ontologists. (St. Anselm, *Proslogion II. Pat. Lat.,* CLVIII, 227 ff.)

[14] Descartes, IIIeme *Medit.* (cf. *Princ. Phil.,* I, 18.). Leibnitz, *La Monadologie,* n. 45.

distinctly conceived must exist. Hence, from a *clear* and *distinct idea* of God, we affirm His *existence*.

Leibnitz' mode of reasoning is more subtle. God is thinkable, therefore possible; but if possible, then he must exist. For if he did not exist, He would not be possible. The reason is that if God did not exist, it would not be possible for Him to begin to be, for a necessary being cannot begin to exist. Therefore if He is thinkable or possible, He must exist.

Perhaps we could sum up these three variants of the same argument in this manner: God is His "To Be." He is, therefore, a necessary being. But a necessary being must exist. Therefore God exists.[15]

We can do no better in answering these difficulties than present St. Thomas' solution. In a celebrated page of the *Summa Theologica*,[16] after proposing St. Anselm's argumentation, St. Thomas begins his refutation by establishing some fundamental principles.

In the first place, he states that a proposition is self-evident to us whenever, from an analysis of the subject, we are able to infer that the predicate is somehow of the essence of the subject. It must be understood that such an inference depends on the analysis of our concept of an essence. Hence, no proposition which affirms existence can be self-evident to us. The reason is that the human mind is not capable of forming a concept of existence. Its knowledge of the "to be" is had by means of a relation to essence. We say that the "to be" is the act of an essence, and we can affirm it of a subject only by means of an existential judgment. Such a judgment results primarily from experience or, at least, from an argumentation based on some antecedent sense knowledge of an existing reality.

---

[15] This argumentation is sometimes called a demonstration, *demonstratio a simultaneo,* sometimes the *ontological argument;* but really it is not a demonstration in the true sense of the word. It might preferably be called an immediate inference resulting from the analysis of a concept. This inference we intend to show is in no way warranted, for it is based on an idealistic postulate that from a concept we can infer the fact, and not merely the possibility, of existence. In a realistic philosophy which bases knowledge ultimately on an existing object, we can never infer the reality of existence from the concept of a being, no matter how perfect. At best, we may conclude to the possibility of existence.

[16] *S. Th.,* I, 2, 1.

Now, when we analyze the proposition, "God exists," we have no objective sense knowledge as a foundation for such an affirmation; for although God is His "To Be," we are not able to know that this "to be" is a fact except by means of a demonstration which begins with an object of sense knowledge. That is the reason why, while anyone with a sane mind cannot deny the self-evident proposition that the whole is greater than the part, not a few, even learned scientists, definitely refuse to accept the existence of God as a fact.

This argumentation would be quite sufficient to solve both Descartes's and Anselm's presentation of our knotty problem. St. Thomas, however, seems to have anticipated Leibnitz' subtle reasoning in the solution to the second difficulty of the same article. There, after proposing the necessity of God's existence from the analysis of a concept, the Angelic Doctor declares expressly that, from the analysis of the concept of an essence, we can never argue to the existence of a being, no matter how perfect, no matter how necessary, even though the essence of this being is supposed to be identical with existence. The reason, as we have stated above, is that the intellect of man does not understand existence in a concept. Hence it cannot analyze such a concept, because it does not form the concept of "to be." No, we can never infer the actual existence of a being unless we know from other sources, either directly from experience or from a demonstration which begins with experience, that such a being exists. These are the words of the Angelic Doctor: "Nor can it be argued that it [such a being, God] exists unless there *actually* exist such a being than which nothing greater can be thought."

We would like to observe again that in this answer, St. Thomas goes much farther in solving the difficulty than in the body of the article. There he had been satisfied to state that we do not know, except from objective reasoning, that God is His "To Be" and, therefore, that without this reasoning we are not warranted in our inference that God exists. Here we deal with a concept of God that is so perfect as to include *all* perfection and, therefore, even necessary existence. The ontological argument is that from the fact that we are able to conceive such a being (and this indicates that it is a possible being), we must infer that He exists. In other words, if the essence of a perfect being which includes all perfection, even necessary existence, is not contradictory, that is, if it is thinkable and therefore possible, such an essence must be.

The solution is most significant, because it so clearly establishes St. Thomas' position as an existentialist. Existence, or rather an existing being, is the primary cause of our knowledge. We can never, therefore, begin with a knowledge divorced from existing reality and conclude to existence. We do not deny the possibility of God. We deny that, from the fact that the concept of a necessary being is thinkable, we can infer that He is. We need either an experience or a demonstration which begins with an existing reality.[17]

---

[17] It seems that this solution of St. Thomas has not always been found acceptable. Not a few scholastic philosophers are willing to grant that God must exist if He is possible. To the celebrated syllogism — "If God is possible, He exists; but God is possible; therefore, God exists" — these philosophers grant the major, and explain that the minor is not known to be true until demonstrated by means of an *a posteriori* argument. Now why a pure act, a pure perfection, a pure "To Be," is not immediately known to be possible is something of a mystery. For if act, perfection, is possible because intelligible, *a fortiori* a pure act which contains no element of contradiction is most possible. Indeed, the possibility, not the existence, of a pure act was established by analysis and not by an *a posteriori* argument in the very first chapter of metaphysics. Through an inference from the intrinsic limitation necessary in a limited being, the principle of the limitation of act by potency states that in any order, even in the order of existence, a being in which there is no passive potency must be infinite and absolute. This principle is certainly not the Leibnitzian argument, for it does not conclude to the existence but to the possibility of a pure act. And let us note that this mode of reasoning to the possibility of a pure act, of a subsisting "To Be," is not an *a posteriori* argument, but an analysis of concept. We conclude that in accordance with the existential theory of knowledge of St. Thomas, we can never from a concept infer the existence of a being, no matter how perfect it be, unless we are already aware of its existence. The words of St. Thomas are strikingly clear: *"Nec potest argui quod sit in re, nisi DARETUR QUOD SIT IN RE."*

S U M M A R Y — Question I

DO WE NEED TO PROVE THE EXISTENCE OF GOD?

ARTICLE I: Is the Existence of God Known Immediately? — Ontologists, Modernists

Refutation.

1. **The Objectivity of Human Knowledge:** Human knowledge begins with a sense experience from which, by means of an objective demonstration, we may rise to the knowledge of a first cause.

2. **The Proper Object of Human Knowledge:** The proper, proportionate, or connatural object of the human intellect is material essences. Hence, according to its natural manner of operation, the intellect of man does not experience God directly.

ARTICLE II: Is the Existence of God Known by an Analysis of Our Concept of God? — Anselm, Leibnitz, Descartes

Refutation.

No Concept of Existence: Our knowledge of existence is not obtained in a concept but by means of an existential judgment. Such a judgment demands a sense experience of an existing being. Hence, to know that God exists, we must begin from such an experience and reason to the necessity of an existing cause for such an existing effect.

Question II

CAN THE EXISTENCE OF GOD
BE DEMONSTRATED?

We may now consider briefly the nefarious theories of those philosophers who claim not only that the existence of God is not evident, but that it can in no way be demonstrated. It will be noted that such an assertion can only terminate in some form of agnosticism.

We shall distinguish two approaches to the position of the agnostic: the materialistic and the idealistic.

Materialistic Agnosticism: The materialist-agnostic makes short shrift of the possibility of proving God's existence. "That which is beyond positive science cannot be reached by the human mind," affirms Littré. In the same vein, Spencer explains that the last reality hidden under appearances is unknown and unknowable. To these we can add the important names of Auguste Comte, Julian Huxley, and their respective schools. This doctrine is not uncommon among modern scientists. Many of these will not admit that there could be a higher science, that of philosophy, whose object and methods differ from those of the empirical sciences and whose conclusions reach a higher level of intelligibility. Everything, they say, must be reducible to the principles of empirical science. Consequently, an incorporeal God is not acceptable as a scientific hypothesis. These scientists fail to realize that, while empirical science deals with phenomena, the philosopher by means of an abstraction far higher than that of the scientist is able to rise to the contemplation of truth even as regards spiritual realities.

Idealistic Agnosticism: Quite different is the position of the idealist-agnostic. Because of his initial subjectivism, Kant, the leader of this important school, destroyed all hope of obtaining certain knowledge of objective reality. With telling cogency, he asserts the impossibility of establishing an objective demonstration of the existence of a God. <u>God, the supreme reality, lies beyond all human scientific knowledge, because such a being transcends the limited value of the Kantian principle of causality.</u> It is obvious that, since Kant posited such an erroneous foundation for his thought, all his subsequent criticisms of the proofs of the existence of God are worthless. The reason is that <u>they are vitiated by the subjective postulates which are the basis of his argumentation.</u>

It seems more than probable from reading his so-called destruction of the arguments of the scholastic philosophers that Kant never knew or, at least, never understood the fundamental principles which underlie the Five Ways of St. Thomas. It would be futile, then, to refute directly Kant's argumentation, based as it is on such subjective notions. Let us rather recall the fundamental truths we learned in metaphysics and in the philosophy of man. These will suffice to indicate the dangerous error in Kant's initial reflection which does away with the objectivity of knowledge.

1. Being is intelligible. It is the adequate object of any intellect.

2. The object and not the knowing subject is the initial cause of human knowledge.

3. The intellect of man is the spiritual faculty of a spiritual living principle, the soul. It is made not merely to know material phenomena, but to understand being. From this understanding of being, the intellect of man is able to form the first metaphysical principles which flow necessarily from an analysis of being.

4. The principle of causality transcends corporeal entities. Indeed, in the course of metaphysics, we established its universality as well as its certitude from an analysis of limited being as such and not from an induction founded upon our experience of corporeal being.[18]

---

[18] Two distinct questions arise regarding the principle of causality. The first is concerned with a psychological inference; the second deals with a metaphysical analysis. (1) The psychological problem is this: How and when do we arrive at our first knowledge of the principle of causality; how do we come to a first realization that every effect has a cause? We answer that, like all first principles, the principle of causality flows from the habit of principles. This knowledge is obtained by means of an induction which is almost immediate and which results from a personal expe-

5. Applying the principle of causality to the consideration of a limited "to be," we are able to rise with metaphysical certitude to the affirmation of a cause that is "To Be."

To the query, "Can it be demonstrated that God exists?" St. Thomas, to whom subjectivism is identical with intellectual suicide, very simply answers: "When an effect is better known to us than its cause, from the effect we proceed to the knowledge of the cause. And from every effect the existence of its *proper* cause can be demonstrated so long as its effects are better known to us; because, since every effect depends upon its cause, if the effect exists, the cause must pre-exist.[19] Hence the existence of God, in so far as it is not self-evident to us, can be demonstrated from those of His effects which are known to us."[20]

---

rience. This realization may be called a quasi-intuition. (Cf. de Tonquédec, *La Critique de la Connaissance*, p. 249 ff.) It is therefore common to all men who have reached the age of reason. The certitude obtained is sufficient for all practical purposes. (2) The philosopher then institutes an analysis of the principle thus obtained; he inquires into the certitude and the universality of this principle. This analysis is not from experience; it is not effected by means of an induction, but by a metaphysical deduction which results from the analysis of a being that is limited, composed, changeable. From such an analysis, we come to understand the absolute validity and universality of the principle of causality. For as we discovered in this analysis, the principle of causality is so linked up with the principle of contradiction that to limit it as Kant does to the world of phenomena is to deny the principle of contradiction; it is to deny all truth.

[19] A proper cause is an existential cause. Consequently, the actual influx of the cause is necessary here and now for the existence of the effect. This will be explained in the following question.

X   [20] *S. Th.*, I, 2, 2, c.

S U M M A R Y — Question II

THE AGNOSTICS CLAIM THAT THE EXISTENCE OF GOD CANNOT BE PROVED

1. Two Positions.

a) **Materialists** hold that nothing exists, nothing can be known, beyond the object of empirical science.

b) **Idealists** have a subjective theory of knowledge. The principle of causality is limited to sensible objects. It cannot suffice to prove God.

2. Refutation.

a) Being is intelligible.

b) Knowledge is caused by the object.

c) The intellect is a spiritual faculty whose adequate object is being.

d) The principle of causality is not limited to sensible objects. It flows from a knowledge of being and is caused by the habit of principles. Its absolute value is made certain by a metaphysical analysis.

e) From a knowledge of the effects, by means of the principle of causality, we are able to rise to certain knowledge of the cause which is God.

Question III

METAPHYSICAL FOUNDATION FOR THE FIVE WAYS OF ST. THOMAS

Division: There will be two articles in this question. (1) We shall show that the true nature of a proper efficient cause *as such* demands that the effect be considered as a prolongation of the property of being-an-agent. Consequently, in the order of existence, the effect, in so far as it is an effect, necessarily depends upon its proper cause here and now. (2) We shall show that the Thomistic concept of efficient cause is derived from the real distinction between essence and "to be." This will be brought into focus by presenting the existential proof from the *De Ente et Essentia,* which proof must be regarded as very helpful to a complete understanding of the Five Ways.

ARTICLE I: The Principle of Existential Causality

The text of St. Thomas quoted at the very end of the preceding question affirms the actual dependence of an effect upon its proper cause. This may be thus expressed under the title of *principle of existential causality:* In the order of existence, every effect necessarily depends actually, i.e., here and now, on its proper[21] cause, in so far as it is its cause.

A. Meaning of the Principle

We should like to establish that the true nature of an existential efficient cause *as such* demands that the effect be considered as a prolongation of the property of being-an-agent. Consequently, in the order of existence, the effect, in so far as it is an effect, must depend *here and now* upon the cause which is now causing. In other words, we mean to say that, regarding its "to be" as well as its becoming, every effect necessarily and actually depends upon its cause.

This metaphysical truth is difficult to establish, because it expresses the very nature of reality in the realm of cause and effect. Aristotle[22] hinted at this principle when he declared: "Causes which

---

[21] By "proper" cause, we mean cause in its most formal sense, that is to say, in so far as it has a *direct* influx on the "to be" of another. It is, therefore, taken in the existential order, i.e., as directly, here and now related to the "to be." Hereafter, in the place of "proper cause," we shall coin the phrase *existential cause.*

[22] The notion of existential cause belongs eminently to the philosophy of St. Thomas. Aristotle really never quite rose to the consideration of the order of

are actually at work and are particular exist and cease to exist simultaneously with their effect, e.g., this healing person with the person being healed, and that house-building man with the house being built."[23]

Commenting upon this difficult passage of Aristotle, St. Thomas explains: "Between causes in act and causes in potency, there is this difference, that the causes which are in act exist and cease to exist with those effects whose actual causes [*causae in actu*] they are, in such manner [i.e., with this limitation; the Latin reads *ita tamen*] that they be considered singular causes [*accipiantur causae singulares, id est propriae*], that is *proper* causes [i.e., in the existential order, here and now]. Thus, for instance, this healing-man [here and now] *exists* [as healing] and *ceases to exist* [as healing] simultaneously with the one *becoming* healed [*cum hoc qui fit sanus*]; likewise, the one building [here and now, *aedificans* not *aedificator*] *exists* [as cause] and *ceases to exist* simultaneously with that which *is being* built."[24] Obviously, then, every effect as regards its mode of existence depends here and now upon its existential cause.

We propose this principle as absolute not only in the line of efficient causality but of material, formal, and final causality as well. The reason is this: A cause, says St. Thomas, is a principle having a direct influx on the "to be" of another. This definition is true of all the four types of causes. Hence, although the manner of causing the influx varies, nevertheless whatever pertains to the very nature of causal influx as such must be attributable to all

---

existence; he is fundamentally an essentialist. On the other hand, the philosophy of St. Thomas is primarily concerned with existence; it is the philosophy of the "to be." Now in this philosophy we define cause as a principle which has a direct influx on the "to be" of another. An existential cause, therefore, looks to the "to be"; it is directly connected with the "to be" of the effect. Let us add that the notion of existential cause is not limited to efficient causality but applies as well to the other types of causes. To be sure, the nature of the influx into the "to be" of another will vary in accordance with the nature of each type of causality, but it should be actual if the effect exists.

[23] *Physics*, Book II, c. 3, 195b, l. 17.
[24] *In II Phys.*, c. 3, lect. 6, no. 9.

true causes. We propose to show that an effect is not intelligible without an actual influx of the cause.

Formal and Material Cause: If we consider the intrinsic causes, namely matter and form, the effect which is the composite cannot possibly exist unless these causes are *actually* causing, having a direct influx upon its existence by the mutual communication of their own reality. There is no Fido, the dog, without its form and its matter being actually united.

Final Cause: We perceive just as clearly that without the *actual* influx of the final cause, that is, without the "to be desired," the agent cannot be determined here and now to this particular action. The reason is that agent as agent does not include a determination to a definite action. Without the determination of the final cause, this or that action would not be intelligible.

Exemplary Cause: The necessity of an actual influx is obviously true in the case of the exemplary cause. For no effect is intelligible without an exemplar according to whose image the effect is determined *in its species* by an intellectual agent. "For the production of anything an exemplar is necessary, in order that the effect may receive a determinate form."[25]

Efficient Cause: In like manner, then, the same must be affirmed in the line of efficient causality. We note, however, that there really are two types of efficient causality in the order of existence, two types of existential causes: the cause of the *becoming* which is generally a creature, and the cause of the "to be" which can only be God. This was established in the philosophy of being[26]

---

[25] *S. Th.*, I, 44, 3, c.

[26] Cf. *The Philosophy of Being*, p. 134. It might prove helpful to recall the mode of procedure in establishing that creatures do not cause the *"to be"* but only the *becoming*. (1) Creatures are real agents; (2) they cannot cause existence; (3) since the effect in the order of existence either *is* or *becomes*, and since moreover creatures are real agents, it follows that they cause the becoming. The third proposition is a necessary conclusion. We need only establish the truth of the first and second propositions.

1. Were we to deny that creatures are real agents, we would be forced to deny the truth of all knowledge and to take a position with absolute skeptics. For since our knowledge of the various beings, of the various natures which surround us, results from our observation of their operations, by denying that these operations are caused

where it was shown that creatures are real agents, that is, existential efficient causes, and not merely necessary conditions. In the same tract, it was shown that their efficiency, however, cannot produce the "to be" but only becoming.[27]

Now it is a matter of constant experience that as soon as the cause of the becoming ceases to act, the becoming itself stops. For example, the wall is being built by the stone mason; the wall is becoming. Were the artisan to stop working, the wall would no longer be being built; it would no longer be becoming. The same inference, then, must be accepted regarding the cause of the "to be." *In a finite, contingent being, the "to be" must be caused here and now by another.*

N.B.: This all-important conclusion regarding the necessity of an efficient cause here and now causing the "to be" of an effect is not obtained by an argument from a scientific analogy but from

---

by the various natures, we would have to deny that we can arrive at a certain knowledge of these natures. (Cf. *C.G.*, III, c. 69.)

2. Creatures, we insist, cannot cause existence. This will be understood if we recall that the limitation, the individuation, the thisness, of an effect is not caused by the virtue of the agent but by the subject in which the effect is received or effected. For an act is not limited by an extrinsic agent, but by an intrinsic potency. Hence, if a creature could cause one "to be," it could cause all caused existence, even its own; and that is a very great absurdity. The reason why it could cause its own "to be" as well as all others is that the causing is the same in all cases, since the "thisness" of the effect, the limitation of the "to be," results not from the agent but from the nature of the patient. It follows that no limited being but only a subsisting existence, only an unparticipated "To Be," can be the cause of a participated existence. (Cf. *S. Th.*, I, 104, 1, c.)

3. We conclude: Creatures are true existential causes, not of complete existence, but causes of motion, of change, of becoming; that is, they are causes of an imperfect form with a flowing "to be" (*esse fluens*).

[27] Cf. *ibid.*, p. 136. N.B. The notion of cause, especially that of efficient cause, is not uncommonly applied, even among philosophers, to former agents that no longer have any influx on the effect. We speak, for example, of the mother cat being the cause of the little cat. Now, strictly speaking, although the mother cat *was* at one time the cause of the becoming of its young, it is no longer its existential cause. For the effect (the little cat) no longer depends upon its former cause (mother) by means of an influx on its existence. If, then, we were to use the term "cause" in the present case, we should be careful to state that the mother cat is not here and now the existential cause of the infant cat; at best, it could be termed an accidental cause (*causa per accidens*).

an inference based upon the definition of cause, a definition common to all four types of causality. The analysis of this definition manifests the necessity of *actual* dependence of effect upon cause. The reason why we began with a reflection upon the causes other than the efficient cause is simply that the actual dependence of effect upon cause is evident in these.

We conclude with St. Thomas: "Every effect depends on its cause, so far as it is its cause. But we must observe that an agent may be the cause of the *becoming* of its effect but not directly of the 'to be.' . . . Therefore, just as the *becoming* of a thing cannot continue when the action of the agent ceases, so neither can the *'to be'* of a thing continue after the action of the agent has ceased, which is the cause of the effect not only in the *becoming* but also in the *'to be.'* "[28]

B. Application of the Principle

The Impossibility of an Infinite Series of Subordinated Existential Causes.

Principle: The principle which we have just established — to wit, *in the order of existence, every effect depends upon its existential cause here and now* — has perhaps its most important application in the Thomistic proof of the existence of God.

An Infinite Series of Existentially Subordinated Causes Is a Contradiction: The proof of the existence of God depends upon the truth of the following statement: In a series of subordinated efficient existential causes in which each member has an influx here and now upon the "to be" of the next cause, and in turn, in the same manner depends on the preceding cause, an infinite number of causes is impossible because contradictory. We must conclude, therefore, to the existence of a first uncaused cause.

Before establishing the truth of this statement, we shall give a

---

[28] *S. Th.,* I, 104, 1. God can, of course, be the cause not only of the "to be" but also of the becoming. Creatures can cause only the becoming.

name to this series of subordinated causes in which each member
is an existential cause. St. Thomas calls these causes *causae per se
ordinatae*. We shall use the phrase *existentially subordinated causes*,
because the dependence is in the order of existence and therefore
immediate.

There are two reasons why such an infinite series is a contradiction. (1) Since the dependence of all the members of the series is in
the existential order and, therefore, simultaneous, in an infinite
series there should exist simultaneously an infinite number of
causes. Now, an *actual* infinite number is clearly a contradiction.
(2) In a series of existentially subordinated causes, the influx of
the first cause looks to the "to be" (that is to say, it has an influx
on the "to be") of all the intermediate members, reaching even
to the last effect.[29] The reason is that the intermediate causes are
actuated here and now by the first cause. If, then, there were no
first cause, these intermediary causes would not be able to act.
Now in an infinite series there is no first cause and, therefore, no
sufficient reason for the actuation of the intermediate cause, no
causing of the last effect, and therefore no effect. This is contradictory, since the effect is there: it exists. Therefore, the series cannot
be infinite.

Accidentally Subordinated Causes: The Thomistic concept of
existential cause and of a series of causes which demands actual
existential and, therefore, simultaneous interdependence of all its
members is not an ordinary and common notion even among
philosophers. What is generally thought of in this matter is a
broken series of causes and effects in which there is no immediate
dependence, as for example, the little cat which scratches me and
was generated at one time by the mother cat, and the mother by
the grandmother. There is no actual dependence of the scratching
done here and now upon the ancestor cats. St. Thomas calls such
a series *causae per accidens ordinatae*. We shall name it a series
of accidentally subordinated causes.

---

[29] Recall the philosophical explanation of instrumental causality. (Cf. *The Philosophy of Being*, p. 141.) "It is necessary that all secondary agents be reduced to the
superior causes as the instrumental to the principal." (Cf. *C.G.*, II, c. 21.)

The Position of Aquinas: St. Thomas bluntly states in several of his works that an infinite series of accidentally subordinated causes cannot be demonstrated to be impossible.[30] If that is the case, then, and if we were to argue, using such a series of causes, to try to prove the existence of God, we would never be able to affirm with metaphysical certitude the existence of a first uncaused cause. To say the least, we might find it difficult to prove God.

Let us, for the sake of argument, admit the possibility of an infinite series of such accidentally subordinated causes. Let us go farther and grant the possibility of an eternal world.[31] What then? The answer is simple and clear-cut. We do not argue on the basis of accidentally subordinated causes, which imply an indefinite broken sequence of causes and changes through the obscurity of the preceding ages of the world; rather, we rise almost immediately to the absolute necessity of a first cause whose existential influx actuates here and now the very last effect, the very being which is the object of our present knowledge, of our immediate experience. Consequently, even if we admit the possibility of an infinite number of successive changes and mutations, even if we grant the possibility of an eternal world, such a world would need to be dependent in the order of existence here and now upon a first and uncaused cause.

The Thomistic proof, therefore, does not reject the possibility of a world existing from eternity; it does not try to answer the difficulty of successive motions and changes without end. The reason is that such a difficulty does not present itself in this proof. Even if an eternity of successive changes were had, we should require a first cause outside of that eternal series, moving here and now, actuating the ultimate effect in the order of existence.

Our argumentation, then, is entirely existential: it deals with the

---

[30] Provided, of course, that these accidentally subordinated causes do not all exist actually but only potentially. (*S. Th.*, I, 46, 2, ad 8^m. Cf. *S. Th.*, I, 46, 2, ad 7^m; *De Ver.*, II, 10.)

[31] St. Thomas states that our knowledge that the world exists in time and not from eternity is a matter of revelation, not of reason. (Cf. *S. Th.*, I, 46, 2.) This point will be discussed in the tract on creation.

influx here and now in the order of the "to be." In this order, precisely because of the immediate dependence involved, an infinite series is a contradiction.

An Eternal World Is Not a Difficulty: Such a contradiction is not so clearly perceived in the essential order in which the "to be" is not considered. In that order, there is no immediate dependence here and now. St. Thomas proposes the example of the multitude of hammers used to drive a nail in the wall.[31a] We insist again: The difficulty of an eternal world which is often brought to bear against the proof of the existence of God has really no meaning in the Thomistic argument. For even if we should grant the possibility of an infinite series of successive and discreet motions, these are not considered in the existential order. There can be no discrete and successive motions in the order of proper causes and, therefore, no infinite series of causes which have a direct influx on the "to be" of the existing effect.

Conclusion: Because every existing effect must depend here and now upon its existential cause, an infinite series of existential causes is unintelligible; it is *non-ens,* nothing. A limited "to be" as well as a motion in the existential order, that is, a becoming, are not intelligible except as related to an existential cause. Hence an argumentation based on accidentally subordinated causes fails absolutely to make this world intelligible, for it fails to account here and now for the becoming as well as the "to be." The mass of errors concerning God which arose in the historical development of human thought generally resulted from an essentialist point of view which failed to realize this profound and difficult notion of causality.[32]

[31a] Cf. *S. Th.,* I, 7, 4.

[32] M. Gilson remarks that the fundamental difference between the position of St. Thomas and that of Aristotle as well as of all the essentialists lies precisely in facing or not facing the problem of existence. There can be no existential problem in a philosophy which accepts an eternal world as *necessary.* A necessary existence presents no philosophical problem. We do not ask, "Why God?" but, "Why an existing world which is contingent?" (*L'être et l'essence,* p. 111; cf. *Le Thomisme.* c. III.)

ARTICLE II: The Existential Proof From the "De Ente et Essentia"

Whence the Philosophical Concept of Existential Causality?:
The Thomistic concept of efficient causality which enables the
philosopher to rise to an affirmation of a subsisting existence is derived from the analysis of the composition of act and potency in
the order of existence, that is, from the analysis of the composition
of essence and "to be" in a limited existing being. We should
recall at this point the fundamental notions learned in *The Philosophy of Being* and in particular the principle of limitation and its
primary application, namely, that limited beings are necessarily
composed of essence and "to be." From this fundamental truth,
from the fact that in such an existing being the "to be" is limited
and, therefore, participated, we perceive almost immediately a
necessary relation of dependence upon another being. This is
clearly expressed in a text already quoted in *The Philosophy of
Being,* but which bears repetition: "The relation (of a participated
being) to the cause," St. Thomas explains, "becomes known by an
analysis of the factors which compose its [constitutive] make-up
[*ratio*]. Because, *from the fact that it is a participated being, it
follows necessarily that it must be caused by another."*[33]

In other words, in predicating the notion of "being" of a limited
subject, I must affirm, not a relation of identity between essence and
"to be," but a real relation,[34] and therefore, a real distinction. For,
since this subject is "being by participation," it is not its "to be,"
but *has* a "to be." Consequently, it is not a necessary being; there
is no reason in the concept of the essence why it should exist. But
it does exist. Why? If the reason for the existence of this being is
not found to be of the very essence, then I must look outside that
essence for a principle of being; otherwise, a limited existing being
would not be intelligible. I conclude, therefore, that an existing limited
and finite being is not sufficiently explained by its intrinsic structure,

---

[33] *S. Th.,* I, 44, 1, ad 1^m.

[34] We shall show later that the knowledge of this relation between the terms of
the predicate results from an existential judgment.

by the composition of act and potency. There must be other principles — extrinsic principles, to be sure — indicating not why these limited beings are such and why they are different from one another (for that is sufficiently explained by the transcendental relation between essence and "to be," matter and form, substance and accident), but simply *why* they *are*. Thus we are brought to the analysis of cause and of causality.[35]

Existential Proof: Let us now propose the existential proof of the *De Ente et Essentia,* a proof which we believe to be necessary for the complete understanding of the Five Ways. The reason for this is that in the celebrated article of the *Summa Theologica* in which the five distinct approaches to the existence of God are expressed, St. Thomas supposes but does not explicitly state the composition of essence and "to be."[36] In the *De Ente et Essentia,* a work of his youth, he is more explicit; for after establishing that in contingent beings essence and "to be" are really distinct, and because of this distinction, he concludes to the existence of a cause which is its own "To Be." There are three stages to this proof. (1) Essence is not identical with "to be." (2) An efficient cause is necessary to explain limited existence. (3) A first cause which is its act of existing is necessary.

1. Essence is not identical with "to be":

Whatever is not contained in the concept of essence or of quiddity comes to it from without and forms a composition with essence, because no essence can be understood without its [constitutive] parts.

Every essence, however, can be understood without understanding its "to be"; for I can know what a man or a "phoenix" is and still remain in the dark as to whether such a being does exist in the world [literally, and not know whether it has a "to be"].

Therefore, it is clear that the "to be" is not the same as [literally, is other than] essence or quiddity, unless perhaps there exist a being whose quiddity is its "to be"; moreover such a being would have to be the One and the First [God]. . . . Consequently it follows in

---

[35] *The Philosophy of Being,* p. 117.

[36] The relation of the world to God is a relation in the order of the "to be." That is the most profound reason for the existentialism of St. Thomas. From his earlier years, the Angelic Doctor realized this profound truth. It is the unifying principle, the vital sap of all his writings.

all other beings, that the "to be" and the quiddity [that is, the nature or form] are distinct [literally, other, different, something else].[37]

All beings, then, except God — if He exists — are composed of essence and "to be."

2. An efficient cause is necessary to explain limited existence: St. Thomas continues:

> Whatever belongs to a being is either caused by the principles of that being's essence[38] or comes to it from some extrinsic principle. . . . The "to be" [in a finite being] cannot be caused by the thing in itself considered formally or in its essence. Here I speak of cause in the sense of efficient cause, for in this case, the being would be its own cause; it would give itself its own "to be," a thing which is impossible. Hence, every being whose "to be" is different from its essence, receives this "to be" from another.[39]

"St. Thomas here declares that since the 'to be' of finite beings is distinct from the essence, it cannot be caused by the essence. For nothing that is caused can be its own cause. Therefore, an extrinsic principle, which is what we mean by an efficient cause, must be the sole reason for the actuation of a finite being in the order of existence. This argument which begins with the real distinction and proceeds from an analysis of the composite 'being' to conclude almost immediately to the existence of an efficient cause, must, like all arguments based on the analogy of proportionality, terminate in a proof of the existence of the Supreme Cause."[40] This is made evident by the application of the principle of existential causality. Because an infinite series of existentially subordinated causes is impossible, we rise to the knowledge of the subsisting "To Be."

3. This first cause is "To Be": St. Thomas concludes:

---

[37] *De Ente et Essentia*, c. V.
[38] Such are the powers of the soul. Cf. *The Philosophy of Man*, p. 60.
[39] *De Ente et Essentia*, c. V.
[40] *The Philosophy of Being*, p. 119.

And since everything that exists because of another [that is, by reason of another as efficient cause] is brought back to that which exists by reason of itself as to the first cause, some being must exist which is the cause of the "to be" in all things, because in itself it is pure "To Be." Otherwise we fall into an infinite series of causes, *since every being which is not pure "To Be" has a cause of its "to be." And this is the first cause, which is God.*[41]

SUMMARY — Question III

METAPHYSICAL FOUNDATION FOR THE FIVE WAYS OF ST. THOMAS

ARTICLE I: The Principle of Existential Causality

1. The principle of causality, which states that an effect requires a cause:

a) Becomes known as a result of *psychological* experience;

b) Is established to be absolutely certain from a *metaphysical* analysis. This analysis shows that an effect without a cause is not intelligible.

2. Definition of Cause: A principle having a *direct influx* upon the "to be" of another.

A reflection upon this definition, which is nothing but another expression of the principle of causality, brings out the necessity of the actual dependence of an effect upon its true cause. This important truth is clearly expressed by the principle of existential causality thus:

3. The Principle of Existential Causality: Every existing effect must here and now depend upon its existential cause.

This is not a new principle; it is a metaphysical expression of the principle of causality as regards any *existing* effect. It is a more profound understanding of the definition of cause.

4. The universality of this principle is made even more evident

---

[41] *De Ente et Essentia,* c. V.

by a consideration of the various types of causes: formal, material, final, exemplary, efficient as regards the becoming.

Although the influx upon the "to be" of the effect varies in each species of causes because the causality is different, nevertheless all the causes have this in common, that the causality of the influx is *here and now.*

From these facts which manifest the true signification of the principle of causality and the true meaning of the definition of cause, we necessarily infer:

5. **The necessity of an Existential Efficient Cause** of the "to be" of an existing effect which causes the "to be" of the effect here and now.

Application of the Principle of Existential Causality

1. The Thomistic proof of the existence of God rests on the *impossibility of an infinite series of existential causes.*

2. Such impossibility appears evident:

a) From the fact that an *actual* infinite number is a contradiction;

b) From the necessity of a *first* cause which actuates here and now the intermediate causes (if there be any) together with the effect.

ARTICLE II: Existential Proof From the "De Ente et Essentia"

1. The principle of existential causality is confirmed by means of a concept of efficient cause which is derived from an analysis of a limited being which is a composite being.

2. The principle of existential causality is then applied to demonstrate the necessity of the First Cause.

Question IV

DEMONSTRATION OF THE EXISTENCE OF GOD
Prologue

The Five Ways: The Five Ways of St. Thomas are metaphysical

demonstrations of the existence of God; they are existential proofs.[42]
They rise from a metaphysical analysis of corporeal existing reality
to a being which is pure act, subsisting existence, absolute necessity, unparticipated perfection, and the end of all that exists. Although the argumentation supposes the fact that our knowledge
depends primarily upon a sensible experience of a corporeal entity,
we do not argue precisely from any individual experience but
from the intellectual knowledge which results from a metaphysical
analysis of limited existing being (1) which is becoming, (2) which
causes another being, (3) which is corruptible, (4) which is imperfect, (5) which is necessarily ordered to an end.

   1. Now a limited being, because it is composed of potency and

---

[42] The Five Ways are existential proofs, and therefore they are metaphysical
demonstrations. They are perhaps the highest moment in Thomistic metaphysics,
because they establish the necessity of a pure existence without which the world
of sensible beings is not intelligible.

It has been stated by some commentators that these proofs and in particular the
First Way are physical, not metaphysical demonstrations, because they begin with
the affirmation of an existing corporeal entity and not — as does the metaphysical
proof from the *De Ente et Essentia* — with an analysis of concepts.

It is true, the proof from the *De Ente* begins with an analysis of concepts, but
in the philosophy of St. Thomas this analysis supposes an objective theory of knowledge. For if we are able to analyze the concept of man and of phoenix, it is because
we have at one time, through some initial sense experience, arrived at a knowledge
of man and bird. Indeed, St. Thomas argues that if such a limited being which is
not its "to be" *exists,* it is only because of an existing cause which is its "To Be."

It is also true that in the First Way we begin with the sense experience of a
moving object. From such initial sense knowledge which is essential in the Thomistic
theory of knowledge, we rise to a *metaphysical* analysis of motion. Then, by means
of the principle of *existential* causality, we conclude with *metaphysical* certitude to a
pure act in the order of *existence.* Let it be said that a demonstration which begins
with a metaphysical analysis, which is concerned with the "to be," in which the
metaphysical principle of existential causality is the middle term, and which terminates in the knowledge of a pure act of existence is not situated in the first degree
of abstraction: it is a metaphysical argument.

Let us note in passing that although the Angelic Doctor uses Aristotelian terminology, he does not, like the Stagirite, remain in the consideration of the essences of
things. He is not an essentialist. St. Thomas is first and last concerned with the
"to be," and the Five Ways are his supreme endeavor to understand the necessity
of a pure act of existence. To declare, then, that that demonstration of a pure
existence which he considers the most evident and the first is a mere physical —
whatever that may mean — argumentation is to miss completely the existentialism
of his philosophy.

act, can be actuated; it can go from potency to act; it can move. That is why there can be motion in this world. Of this we are aware by constant experience. From the fact of the reality of motion we argue to the Supreme Unmoved Mover that is pure act.

2. Moreover, a limited being which is an efficient cause of another being cannot be the cause of its own existence. From this realization we argue to the necessity of a first efficient cause that is its own "To Be."

3. It is also our constant experience that sensible realities, because of their composition of act and potency in the order of essence, are corruptible. The fact that such beings exist postulates the existence of an absolutely necessary being.

4. Again, a limited being, because it is limited, implies participation in a being that is absolutely perfect.

5. Finally, limited beings must have for their ultimate final cause a being that is its own end.

Five Distinct Proofs: Are the Five Ways five distinct and complete demonstrations of God, or should we consider them as integral parts of one and the same proof? If by parts of the same proof we understand that each of the Five Ways is not a complete argumentation and that it does not conclude to a metaphysical certitude of the existence of God, then we must deny that they are parts of a whole. For as we shall establish, each way is an absolute demonstration. On the other hand, we are more than willing to grant that the Five Ways form a well-knit unit and that, taken together, they give a rounded and a more complete understanding of God. Indeed this point should be stressed: each of the Five Ways considers a different formality of limited reality — motion, caused existence, corruptibility, participation, finality. Consequently, the term of each proof envisages God from a different point of view, viewing Him now as Pure Act, now as "To Be," now as Necessary Being, now as Absolute Perfection, now as Supreme End.

No Succession in Time: The Five Ways transcend time, the *hic et nunc*. There is never question of a regression of causes in the succession of consecutive duration. The series of causes considered is always existential; hence the first cause actuates here and now the effect which is presently produced. Consequently, even if we were to grant, for the sake of argument, the erroneous hypothesis of eternal motion, of an eternal world, the Five Ways would conclude just as well. The reason is that the notion of creation does not deny the possibility of the eternity of the world; rather it denies the necessity of such an eternity.[43]

ARTICLE I: The First Way[44]

The Existence of an Unmovable Mover Is Proved From the Fact of Motion: Motion, the formal aspect of reality upon which this proof is based, is not restricted to any particular kind of motion such as, for example, local motion. Indeed this demonstration is founded on motion as such, the concept of which is applicable to all types of motion, whether corporeal or spiritual; in short, it is founded on becoming.

> The first and more manifest way is the argument from motion. It is certain and evident to our senses that some things are moved in this world. Now whatever is moved is moved by another, for nothing is moved except as it is in potency to that to which it is moved; whereas a thing moves something inasmuch as it is in act. For to move is nothing else than to reduce something from potency to act. But a thing cannot be reduced from potency to act except by a being in act. Thus that which is actually hot, as fire, makes wood which is potentially hot to be actually hot, and thereby moves and changes it. Now it is not possible that the same thing should be at once in act and potency in the same respect, but only in different respects. For what is actually hot cannot simultaneously be potentially hot, but it is simultaneously potentially cold. It is therefore impossible that in the same respect and in the same way a thing should be both mover and moved, i.e., that it should move itself. Therefore, whatever is moved must be moved by another. If that by which it is moved be itself moved, then this being itself must needs be moved by another, and that by another again. But this cannot go to infinity, for then there would be no first mover and, consequently, no other

---

[43] Cf. *S. Th.*, I, 46.
[44] Cf. *C.G.*, I, c. 13; cf. Aristotle, *Physics*, Book VII.

mover, because second movers do not move except through this, that they are moved by a first mover, as a staff does not move unless it is moved by the hand. Therefore it is necessary to arrive at a first mover moved by no other; and this everyone understands to be God.[45]

Analysis of the Text: First, the fact of motion is stated. It is a fact which no one can deny unless the validity of all sense knowledge be rejected and, as a consequence, some form of skepticism implied. Following this, the principle of causality is stated in terms of motion: *"Whatever is moved must be moved by another."* This principle then is analyzed and its truth established, for it is shown to rest upon the principle of contradiction. This is made evident in the following manner. First a metaphysical analysis of motion is proposed. Motion is the passage from potency to act. In order to go from potency to act, the moving subject must be moved, that is, be put in act, by another being which is in act. For *nothing can be reduced from potency to act except by a being which is in act.* This statement is a metaphysical expression of the principle of causality which had been proposed before in terms of motion: "Whatever is moved must be moved by another." The reason for such metaphysical expression in terms of act and potency is to make it self-evident. For to affirm that a being which is in potency to a certain act moves itself to that act without being moved by another is to say that it is both in act and in potency simultaneously and regarding the same perfection; it is a denial of the principle of contradiction. Hence the argument:

Whatever is moved must be moved by another.

But we cannot proceed to infinity regarding moved and mover, since we are dealing with existential causes.

Therefore we must come to an unmoved mover, and that is God; for only a being without potency, that is, pure act, is not moved because not movable.[46]

---

[45] *S. Th.,* I, 2, 3, c.

[46] Let us not forget that this argument is not in the order of essences but of existence. Hence the conclusion affirms a pure act of existing as the source of all becoming.

The major has just been established;[47] to deny it is to deny, at least implicitly, the principle of contradiction.[48] The minor was explained in a previous question.

No Successive Motions: It is sufficiently evident that in this proof St. Thomas in no way considers successive motions. That is why a difficulty based on the eternity of successive changes, which might prove fatal against an argument which rests upon a series of accidentally subordinated causes, does not present itself. Even if such an eternity were had, we should require outside of that infinite series of unrelated becomings a first mover moving here and now and causing this present motion, either immediately or through the instrumentality of intermediate causes.[49] This proof, then, does not reject the possibility of a world existing from eternity; it transcends this possibility, because it is an existential proof.

No Mere Aristotelianism: The First Way goes far beyond mere Aristotelianism. Aristotle concludes to a first cause which moves only in so far as desired in the order of efficient causality. Indeed it is not an easy matter to know just what Aristotle understands by efficient cause.[50] St. Thomas, on the contrary, posits the existence of a first unmoved mover *which by its action here and now* has an influx upon any actual motion.

ARTICLE II: The Second Way

The second way is from the nature [*ratione*] of efficient cause. In the world of sensible things we find there is an order of efficient causes. It is not found, neither is it possible, that something be the efficient cause of itself, for so it would be prior to itself which is impossible. Now in efficient causes it is not possible to

---

[47] Cf. also *The Philosophy of Being*, p. 121.

[48] A difficulty sometimes proposed against the universality of this principle is that living beings, because they move themselves, cannot be moved by another. The answer is that the operation of life, although immanent, presupposes in a limited living being that it be actuated by an extrinsic cause before it can act immanently.

[49] "*Oportet omnes causas inferiores agentes reduci in causas superiores sicut instrumentales in primarias.*" (*C.G.*, II, c. 21.)

[50] Cf. Gilson, *Le Thomisme*, pp. 98-99.

go to infinity, because in all [existentially] subordinated causes, the first is the cause of the intermediate cause, and the intermediate is the cause of the ultimate cause, whether the intermediate causes be several or one only. Now should the cause be removed, the effect would cease. Therefore, if there be no first cause among efficient causes, there will be no ultimate nor any intermediate cause. But if in efficient causes it is possible to go to infinity, there will be no first efficient cause; neither will there be an ultimate effect nor any intermediate efficient causes, all of which is plainly false. Therefore it is necessary to admit a first efficient cause, which all name God.[51]

Exposition of the Proof: The second demonstration is founded on the notion of efficient cause.[52] Here, as in the First Way, we begin with a fact of experience. We observe in the world around us that there is an order of efficient cause and effect; that is, certain beings are the reasons why other beings exist. But what of the cause itself? St. Thomas argues:

It is inconceivable that a limited being be its own efficient cause, since it would have first to exist in order to cause itself to exist. In other words, no being can cause its "to be." It needs another cause.

But we cannot proceed to infinity in a series of existentially subordinated efficient causes. The reason given by St. Thomas shows clearly that he is referring to existentially subordinated causes. He actually says: "If the cause were removed, the effect would cease."[53] Hence if there were no first cause, there would be no present effect.

Therefore, we must posit a first efficient cause which is uncaused because first and which, because uncaused, must be its own "To Be."

Difference from the First Way: It has been suggested by some philosophers that this Second Way is a repetition of the First with this minor difference, that the starting point in the second is being and not becoming. In the first, we consider motion; in the second, an existing substance.

---

[51] *S. Th.*, I, 2, 3, c.

[52] Cf. Aristotle, *Met.*, II, 2, 994a, 1. In this text, Aristotle does not actually prove the existence of God but merely states that an infinite series in any of the four types of causes is an impossibility.

[53] *"Remota autem causa, removetur effectus."* (*S. Th.*, I, 2, 3, c.)

The Second Way, to be sure, has a great deal in common with the first: existential order, efficient causality, impossibility of an infinite series. There are, however, essential differences which place each proof under a distinct formality. The First Way considers the passivity of beings, their becoming as they are moved; it considers motion. The formal aspect of the Second Way, on the contrary, is activity. This proof studies a limited being in so far as it is a cause, that is, in so far as by its *action* it is the efficient cause of another. This limited efficient cause of another, we find, cannot be its own cause, because it is not its own "to be"; and therefore, we must rise to a higher cause.

It is true that only God can be the adequate efficient cause of existence in all its plenitude; all other causes only prepare by causing the becoming.[54] Nevertheless, it is often through the intermediate efficiency of these secondary causes, which must be called instrumental, that the principal cause, God, effectively gives the "to be" to the present effect.

Hence: (1) the Second Way does not analyze being because it is passive or becoming, but because it is active and causes an effect by its action. (2) That is why, in the First Way, we rise to the affirmation of a being in which there is no passivity, no potency, and therefore of a being which is pure act; whereas in the Second Way we conclude to a cause that is so perfect in its activity that it is "To Be."

ARTICLE III: The Third Way[55]

The third way is taken from the possible and the necessary and runs thus. We find in things some that are possible to be and not to be, since they are found to be generated and to be corrupted; and consequently, it is possible for them to be and not to be. But it is impossible for these always to exist, for that which can not-be [*possibile est non esse*] at some time is not. Therefore, if every-

---

[54] *Supra*, p. 19, n. 24.
[55] Cf. *C.G.*, I, c. 15.

thing can not-be, then at one time there was nothing in existence.
But if this were true, nothing would exist now, because that which
does not exist does not begin to be except through something which
is. Therefore, if at one time no being were in existence, it would
have been impossible for anything to have begun to be; and thus
even now nothing would be in existence, which is evidently false.
Therefore, not all beings are merely possible, but there must be
some necessity in things. But every necessary thing either has its
necessity caused by another or not. Now it is impossible to go to
infinity in necessary things which have their necessity caused by
another, as has been already proved in regard to efficient causes.
Therefore we cannot but admit the existence of some being which
is of itself necessary, not having the cause of its necessity from
another, but which is the cause of necessity in others. This all men
call God.[56]

Terminology: St. Thomas uses the word "possible" here in a
technical sense. By possible being, he does not mean anything that
is not God, that is, whose "to be" is distinct from its essence;
rather, he means beings which, because of their nature, have a
potency not to be — that is to say, they can be generated, and they
can corrupt. Any corporeal substance, then, because its matter is
in potency to all other material forms, is a possible being in this
technical sense. A dog, for example, has a capacity to cease being
a dog; it can cease to exist. Because of the ambiguity of the word
possible, we shall use in its stead the term *corruptible.*

On the other hand, by the expression *necessary being having a
cause for its necessity,* St. Thomas designates a being whose essence,
because fully actuated by a distinct "to be," has no capacity, no
potency, to cease to exist. Such is a spiritual form; such also, as
thought medieval philosophers, were the celestial bodies. These
beings are necessary, that is, incorruptible. Nevertheless, since the
"to be" is really distinct from their essence, they are not absolutely
necessary beings in the order of existence, but their necessity depends
upon the active potency of an extrinsic agent.

By an absolutely (*per se*) necessary being, St. Thomas understands

---

[56] *S. Th.,* I, 2, 3, c. The elements of this proof were proposed first by Avicenna
and developed later by Maimonides. St. Thomas adopted it but transformed it by
placing it in the order of existence.

a being which has no cause for its necessity, because the "to be" is the essence; it simply *is*. Such a being is God.

Why an Eternal World?: The Third Way is proposed in the hypothesis of an eternal world. It is true that St. Thomas, the Christian theologian, was aware that the world was created in time. Why, then, such an erroneous hypothesis? The reason is that to one who denies the existence of God an eternal world is presupposed. Now if we accept this supposition, that is, an eternity of successive changes, all possibilities — even that of corruption in a corruptible being — would necessarily come to pass. The reason is that a corruptible being is one which has the possibility of corrupting; it has a potency for ceasing to exist. Hence, given an infinite duration, all possibilities, even that of non-existence, would necessarily happen at some time, and not only for one but for every corruptible being. Sooner or later, then, during this infinite succession of time, the world of material beings would cease to exist; it would disappear; there would be nothing left; and from nothing, nothing could ever become. But the world exists today. Therefore, to explain the fact of an existing world of corruptible beings, we must posit the existence of some incorruptible, some necessary being.

St. Thomas then proposes a series of distinct steps to reach God.

1. A necessary being is the only explanation for the actual existence of an eternal world of corruptible beings.

2. This being has the cause of its necessity either from another or not.

3. There cannot be an infinite series of necessary beings whose necessity is caused by another, for these causes are existentially subordinated.

4. Therefore, there must exist a necessary being whose necessity it not from another but from itself, and this is God.

This argumentation may be put in syllogistic form thus:

If all existing beings were corruptible, in the supposition that this world is eternal, at a given moment everything would cease to be and nothing would exist today.

But the conclusion is false.

Therefore, the antecedent must be false. Consequently, we must posit a necessary being whose necessity does not depend upon another.

Difficulty: It might be objected that matter does not corrupt but, after each corruption of the substantial form, it continues to exist united with another form just educed from its potency. The answer, of course, is: If that is so, then matter must have some necessity not of itself, since it is distinct from its existence,[57] but from another. And that is precisely our argument. An eternal world of corruptible beings is not intelligible without a being that has some necessity either from another or from itself. St. Thomas seems to have foreseen this difficulty when he remarked in the Commentary on the work of Aristotle, *On the Heavens:* "It is impossible that what is corruptible is not at some time corrupted, because if it is not corrupted at some time, it can not-be-corrupted, and so it will be incorruptible."[58]

To Conclude: The First Way establishes God the Immovable Mover in whom there is no potency. He is pure act. The second posits God the First Efficient Cause of all existence. He is the "To Be." In the third, God is proposed to us as the reason for all necessity, for He is in an absolute sense the Necessary Being. This last deduction is an important concept in Thomistic thought.

ARTICLE IV: The Fourth Way

This proof will appeal to certain types of thinkers, to those gifted with a poetical, an artistic insight into reality. Thomas puts it in the fourth place and does little more than state it bluntly, ending with the evident fact that the exemplar of the multitude of participated true, good, and beautiful which exist must necessarily be their efficient cause.

---

[57] This appears from the changes which occur in corporeal substances. These changes necessitate successive actuations in the order of existence.

[58] "*Impossibile est id quod est corruptibile quandoque non corrumpi, quia si quandoque non corrumpitur potest non corrumpi, et ita erit incorruptibile.*" (*In I De caelo et Mundo*, lect. 29.)

The fourth way is taken from the gradation to be found in things. Among beings there are some more and some less good, true, noble, and the like. But *more* and *less* are predicated of different things according as they imitate in their different ways something which is the maximum, as a thing is said to be hotter according as it more nearly imitates that which is hottest; so that there is something which is truest, something best, something noblest, and, consequently, something which is most being, for those things that are most true are most fully being, as it is written in *Metaphysics,* ii. Now the maximum in any genus is the cause of all in that genus, as fire, which is the maximum of heat, is the cause of all hot things, as is said in the same book. Therefore there is something which is to all beings the cause of their "to be," goodness, and every other perfection; and this we call God.[59]

Analysis of the Text: The Fourth Way is a proof from exemplarity and, therefore, in the line of formal causality. It begins with the statement that the beings which are immediately known to us are many; consequently, their perfection is limited. Because limited, this perfection is participated. This is evident especially when we consider the order of the transcendentals. Each of the limited beings with which we come in contact is a participated true, a participated good, a participated being. But a participated reality supposes the existence of that which is unparticipated, that is, of a being which is absolute Truth, absolute Goodness, absolute Beauty, and, therefore, absolute Being. This reality we call God.

The argument may be put in syllogistic form thus:

The more or less are predicated of various things according as they resemble that which is absolute.

But we note that the things which exist around us are more or less true, more or less good, more or less being.

Therefore there exists a being which is absolute Goodness, absolute Truth, absolute Being, and that being is God.

The Principle of Exemplarity: Undoubtedly there must be in this argumentation an implicit principle which the major premise supposes, and upon which it rests. There is such a principle. We

---

[59] *S. Th.,* I, 2, 3, c.

shall call it the principle of exemplarity, and we shall express it thus: *Every limited perfection of the existent is a participation of the absolute which must exist.* The Angelic Doctor states this principle in several of his works, but in the knowledge of the author, he has never attempted to establish its truth; to St. Thomas it must have been evident. Indeed, he never discusses it, far less, questions its evidence; he simply affirms it. Let us quote his own words.

> Everything which is according to participation is reduced to something which is by its own essence.[60]

And again,

> Where something is found diversely participated by several things, it is necessary that, from that in which it is found most perfectly, it be attributed to all those in which it is found imperfectly.[61]
>
> For if something is found in something through participation, it is necessary that it is caused in it by that to which it belongs essentially.[62]
>
> For what is such by participation, and what is movable, and what is imperfect, always requires the pre-existence of something essentially such, immovable and perfect.[63]

If this principle is understood and accepted, the conclusion follows rigorously. It has been said that the acceptance of this principle depends upon a sort of quasi-intuition; it is certainly not a real intuition, for in understanding this principle, we do not *see* the unparticipated exemplar; rather, from the knowledge of participated beings which exist, we understand the necessity for the existence of the absolute.

Analysis of the Principle of Exemplarity: Although St. Thomas

---

[60] "*Omne quod est secundum participationem reducitur ad aliquid quod est per suam essentiam.*" (*In Ioannem Evangelistam Expositio, Prologus, in medio.*)

[61] "*Quum aliquid invenitur a pluribus diversimode participatum, oportet ab eo in quo perfectissime invenitur attribuatur omnibus illis, in quibus imperfectius invenitur.*" (*De Pot.*, III, 5.)

[62] "*Si enim aliquid invenitur in aliquo per participationem, necesse est quod causetur in ipso ab eo cui essentialiter convenit.*" (*S. Th.*, I, 44, 1, c.)

[63] "*Semper enim quod participat aliquid, et quod est mobile, et quod est imperfectum, praeexigit ante se aliquid, quod est per essentiam suam tale et quod est immobile et perfectum.*" (*S. Th.*, I, 79, 4, c.)

Christus   Father Robert L. Heim, C. S. Sp.

B-C 508

CHRIST, OUR MODEL AND FRIEND

"The mind may photograph Christ, but little spiritual meaning or comfort comes that way. Instead, we must stop and analyze Him, and paint on the canvas of the imagination such a picture of warm colors, lifelike motion, eloquent features and deep interpretation that the soul, gazing on it, walks again with Him through Palestine."

Fr. I. O'Brien.

EUGENE C. BRAUN

Ordained a Priest
May 1, 1957

has not given us a formal demonstration of this principle, it is possible by means of an analysis of the nature of exemplary causality to establish that this principle is self-evident.

To begin with, we should note that an exemplary cause supposes an intellectual agent. The reason is that an exemplary cause does not by its action produce an effect directly; rather, through the action of the efficient cause, and therefore only mediately, it determines the perfection, the intelligibility, the nature, of the effect. The perfection and intelligibility of an effect, as well as the finality which we observe in the various natures, manifest the necessity of an agent which is intellectual, which operates through intellect and will. The reason is that these two types of causality — exemplary and final — are in the intentional order, since they are the *effect as understood and willed*. Hence, the agent must needs be intellectual.

Consequently, no effect, no limited being, is intelligible without an exemplary cause which supposes an intellectual agent. The reason is that an agent which acts through intellect and will cannot act without the knowledge of the effect (exemplary causality) and without the will to produce the effect (final causality).

Beginning, then, with the experience and consideration of limited perfection which exists, we rise immediately to the need of an exemplary cause in an intellectual agent. Now, either this exemplary cause is identical with the agent, and then we speak of an absolute, unparticipated perfection which is pure existence, or the exemplary cause is distinct from the agent, and then the cause is another limited being, another participated perfection, and therefore another effect which demands another, a higher exemplary cause.

But because we cannot proceed *ad infinitum* in existential subordinated causes, we must conclude to a Supreme Exemplar which, being identical with the agent, is the absolute, unparticipated perfection we call God.

N.B.: We shall study in the treatise on the operations of God that knowledge of a possible effect is, in the intellect of God, the knowledge of an essence, a *ratio*. This knowledge is called an *exemplar* (exemplary cause) when connected with the will (efficient cause) which causes the existing effect.

Not a Proof From Efficient Causality: The Fourth Way has been a source of endless controversy among interpreters of the Angelic Doctor. Some have even asserted that this argumentation is not from exemplarity but from efficient causality as is evidenced from the second part of the proof. There, they explain, St. Thomas shows plainly that God is the efficient cause and, therefore, the First Exemplar. It is sufficient to read the Fourth Way to realize that St. Thomas says nothing of the kind. He points out, on the contrary, that the First Exemplar must be the efficient cause, a truth which he has repeatedly expressed in most of his works. The complete proof of the Fourth Way actually ends with the words, ". . . and consequently, something which is most being (*maxime ens*)." This is a definite affirmation of the existence of the Supreme Being. Having stated the conclusion of his argument, Aquinas proceeds to explain that the Supreme Exemplar is, of course, the Supreme Efficient Cause. And that is evident enough.

The Fourth Way and Platonism: It is undoubtedly true that the Fourth Way is related to Platonism. It is not, however, a Platonic argument put in scholastic terminology. Indeed it profoundly differs from the Platonic proofs of the supreme exemplars. Plato begins with the concept and ends with the idea; Thomas begins with existing reality and proves an existing God. The exemplar of Plato is a universal idea in which the individual is not understood, since the individual is not understandable. This Platonic exemplar causes an effect seemingly without an efficient cause. On the other hand, the exemplar according to St. Thomas is the *idea of the individual* in the intellect of God which God *wills* (efficient cause) to create. This idea, although identical with the divine "To Be" manifests the distinct individual, for it is the individual not the universal which is real and, therefore, intelligible. Plato remains in the world of essences; Thomas looks at the existential order and reaches the "to be." Plato's proof rests on a fundamental idealism; Thomas is a realist who loves existence.

It is true, the notion of participation in the Fourth Way signifies a fundamental exemplarity. And we are willing to grant that this is an element which Aquinas borrowed from Platonism; but how completely did the Christian theologian, with his knowledge of the fact of creation, transform the thought of Plato! No longer must we accept the notion of exemplarity from the point of view of a fundamental idealism, but we understand it with the profound insight of a Christian realism which is the philosophy of St. Thomas. That there is no lurking idealism in the Thomistic theory of participation appears from the fact that we do not consider a thought in the abstract and postulate, with Plato, its absolute existence; rather, we begin with the existing, concrete, sensible reality which has limited perfection, limited beauty, limited "to be." This existing reality manifests the Exemplar which is absolute perfection, infinite beauty, the *Maxime Ens*.

Not the Ontological Argument: For the same reason this proof differs from Anselm's ontological argument, which consists in concluding to the existence of God from the analysis of the concept of God. There is no analysis of the concept of God in the Fourth Way; there is only an affirmation of the existence of the perfect exemplar from the known fact of the existence of the exemplate.

ARTICLE V: The Fifth Way

The fifth way is taken from the governance of things. For we see that things which lack knowledge, such as natural bodies, act for an end which appears from this, that they act always or nearly always in the same way, so that they attain that which is best; whence it is clear that they arrive at their end not by chance, but by intention. Now those things which do not have knowledge do not tend toward an end unless they be directed by some being endowed with knowledge and intelligence; as the arrow is directed by the archer. Therefore some intelligent being exists by whom all natural things are directed to their end; and this being we call God.[64]

Analysis of the Text: The Fifth Way is the way of finality. It begins with the analysis of a nature, a corporeal being, *res naturae,* that is, of a limited being which, because it is a nature, a principle

---

[64] *S. Th.,* I, 2, 3, c.

of action, is necessarily ordered to its end.[65] Nature, St. Thomas explains, is endowed with a *natural*, a *necessary appetite* to its end. This is a philosophical law; we might call it a dynamic definition of nature. Because nature must seek its end, it does not possess it but is in potency to and distinct from the end. Now the most profound reason why such a nature is not identical with its end is that the essence and "to be" are really distinct. For if there were no such distinction, a nature would possess all perfection and would be, consequently, its own end. A *res naturae,* then, is necessarily ordered to a distinct end. Now determination to an end requires an intellect.[66] A limited nature, therefore, is not intelligible regarding its natural appetite to an end without an intellectual extrinsic agent which determines the nature to its end, and which, being its own existence, is its own end.

It might seem that St. Thomas leaves out a definite step in going from a nature which in its primary manifestation is a corporeal substance to an intellectual substance that is God. Why could not the extrinsic intellectual agent which determines finality in a corporeal nature be a limited intellect, such as an angel?

The reason is that a limited intellect is not its own end, because it is not its own "to be." Like the corporeal entity, when viewed in its most fundamental aspect, the limited intellect is a *res naturae* which is necessarily inclined to an end distinct from itself. This necessary inclination, whether known or not, is what we call the natural appetite. All limited natures have it; all finite beings, whether they know it or not, have a natural desire to their end. They are all *res naturae* in the most profound sense. The stone tends necessarily to fall to the ground, the tree to grow and bear fruit, the intellect to know, the will to love. Even man, possessing as he does the freedom of judgment (*liberum arbitrium*), can choose what he may know and whom he may love; but he cannot destroy the natural appetite of his intellect to know the

---

[65] This important truth, *a nature is necessarily ordered to its end,* was discussed in *The Philosophy of Being,* p. 146.

[66] Cf. *ibid.,* p. 148. The end is in the order of intention, that is, of intellect and will, for it is the effect *as desired.*

truth nor the natural appetite of his will to love the good. He is necessarily ordered to his end by the appetite of his nature. The reason for this fundamental urge is, as we have stated, that he is not his existence. He is limited and, therefore, necessarily ordered to an end. Any limited intellectual nature, then, no matter how perfect, is not its own end. It cannot even determine that end. But, as a *res naturae,* it has a profound and necessary determination to the end; and for such a determination it must depend upon a higher intellectual agent.

Because, however, an infinite series of existentially subordinated causes is impossible, we must affirm the existence of an extrinsic intellectual agent which is in no way a *res naturae:* an intellectual agent which does not seek its own end because, being its own "To Be," it is its own end. This is God, the Final Cause of all finite nature, the End of all reality.

Argument: We may state the argument thus:

All finite natures (including limited intellects) have necessarily determined natural appetites to an extrinsic end.

But a necessary determination to an extrinsic end is not intelligible without an intellectual agent which is its own end.

Therefore, there exists an intellect which is its own end, because it is its own "To Be," and that is God.

N.B.: St. Thomas points out that the Fifth Way is founded upon the notion of governance (*gubernatio*) of things. The word "government" has sometimes been misunderstood because, no doubt, of our modern usage. In such a notion, St. Thomas does not consider precisely the efficient action of those who govern, but presents the idea of natural inclination of the thing governed to a determined end. This natural inclination is, as we have explained, the formality under which the Fifth Way establishes the existence of God.

It would appear from many textbooks that the Fifth Way is often presented from a different point of view. The element stressed in these treatises is not the order, the natural appetite, which any nature has necessarily to an end; it is not the "to be desired" which is the essential aspect of finality; but it is, rather, the efficient action of a supreme cause. With St. Thomas, even if there were only one finite nature, we could argue to and prove with metaphysical certitude the existence of a being that is its own end. St. Thomas argues that the appetite of nature to its end is not intelligible without a supreme nature which has no appetite to its end, because it is its own end. With these authors, on the contrary, such is not the case. They argue, not from the appetite of a nature, but from the admirable complexity of the created world. Beginning with the stars and planets and coming down to the infinitesimal atom and electron, they describe in long and beautifully written pages the grandeur of the universe and its marvelous order. Once we have been duly impressed by such poetical magnificence, they proceed to an argument from scientific analogy. Just as, they reason, the complexity of a watch demands a watchmaker gifted with some intelligence, just as the order of the city demands some capable policemen, just as the skyscraper supposes some architect or other, so *a fortiori* does this marvelous order of the world postulate a God.

This is an impressive argument and quite satisfying to a certain type of mind. We should like to state, however, (1) that it is by no means the Fifth Way of St. Thomas; (2) that, while we are willing to grant that this argument establishes a God who is a super-watchmaker, a super-policeman, a super-architect, we cannot help but wonder whether such a super-being is its own end, because it is its own "To Be" or, in other words, whether such a being is God.

Conclusion

The Five Ways Establish That the Most Profound, the Most Radical Expression of the Whatness of God, of His Essence, Is Subsisting "To Be": As a necessary deduction from the conclusions of the Five Ways, we must affirm with St. Thomas that God is the Subsisting "To Be." The essence of God, therefore, is the "To Be."

The most fundamental, the most profound, the most radical

knowledge that we have of God is that His essence is "To Be."[67] Upon this great truth we must base whatever else we may learn about the essence of God. Any additional knowledge which we may derive from the consideration of created perfections can be affirmed of God only in so far as we understand this fundamental fact that His essence is "To Be." For whatever we attribute in truth (*secundum veritatem*) to God, must be predicated of a subject which is the "To Be."

The "To Be" belongs to God according to His nature. Hence the "To Be" of God is His substance. The proper name of God, then, is *He Who Is,* because to Him alone is it proper that His substance be His "To Be."[68] This is the sublime truth, points out St. Thomas, which was revealed to Moses when he asked the Lord God what His name was. And the Lord answered: "I am Who am. . . . Tell them, 'He Who Is sent me to you.'" The true name of God, therefore, is He Who Is. Now, a name signifies a nature, that is, it signifies the essence of a being. Hence the nature or essence of God is "To Be."[69]

Obviously such an affirmation could be made only by a pure existentialist. It is not surprising, then, that many philosophers do not admit that the most profound, the most radical, the most pregnant understanding of God's essence is that it is "To Be." The reason is that these writers are essentialists; hence they fail to grasp the meaning of this all-embracing truth. It is because of this essentialism that these authors place the first constitutive note

---

[67] Scholastic writers term such a knowledge "the metaphysical essence" of God. The word "metaphysical" does not seem a happy choice. We prefer to say with St. Thomas, *"Essentia Dei est esse."* That is quite enough.

[68] *"Ipsum esse competit primo agenti secundum propriam naturam: Esse enim Dei est eius substantia. . . . Hinc est quod Exodi III, 14 proprium nomen Dei ponitur esse Qui Est, quia eius solius proprium est quod sua substantia non sit aliud quam suum esse."* (C.G., II, c. 52.)

[69] *"Hanc autem sublimem veritatem Moyses a Domino est edoctus: qui cum quaereret a Domino, Exod. III, 13, 14, dicens: Si dixerint ad me filii Israel, Quod nomen eius? Quid dicam eis? Dominus respondit: Ego sum qui sum. Sic dices filiis Israel: Qui est misit me ad vos, ostendens suum proprium nomen esse Qui Est. Quodlibet autem nomen est institutum ad significandum naturam seu essentiam alicuius rei. Unde relinquitur quod ipsum divinum esse est sua essentia vel natura."* (C.G., I, c. 22.)

of the essence of God in various other perfections such as immutability, aseity, infinity, eternity, and the like. These philosophers, having failed to understand that existence is the supreme perfection,[70] cannot realize that any perfection which we attribute to God is divine because identical with the Subsisting "To Be."

We grant, of course, that without a thorough understanding of the metaphysics of St. Thomas, without an understanding of the limitation of act by potency and of the real distinction between essence and "to be" in creatures, the fact that God is the *Ipsum Esse Subsistens* would seem of little or no importance.

In order to prepare us to face the problem of our knowledge of the attributes of God, let us recall briefly the conclusions of the Five Ways in terms of God's essence.[71]

1. In God there is no potency; there is nothing but pure act, and that is "To Be." God's essence, then, is His "To Be."[72]

2. Any being whose essence is not the "to be" must be caused by another. Because, however, God is the uncaused cause, His essence is the "To Be."[73]

3. A being which is not its "to be" cannot be an absolutely necessary being, since its necessity is not from its essence but from another. Because God is absolutely (*per se*) necessary, His essence is His "To Be."[74]

4. A participated being does not exist by its essence but by participation. But God, the Supreme Exemplar, is unparticipated.

---

[70] "*Esse est perfectio perfectionum.*" (*De Pot.*, VII, 2, ad 9^m.)

[71] *C.G.*, I, c. 22; cf. *S. Th.*, I, 3, 4.

[72] "*Si ergo divina essentia est aliud quam suum esse, sequitur quod essentia et esse se habeant sicut potentia et actus. Ostensum est autem in Deo nihil esse de potentia, sed ipsum esse purum actum. Non igitur Dei essentia est aliud quam suum esse.*" (*C.G.*, I, c. 22.)

[73] "*Si autem illi conveniat per aliquam aliam causam; omne autem quod acquirit esse ab alia causa, est causatum et non est causa prima; Deus autem est prima causa non habens causam, ut supra demonstratum est; igitur ista quidditas quae acquirit esse aliunde, non est quidditas Dei. Necesse est igitur quod Dei esse quidditas sua sit.*" (*Loc. cit.*)

[74] "*Unumquodque est per suum esse. Quod igitur non est suum esse, non est per se necesse esse. Deus autem est per se necesse esse. Ergo Deus est suum esse.*" (*Loc. cit.*)

Therefore, God exists by His essence; that is, God's essence is "To Be."[75]

5. Finally, the supreme end, the "why" of all existing beings, must be an intellectual nature which is pure existence. God's essence is "To Be."

Scholion

Atheism: Is it possible for one to be a sincere atheist? To answer this we must first of all understand what we mean by the term "atheist." An atheist in general is one who does not admit that there exists a supreme being whom we call God and who is the cause of all reality. This definition, however, is susceptible of various interpretations in its application. Let us, then, distinguish between various types of atheists.

In general, we may speak of *practical* and *theoretical* atheists. The first class admit God, but their lives are altogether at variance with their knowledge. They live as if there were no God. There is no metaphysical problem regarding these. Theirs is a moral difficulty.

We are concerned with the *theoretical* atheists who do not admit God in their minds and hearts. There are various types of these.

1. The *negative* atheists are those who simply do not know that there is a God. The reason is that they have not reached the age of reason and have not been told about God. Just when it is that an individual reaches the age of reason is a matter which has been widely discussed and about which there are various opinions that need not be discussed in this treatise.

2. The *positive* atheist who does not admit God is either a *dogmatic* atheist or an *agnostic*. The dogmatic atheist denies the existence of a supreme being and tries by means of sophistical argument to prove his point. The *agnostic* or *skeptic* claims ig-

---

[75] *"Omnis res est per hoc quod habet esse. Nulla igitur res cuius essentia non est suum esse, est per essentiam suam, sed participatione alicuius, scilicet ipsius esse. Quod autem est per participationem alicuius, non potest esse primum ens: quia id quod aliquid participat ad hoc quod sit, est eo prius. Deus autem est primum ens, quo nihil est prius. Dei igitur essentia est suum esse."* (*Loc. cit.*)

norance and uncertainty. He affirms that there is no valid argument for the proof of the existence of God.

The question may be asked, is it possible for a man of intelligence to deny in his mind the existence of God? The answer is yes, this is quite possible. The reason is that the fact of God's existence is not immediately evident to us. Consequently, there is always the possibility of an imprudent doubt which can be bolstered by the act of the will. The will of man can freely move the intellect to consider sophistical arguments. A denial of God's existence is the conclusion.

Moralists agree in stating that positive atheism is not without guilt. The question of moral obligation is discussed at length in ethics, and we shall not consider it here.

CHAPTER II

MAN'S KNOWLEDGE OF THE ESSENCE OF GOD

Prologue

The problem of man's knowledge of the essence of God is discussed in the *Summa Theologica* from question III to question XIV. The discussion is a unit and should be studied as a unified whole. The order followed by St. Thomas is: (1) What the essence of God is not (questions III to XII). (2) Why cannot man have a connatural knowledge of the essence of God (question XII)? (3) What do we understand when we predicate directly of God perfections which we discover in creatures (question XIII)?

It would be difficult to read intelligently some of the articles in the first section (questions III through XI) unless we already possessed a fundamental knowledge of the principles proposed in the twelfth and thirteenth questions, for while explaining what God is not, St. Thomas often states what He is. Because of this, it seems advisable that there be presented first a general introduction to the problem of our knowledge of God's essence in which the unity of the treatise is stressed, the fundamental principles are stated, and an approach to the solution is indicated. After this introduction, some of the more important attributes will be analyzed briefly.

Having demonstrated in the Five Ways that God is first mover, uncaused cause, pure act, unparticipated existence, and the end of all things, it is not difficult for us to establish that the various perfections called the divine attributes are properly said of Him, that He is simple, infinite, immutable, and the like. Indeed, these attributes may easily be inferred from the fact that the essence of God is "To Be." Hence in the treatise on the attributes of God, after such inferences, St. Thomas devotes his best efforts to solving a far more difficult question. It is this: what do we really understand when we say that God is simple, infinite, immutable, and the like? The purpose of this chapter, then, is to endeavor to understand, in so far as we can, the whatness of God, that is, the divine essence.

Question I

GENERAL PRINCIPLES

This question is divided into three articles: (1) Can we have a true and positive knowledge of God's essence? (2) Just what do we understand when we attribute a perfection to God? (3) What sort of analogy does such predication imply?

ARTICLE I: Can We Know the Essence of God?

The Problem: Is man capable of knowing what God is? Is it possible for the human intellect to arrive by its own natural resources at a true knowledge of God's essence? We know, of course, that God's essence is "To Be"; hence whatever we attribute to God by direct predication in answer to the question, "What is God?" is identified with absolute existence. Does such predication give us any true knowledge of God; or, to put it succinctly, can we understand the essence of God?

To this question St. Thomas gives a clear and decisive answer: "We cannot know what God is but only what He is not."[1] This knowledge, however, although negative, is not futile, for it enables us to distinguish God from other beings; although imperfect, this knowledge is true and precious, for it enables us to do away with many false notions about God.

---

[1] *S. Th.,* I, 3, *Proemium.*

Difficulty: As we examine this clear-cut statement that we can only know what God is not, we are faced with a difficulty. It is this: there is no such thing as purely negative knowledge, since any negation presupposes an affirmation. We say, for example, that Peter is not an ass because he is a man. In like manner, when we deny that God is composed of parts, we affirm at least implicitly that He is simple; when we reject any limitation, any imperfection in His essence, we conclude that He is infinite and absolutely perfect. It would seem, then, that our knowledge of God's essence is not merely negative.

To make matters worse, St. Thomas himself affirms repeatedly, and sometimes immediately after stating that we cannot know what the divine essence is in itself, that we know God by way of causality, and supereminence.[2] Indeed he devotes an entire question to the divine names, that is, to the perfections that can be predicated of God directly.

Two Types of Knowledge, Connatural and Non-Proper:[3] In order to understand the solution of this arduous question, we should explain that in finite beings there are two distinct types of knowledge, depending on the mode of existence of the object. If the mode of existence of the object is proportioned to that of the knowing subject, that is, if they are both of the same species or of the same proximate genus (e.g., corporeal substances), then the knowledge is natural (*connaturalis*) and proper; that is, the object can be known *as it is in itself*. If, on the other hand, the mode of existence of the object is superior to the existential perfection of the subject, then the knowledge is not connatural but non-proper, that is, it is obtained indirectly from the knowledge of beings whose mode of existence is proportioned and connatural to the knower. Accordingly, we do not understand the object as

---

[2] Cf. *S. Th.*, I, 12, 12; I, 13, 1; I, 13, 8, ad 2m.

[3] By *connatural knowledge* of man we mean the knowledge of the proper object of the intellect of man, namely knowledge of material essences. By *non-proper knowledge* of man we mean the imperfect and indirect knowledge of an object not proportioned to the intellect of man, e.g., knowledge of an immaterial essence.

it is in itself. This knowledge is indirect, imperfect, and it is called non-proper knowledge.[4]

No Positive Connatural Knowledge of God's Essence: St. Thomas points out that we can never have connatural knowledge of the essence of God as It is in Itself. The most profound reason for this fact is, of course, that the essence of God is "To Be." Now even a limited "to be" cannot be grasped by the human intellect. At best we affirm it in the existential judgment as the actuation of an essence.[5] We know, of course, that existence is the perfection of perfections; we know that the essence of God is pure existence; but the knowledge resulting from such an affirmation could in no way be called connatural knowledge. The reason is this: the human intellect is primarily a passive potency; it needs to be actuated by an intelligible species in order to give forth the act of knowledge. Now no created intelligible species which is the natural actuation of the human intellect is its own "to be." Hence, no created form can properly represent God's essence which is pure existence. Consequently, the intellect of man is not capable of arriving naturally at a proper and positive knowledge of God's essence.[6]

This argument is presented in the *Summa Theologica*, I, 12, 4. Knowledge, St. Thomas points out, is had according as the known is in the knower. Now the known is in the knower according to the manner of existing of the knower, since whatever is received in a subject is received in accordance with the mode of being of the receiver. Hence, if the manner of existing of the known is

---

[4] Such is our knowledge of things spiritual. (Cf. Henri Renard, S.J., *The Philosophy of Man* [Milwaukee: Bruce, 1948], p. 151.) Although this knowledge is partly negative, e.g., an immaterial substance is a substance that is not material, nevertheless the concept of such a substance is not merely negative, for it indicates a very great perfection, namely, independence from matter in its mode of existing. The concept obtained is then positively predicated of the subject. It is positive knowledge of the subject but not connatural knowledge. To give an example, we do not know the soul directly, that is, by means of an intelligible species proportioned to the nature of the soul, but only through our knowledge of material essences.

[5] *Ibid.*, p. 145.

[6] "Connatural" and "non-proper" knowledge refer primarily to the concept. "Positive" and "negative" knowledge refer to the judgment which is affirmative or negative.

superior to that of the knower, it becomes known not as the known *is* in itself, but in accordance with the manner of existing of the knower.

Now God's mode of existence is that He is "To Be." On the other hand, not only is man not his "to be," but his soul is the substantial form of matter. Hence, the only objects which we know connaturally, that is, according to their proper mode of existing, are material essences.

It is clear, then, that to know God by a knowledge that is connatural l̶ ̶ ̶ ̶ ̶s̶ ̶ to God alone. No created intellect, no matter how perfect ̶ ̶ ̶ ̶ ̶ ̶own "to be" but has a participated "to be," ca ̶ ̶ ̶ ̶ ̶ the divine essence as It is in It̶

Negativ̶ ̶ ̶ clude: Because
it is imp̶ ̶ ̶nnaturally at a
knowled̶ ̶ ̶lows — and this
is extrer̶ ̶ ̶wledge we have
about t̶ ̶ ̶aturally must be
simply̶ ̶ ̶understand what
St. T̶ ̶ 'We cannot know
the d̶ ̶ t It is," and, "We
cann̶ ̶ ̶."8

P̶ ̶ can arrive at a true
but̶ ̶ 'by way of *eminence*,

---

7 In ̶ ̶ ̶ ̶ ̶ are able to contemplate the essence of God as it ̶ ̶ ̶ ̶r, is not connatural to man but results from a supernatural ̶ ̶ ̶

8 This is simply true of any corporeal per̶ ̶ ̶ since such a perfection necessarily implies limitation. God is simply not that. "Although in the remotion of some (predicates) from God, the predication of the same of God by eminence and causality is simultaneously understood; nevertheless some perfections are only denied of God and in no way predicated, as when it is said, 'God is not a body.' " (*De Pot.*, IX, 7, ad 2ᵐ.) "There are some names which signify these perfections flowing from God to creatures in such a way that the imperfect manner in which creatures receive the divine perfection is part of the very signification of the name itself, as *stone* signifies a material being; and names of this kind can be applied to God only in a metaphorical sense." (*S. Th.*, I, 13, 3, ad 1ᵐ.)

causality, and *negation.*"[9] "We can be led from the effects of God to what must necessarily belong to Him as the First Cause of all things *caused* by Him, because His effects are *removed* from Him as the cause of all things, *exceeding* all things caused by Him."[10] We are able, therefore, from our knowledge of creatures, to rise to a positive knowledge of the divine essence. This knowledge is, of course, not connatural but non-proper, that is, it results not from an immediate vision of the divine essence but from our knowledge of created perfections. In order to predicate of God the perfections which we discover in creatures, we must remove from them all limitation, all imperfection, and attribute them to their supreme cause by identification with the "To Be."

SUMMARY—ARTICLE I: Can We Know the Essence of God?

After distinguishing clearly between our *connatural* or *proper* knowledge of corporeal beings, and the *non-proper* knowledge of immaterial perfections, a knowledge which is imperfect and in-direct, we may state:

1. Problem: Can we know the essence of God?

2. Answer.

a) We have only negative knowledge of God's essence as it is in itself, i.e., we must deny that we have *proper* and *connatural* knowledge of the divine perfections.

b) We have positive knowledge of God's essence, not as it is in itself but by a knowledge that is indirect, imperfect, because it is *non-proper.*

3. Explanation.

a) We can never attribute to the divine essence the material

---

[9] *S. Th.,* I, 13, 8, ad 2^m.
[10] *S. Th.,* I, 12, 12, c. "God is known by us from creatures because of a relation to their principle and also by way of excellence and remotion." (I, 13, 1, c.)

perfections of the creatures which we know connaturally. We must always deny that God is material. This we call our *negative* knowledge of God.

b) We can, however, predicate of God's essence the *non-proper* knowledge of immaterial perfections which we obtained indirectly. In doing so, it is necessary to remove from our concept of such perfections the limitations of the creature. This is our positive but non-proper knowledge of the essence of God.

c) There are, therefore, three steps to be observed in our positive knowledge of God's essence:

1) *Causality.* God is the cause of this perfection.
2) *Remotion.* We must remove the limitation found in created perfection.
3) *Supereminence.* In predicating this perfection directly of God's essence, we identify it with pure existence and thereby affirm its absolute perfection.

The deeper signification of the knowledge resulting from such predication will be examined in the following article.

ARTICLE II: The Divine Names

The Problem: What do we understand when we predicate directly a perfection of the essence of God, that is, when we affirm that God is this; or, to use the language of St. Thomas, what do we mean when we name God?

The Divine Names: We name an object by means of a judgment when we attribute to it a perfection expressed by a word. We say that Peter is a boy; that Peter is wise. Words, however, are signs of the things understood. They manifest our concepts, and these are the images of reality: words, then, manifest our knowledge. We are able to name a thing according to the knowledge which we possess. Now since our knowledge of God is obtained from creatures, it follows that any name we attribute to God does not express the divine essence as It is in Itself. What, then, do we understand by such predication?

This difficulty is rendered more acute if we consider that God's essence is pure existence. Existence, however, is not intelligible to us. We cannot have a true concept of the "to be," since the proper object of man's intellect is material essences. We reach some sort of knowledge of existence only in the existential judgment in which we affirm that an individual supposit exists.[11] What of the essence of God which is "To Be"? What knowledge can we have of such an essence, and what does the affirmation which states the identity of a predicate, a given perfection, with the subject, Pure Existence, signify? We know that every true affirmative proposition — in which God is the subject — is a pure judgment of existence. We affirm Existence of Itself. What does that mean?

Erroneous Solutions: Various answers have been given to this question. Two especially must be examined and refuted before we can propose a true solution.

Maimonides (1135-1204) thought that these names or perfections are attributed to God only in order to remove some imperfection; they do not in any way affirm a perfection in God. When we declare, for example, that God is a living being, we mean to say only that He is not an inanimate being. What life really is in God we do not see and cannot know. Such an opinion is, of course, fundamentally that of an agnostic. St. Thomas attacks it vigorously in several of his works. It will be sufficient to state that this erroneous position leads us to deny that we can have any knowledge of God. It denies implicitly, at least, that God is Being.

The other opinion is widespread and seems to have found favor even with several Neo-Thomists. It may be stated thus: any predication of a perfection indicates only that God is the cause of that perfection. Our knowledge of God, then, is nothing more than an affirmation of divine causality. God is good because He is the cause of the goodness of creatures. Beyond this fact, to attribute goodness to Him is meaningless.

---

[11] Cf. *The Philosophy of Man*, p. 145.

This last position is not reasonable. In the first place, if all that we learn from attributing a perfection to God is that God is its cause, since God is the cause of all perfection, we should have to predicate of Him every perfection even when it implies in its very definition the fact of participation and, therefore, of limitation. We should have to say not only that God is good because He causes goodness, but that He is a body because He is the cause of bodies.

St. Thomas proposes a second and more profound argument. In the analogy in which we predicate various attributes of God and creature, God is necessarily the prime analogate. Now if it were true that when we predicate a perfection of God we do so merely because He is the cause and not because that perfection is in Him, then in the analogy between God and creatures, God would not be the prime analogate. For in the analogy between healthy drug and healthy man, we attribute health to the drug, not because it has health but because it causes health and, therefore, not as the first analogate (*non per prius sed per posterius*).[12] Likewise in this case any perfection (e.g., intelligence) would be predicated of God not because He has intelligence but merely because He causes intelligence in man. Indeed we would have to deny that God is being, since He is the cause of all beings. Finally, if God is being, to deny that we can know even imperfectly what He is is to deny that being is intelligible.

Another reason for rejecting both errors mentioned above is that either position will lead us into skepticism, for if we understand that God is not what we say He is, then direct predication is meaningless. This argument is a clear statement of Thomas' objective realism regarding the truth of the judgment.

We do not affirm, therefore, that God is good merely because

---

[12] This is a clear indication that when St. Thomas, in a following article (article five), uses the example of the analogy of health to explain the analogy between God and creature, he in no way intends to affirm that the analogy between God and creature is an analogy of attribution; for in such an analogy the creature would be the first analogate (*per prius*). He merely wishes to indicate that the analogy between God and creature must express causality as that of health when affirmed of the drug.

He causes goodness in creatures; rather we say that because God is good, He is the cause of goodness in creatures.

Conclusions: Consequently, we must state that: (1) These names *really signify* the divine essence. (2) They are predicated directly and therefore *attributed substantially* to God's essence. (3) They fail, however, *to represent* the divine essence as It is in Itself. Just as creatures represent God imperfectly, so these names — which are derived from our knowledge of creatures — represent the divine essence imperfectly.

> Therefore we must hold . . . that these names signify the divine substance and are predicated substantially of God, although they are deficient as representations of Him. Which is proved thus. These names signify God so far as our intellects know Him. Now since our intellect knows God from creatures, it knows Him as far as creatures represent Him. But it was shown above that God, as simply and universally perfect, prepossesses in Himself all the perfections of creatures. Hence every creature represents Him and is like Him, so far as it possesses some perfection, yet not so as to represent Him as something of the same species or genus but as the excelling source from whose form the effects fall short, although they have some likeness thereto, even as the forms of inferior bodies represent the power of the sun. . . . Therefore, the aforesaid names signify the divine substance, but imperfectly, as creatures also represent it imperfectly. Consequently, when we say, "God is good," the meaning is not, "God is the cause of goodness," or, "God is not evil"; but the meaning is, "That goodness which we predicate of creatures pre-exists in God, and in a higher way." Hence it does not follow that God is good because He causes goodness; but rather, on the contrary, He causes goodness in things because He is good. As Augustine says, "Because He is good, we are."[13]

Corollaries

1. Our Knowledge Is Not Merely of a Causal Relation: We do not deny, of course, that our affirmation of the various names results from knowledge of causality, of the fact that all created perfections proceed from Him who is their cause. But we hasten

---

[13] *S. Th.*, I, 13, 2, c.

to add that, having removed the limitation of the created perfection, what we affirm primarily in the affirmative proposition is not causality but *what* God really is. Because, however, of the mode of representation which is that of creature, our affirmative proposition is an expression of a knowledge not connatural but imperfect. For the intelligible species in the human intellect can represent only a created perfection.

2. Both Concrete and Abstract Predication: Because of this imperfect mode of representation, we attribute to God both concrete and abstract names; e.g., we say that God is wise and that He is Wisdom. In this twofold predication, the concrete name is used to signify His subsistence and perfection, because a concrete name is predicated of a subsisting being; the abstract name is used to signify His simplicity. Both names, however, fail to express His mode of existing, for such a mode is truly beyond our comprehension.[14]

3. Not Metaphorically but Truly Attributed to God: We insist, therefore, that these names — which in themselves do not signify participation and, therefore, limitation and which are attributed to God both as concrete or as abstract denominations — are not predicated of Him metaphorically but are truly attributed to Him. Indeed, if we distinguish between what these names signify and the manner or mode of signification, we must declare that each of these perfections is attributed more properly to God than to creatures,[15] for we declare that God *is* this perfection; God *is* Wisdom, whereas man has wisdom only as an accidental form.[16]

4. Not Repetitious: The various names which we attribute to God are not repetitious; they are not synonymous, for they enable us to understand the essence of God more completely though in an imperfect manner. The intelligible content varies with each predication. It is true, in each predication we affirm the identity

---

[14] Cf. *S. Th.*, I, 13, 1, ad 2[m].

[15] By "proper," here, we do not mean proper or connatural knowledge but that which truly and "properly" belongs to a subject, as opposed to "metaphorically." In other words, these perfections are attributed absolutely to God.

[16] *S. Th.*, I, 13, 1, c.

of each predicate with the subsisting "To Be." But these various perfections are intelligible to us and, therefore, their intelligible content gives us a more complete though imperfect understanding of the essence of God. It is as if we viewed the same object from different points of vantage. St. Thomas has these illuminating words: ". . . And although these names which are attributed to God signify one identical being, nevertheless, because they signify this being under various aspects [*sub rationibus multis et diversis*], they are not synonymous."[17]

S U M M A R Y — ARTICLE II: The Divine Names

1. Problem: What does a direct predication of a perfection (a name) mean regarding the divine essence?

2. Error: The direct predication of a perfection is not a mere indication of causality in God; nor does it signify that we remove a certain imperfection from God. Such theories lead to agnosticism and skepticism, for they imply either that God is not being or that being is not intelligible.

3. Solution: This direct predication:

  a) Signifies God's essence;

  b) Implies a substantial predication;

  c) Represents God according to the mode of creatures.

4. Corollaries.

  a) We do not deny causality as the initial moment of our search, but in the predication we do not merely affirm causality. We come to a true, albeit imperfect, non-proper knowledge of the divine essence.

  b) In an effort to express the perfection of the divine essence, we make use of abstract as well as concrete predication.

  c) This knowledge is not metaphorical. The perfection is more truly affirmed of God than of the creature.

---

[17] *S. Th.,* I, 13, 4, c.

d) This knowledge is not repetitious. It signifies God under various aspects.

ARTICLE III: The Analogy of the Divine Names

Problem: In the preceding article, when we established the substantial predication of the names of God, we proposed a distinction between *what* the names signify and their *mode of representation.* The question now is what is the meaning of such a predication in which, although the perfection is truly and substantially attributed to the essence of God, the manner of representation in the concept is that of the creature. In order to clarify our understanding of this statement, St. Thomas proposes the celebrated question of the analogy by means of which the same name, the same perfection, is attributed to God and to creatures in a different manner.

There are, as everyone knows, three ways in which the same term may be predicated of various subjects: univocal, equivocal, and analogous predication.

Not Univocal: Now it is obvious that these perfections are not attributed to God and to creatures univocally. The reason is that whenever an effect which does not equal the virtue of an agent receives the similitude of an agent, its likeness to the agent fails in its content to reproduce the perfection of the agent.[18] For example, in stating that God is wise and man is wise, I imply that wisdom in God is identical with His essence because of His simplicity, while in man it is a distinct accident. Hence in God wisdom exceeds the signification of human wisdom. That is why the same name when predicated of creatures defines and comprehends the perfection predicated, while when predicated of God it leaves the perfection not fully understood (*incomprehensus*).

---

[18] God is the cause of the perfection of the creature, that is, the cause of the complete form with its "to be." If, then, the perfection were predicated univocally, this would indicate that the form is in both analogates according to the same species. Now no being can cause a complete existing form similar in species to its own. Moreover, since God is "To Be," He is not under any genus. Hence any direct predication which identifies a perfection with absolute existence cannot be in any species.

Such a signified perfection — which is made identical with the "to be" in an affirmative proposition — transcends the meaning of the word used, because it transcends our connatural knowledge. Clearly then, when we predicate wisdom of God and of man, we do not predicate it univocally. For wisdom in God is "To Be," while in man it is an accidental perfection.

Not Equivocal: Nor can such predication be purely equivocal. This truth was established when we refuted the error of Maimonides. Let us recall that the foundation for such refutation is the objective realism of Thomas to whom the fact that being is intelligible is fundamental. Now God is being. To deny this, of course, is to affirm agnosticism; and in the last analysis, it is an implicit assertion of skepticism.

Analogous: The predication of the same perfection, when attributed to God and creatures, cannot be univocal or equivocal. We conclude, therefore, that such predication must be analogous.

The question of analogy in general has been sufficiently discussed in the philosophy of being.[19] There are, however, several points regarding the analogy between God and creature which require further explanation.

Every analogous predication supposes some sort of similarity between the various subjects of predication and, in our case, between God and creatures. Indeed in an analogous predication, the predicate which is attributed to the various subjects is said to be "simply different and somewhat the same." It is evident, of course, that a predicate which is identified on the one hand with subsisting existence, and on the other is shown to be really distinct from the "to be" has to be *simply different*. In order to clarify our knowledge of God's essence, we are interested, of course, in determining as exactly as we can just what is meant by the phrase "somewhat the same." Hence, before giving our definite solution, we should like to indicate, first, the foundation for the likeness of the creature to God; second, the nature of this similarity.

The Foundation for Similarity: The foundation for the similarity

---

[19] Cf. *The Philosophy of Being*, p. 92.

between creatures and God is due to two facts: first, God is the analogous[20] cause of all created reality; second, and the most profound reason, God is His own "To Be."

1. Because an agent must be in act in order to act, it follows that all the perfections of creatures must be found in God, their efficient principle. Now God cannot be a univocal cause, since He is not in any genus.[21] He is, therefore, an analogous cause. Hence, the perfections of creatures must be in God, their analogous cause, eminently, that is, in a far more perfect manner.

2. The perfection of perfections is the "to be." Other perfections are limited, participated modes of existence, for they are perfections precisely, as St. Thomas puts it, because they have "to be" in some respect.[22] Therefore, God possesses the perfections of all creatures absolutely. This is the foundation for the similarity between God and creatures.

The Nature of This Similarity: Now in what does this similarity consist? Any similitude (likeness) supposes some sort of communication of *form*. Sometimes the form which is communicated is of the same species or, at least, of the same genus. In such a case, the same perfection is attributed to various subjects in a univocal manner. Sometimes, however — and this happens in the case of analogous agents — the perfection which is communicated is not of the same genus. In such a case, the perfections will need to be attributed to the various subjects by means of an analogy. Thus, the likeness will not be a univocal but an analogous similarity. The similarity here, then, consists in an *analogous communication of form*.

Analogy of Proportionality: St. Thomas adds these significant

---

[20] The word "equivocal" is sometimes used by the medievalists in the sense of analogous. As a rule they distinguish two types of equivocation: one which they call "chance equivocation" (*a casu*), and it is absolute equivocation; the other is had by design (*a consilio*), and it is precisely what we generally term "analogy." This should be kept in mind when interpreting the text of St. Thomas.

[21] God is not in a genus, because He is "To Be." (Cf. *S. Th.,* I, 3, 4.)

[22] All perfections are a participation in the "To Be." They are limited modes of existing, and their perfection is in accordance with the "to be" which they limit. Indeed the reason why a being is not necessarily a living being, a wise being, is the limitation of the "to be." (Cf. *S. Th.,* I, 4, 2, ad 3m.)

words which indicate that the analogy referred to in the case of God and creatures is one of proportionality, that is, the analogy in which all predication of perfections to the first analogate is had by identity with the subsisting "To Be." The form which is communicated is identical with existence in God. It is, therefore, infinite, absolutely perfect. In creatures, it is distinct from the "to be." It is therefore a limited, a participated form. This is what we call the analogy of proportionality.

> . . . If there is some agent which is not contained in a genus, its effects will still more remotely approach to a likeness of the form of the agent, not, that is, so as to participate in the likeness of the agent's form according to the same specific or generic formality, but only according to some analogy, just as *existence is common to all.* In this way, those things which are from God are assimilated to Him, in so far as they are beings, as to the *first* and *universal principle of the whole "to be."*[23]

These words clearly imply that any perfection which is predicated of the essence of God is identified with "To Be." In creatures, on the other hand, all perfections, whether substantial or accidental, are really distinct from existence. This is a clear expression of what we call the analogy of proportionality.[24]

The Analogy of Proportionality Is Based Upon an Existential Judgment in the First Analogate: The analogy of proportionality — in which the first analogate is pure existence — is not had by means of changes in the concept of the perfection which is predicated of the various analogates. It is found in a judgment which only in the first analogate must express identity between subject and predicate. Since God is "To Be," this identity is expressed by the judgment of existence. In other words, the most profound reason for this analogy lies in the fact that *any direct predication in which the subject is the "To Be" indicates existential identity,* that is to say, the perfection is identified with "To Be." Consequently, our knowledge of God must remain imperfect, for our

---

[23] *S. Th.,* I, 4, 3, c.
[24] Cf. *The Philosophy of Being,* p. 92 ff.

intellect, proportioned as it is to the knowledge of material essences, can never comprehend such existential identity.

This Analogy Can Be Found Only Between God and Creatures: It appears from this that the analogy by means of which the same perfection is attributed to God and to creatures is unique: it is an analogy which can be had only between God and creatures. Only regarding the subject, God, can we have an existential judgment of identity; and consequently, only by means of the analogy of proportionality can we truly predicate a perfection of God and man. Hence any other type of analogy between creatures which may be proposed to explain predication of perfections of God and creatures is used only as an example and to explain a phase of this predication. It cannot be the true analogy between God and creatures, for the analogy of proportionality, from its very nature, can be found only between God and creatures.

The Analogy of Proportionality Presupposes an Implicit Judgment Between the Terms of the Predicate: It may well be asked how the predication of perfection which is attributed directly to God, "God is Wisdom," and indirectly of creatures, "Man has wisdom," can be an expression of the analogy of proportionality. The reason for asking this is that this analogy, as we studied in the philosophy of being, is had when the perfection is predicated *directly* of all the *analogates*. God *is* being; creature *is* being. The difference, we explained, lies in the ratio between the terms of the predicate which varies in every distinct predication. How, then, can we affirm that the direct and indirect predication of the same identical concept of a perfection is an expression of this analogy? The answer is, of course, that the perfect form of the analogy of proportionality is found in a direct predication but that this form presupposes an implicit judgment in the predicate. This judgment is nothing else but an expression of the transcendental relation between "to be" and the perfection.

This Implicit Judgment Is Direct as to the First Analogate, Indirect as to the Others: We may recall that this implicit judgment (transcendental relation) is one of identity between the components of the predicate in the case of the prime analogate. It is an indirect predication for the others. An example will clarify this point. When I declare that God is being, I affirm implicitly that in God the components of being, essence and "to be," are one: the essence *is* "To Be." That is the kind of being God is. On the contrary, in the proposition, "Creature is being," I implicitly understand that the essence *has* a "to be" and is, therefore, really distinct from its "to be." The direct or indirect predication which is implicit in the terms of the predicate is really the very essence of the analogy of proportionality. It is because of this that the ratio which is discovered by the determination of the relation between essence and existence establishes that the predicate, being, is attributed to the various subjects according to a content which varies with each predication. Hence the predicate, being, is attributed analogously to the various subjects because of this implicit judgment between the components of being, essence, and "to be."[25]

Conclusion: This will suffice to solve our difficulty regarding the names of God. If we attribute to God and creature a perfection as such (in the abstract), we must predicate it directly of God and indirectly of creatures. God is Wisdom; man has wisdom. This mode of predication expresses God's simplicity. If, on the contrary, we consider the perfection in the concrete, that is, as we find it in a being that is subsisting and *complete,* we shall predicate the complete subsisting reality directly of God and also directly of creature; we shall say that God is wise (a wise being), and man is wise (a wise being). This direct predication, to be true, supposes a ratio between the factors of the predicate. God is a wise being, that is, God is a being whose "To Be" is identified with wisdom; man is a wise being, that is, man is a being whose wisdom is really distinct from his "to be."[26] Or, according to the manner

---

[25] We do not mean to say that, in the predicate, being, we have a concept of "to be" as it is in itself, since "to be" is not intelligible to the human intellect. We understand it in this implicit judgment only as the actuation of essence, an actuation which is either identical with the subject of actuation in the case of God, or really distinct as in creatures.

[26] We may add that the judgment which, regarding the unparticipated cause, takes place between the components of the predicate is always a judgment of existence, since the perfection in God is identical with the "To Be."

of expression of the Angelic Doctor: God *is* Wisdom; man *has* wisdom. God is "To Be"; man has a "to be."

Now we understand clearly why the direct and indirect predication regarding God and creatures, which St. Thomas uses so frequently, is but an expression of the analogy of proportionality.

The Analogy of Proportionality Manifests Causality: The indirect predication expressed in attributing a perfection to an existing creature indicates that the subject is not its own "to be"; it is not its own actuation in the order of existence. This manifests the necessity of an efficient cause. For an existing being which is not its "to be" is not intelligible without a cause of its existence which is pure existence. The participated perfection demands the unparticipated cause.[27] *The analogy of proportionality is really a metaphysical expression of the principle of causality.*

Doctrine of St. Thomas: There has been considerable ado about the question of analogy in connection with the text of St. Thomas. The assertion has been made that the analogy of proportionality is nowhere to be found in the writings of the Angelic Doctor. Is such a statement correct? If such a declaration signifies only that the expression "analogy of proportionality" is not mentioned, we heartily agree;[28] if, on the contrary, the statement means that the substance of such an analogy is not in St. Thomas, we no longer agree. Indeed it is our contention that this analogy — which is based on direct and indirect predication of various perfections, direct for God and indirect for finite beings — plays a most important part in the natural theology of St. Thomas. For when we say that God is being, that man is being, we imply that God is His "To Be," while man has a "to be." Now this affirmation, that God is "To Be" while creatures have existence, which is so often found in St. Thomas, is the clearest and most profound expression of what we today term the "analogy of proportionality."

The difficulty in interpreting the text of St. Thomas is caused

---

[27] Cf. *S. Th.*, I, 44, 1, ad 1ᵐ.

[28] The expression is that of Thomas de Vio Cajetan (1469–1534), who fully developed the Thomistic doctrine of the analogy of proportionality from principles found in St. Thomas.

largely by the fact that Aquinas never calls this predication by the name of analogy. He reserves such a title to that which we term the analogy of attribution. The example which he gives most frequently is that of health as predicated of the health-giving drug and of the sick person who is made healthy. Thomas insists again and again that this is the analogy between God and creatures. We predicate of God a perfection which we find in creatures, for example, wisdom, because God is the cause of the created perfection. The natural inference from a superficial reading of the text is, of course, that St. Thomas teaches that the analogy between God and creatures is not one of proportionality but of attribution.

Nothing could be farther from the truth. To begin with, St. Thomas' usage of the analogy of proportionality (a phrase which he never knew) consists in attributing a perfection to God and creatures in a different manner: directly of God, indirectly of creatures. God is "To Be"; God is Wisdom. Man has "to be"; man has wisdom. This he constantly repeats without bothering to explain. The reason is that to him this mode of predication is a necessary and immediate deduction in the application of the profound philosophical law that act is limited by potency.

Moreover, the Angelic Doctor also remarks in not a few places[29] that a participated perfection supposes an unparticipated cause. Indeed his metaphysical analysis of the principle of causality rests upon the real distinction,[30] that is, on the fact that a participated perfection, and clearest of all a participated "to be," is distinct from the essence of the subject which limits it. This analysis, as everyone knows, leads to a characteristically Thomistic proof of the existence of God.[31] In other words, causality between God and creatures is most profoundly understood in the use of the analogy of proportionality and, in turn, such causality is an expression of this analogy.

Why the Example of Healthy Drug Which Indicates Analogy of

---

[29] E.g., *S. Th.*, I, 44, 1; *De Ente et Essentia*, c. V.
[30] Cf. *S. Th.*, I, 44, 1; *The Philosophy of Being*, p. 116.
[31] *De Ente et Essentia*, c. V.

Attribution?: Now when, after several questions which deal with those attributes such as simplicity, infinity, and the like — attributes which are known to us by way of negation — the difficult problem of our positive knowledge of God's essence is finally proposed, only then is the solution by means of analogy affirmed. At this juncture St. Thomas points out that such positive knowledge is neither purely equivocal (*a casu*), which is no knowledge at all, nor univocal, which implies pure pantheism, but analogous. Obviously, at this point he is not in the least concerned with showing that whatever is predicated of God and creatures is predicated of God by identity with His "To Be," that is, directly, and predicated of creatures indirectly. That was established when he demonstrated that God *is "To Be,"* whereas creatures *have* existence. Aquinas is concerned, rather, in showing that the essential aspect of such predication implies an analogy of *cause* and *effect,* since we know that these perfections are in God because He causes them in creatures.

To exemplify the fact that the analogy by which we predicate a perfection of God and creatures expresses causality, St. Thomas looks to an analogy which is found between creatures and which expresses causality. Now, the analogy of proportionality is never found between creatures as an expression of causality. The reason is that such an analogy, being based on the real distinction, supposes a prime analogate which is "To Be." Hence Aquinas chooses an analogy of attribution which manifests causality of one creature to another. This explains why, after examining the analogy of two to another (*duo ad unum*) which does not manifest causality, he rejects it and adopts the other analogy of one to another which does.

It seems to me, therefore, that St. Thomas does not question the fact that these perfections will be predicated directly of God and indirectly of creatures, which is exactly what we mean by the analogy of proportionality. That is taken for granted. His problem here is to show that the analogy between God and creatures is based on efficient causality, and the example used shows that fact beyond doubt.

Analysis of the Text: In a text[32] which has been so often mis-understood, even by some of his followers, St. Thomas explains that these names are predicated of God and of creatures according to analogy, that is, according to a proportion. Here let us remark that the word "proportion" indicates relation and, of course, every analogy is founded on a relation to another. We observe, continues Aquinas, that there are two types of such proportions or relations regarding predication of names. One is found between two subjects of which a predication is had because of their varied relation to a third being. The classic example is the attribution of "healthy" to drug and to complexion because of the relation they have to animal. The analogy between these two, namely drug and complexion, is certainly not that found between God and creatures. The reason is obvious: creatures are not referred to God because of another being.

The second type of analogy manifests direct causality. "Healthy" is predicated of drug and of animal, because the drug is the cause of the health which is in the animal. This is the type of analogy, insists Thomas, which we find between creatures and God.

> And in this way some things are said of God and creatures analogically, and not in a purely equivocal nor in a purely univocal sense. For we can name God only from creatures. Hence, whatever is said of God and creatures is said according as there is some relation of the creature to God as to its *principle* and *cause,* wherein all the *perfection* of things *pre-exist* excellently.[33]

In a preceding article (article two) as well as in the following article (article six), St. Thomas insists that a name cannot be attributed to God *per posterius* as in the case of health which is attributed to a drug because of its relation to the animal. In view of this fact, no one should imagine that in the present article St. Thomas means just the opposite. What he means here is, as we have remarked above, that the analogy between God and creatures should manifest causality; it should indicate that God is the principle of

---

[32] *S. Th.,* I, 13, 5.
[33] *Loc. cit.*

the created perfection. The virtue of a drug which restores health to the animal exemplifies this excellently. It helps us to understand the fact that the analogy between God and creature must express causality.

Finally, St. Thomas insists that the perfection is said of God according to *what* it signifies. Now, no one will suspect that health, which is a property of living corporeal being, is in the drug. The term "health," when attributed to the drug, does *not signify* the perfection of health. It is said merely because the drug possesses a virtue which can help to restore health. The animal has health; not so the drug. On the contrary, God is wise and does not merely cause wisdom. To affirm that the analogy of attribution is the solution offered by St. Thomas is to indicate, not only that Thomas has contradicted himself on every page but that he holds the very position which he has so constantly and so vigorously attacked, the position of the agnostic.

S U M M A R Y — Article III: The Analogy of the Divine Names

1. **Problem:** The meaning of a predication:

   a) Which signifies the essence of God;

   b) Which is substantial;

   c) In which the mode of representation is that of creatures.

2. **Solution:** This predication is:

   a) Not univocal. God is not a univocal agent, because He causes the form with its "to be"; moreover, because God is "To Be," He is not under any genus.

   b) Not equivocal, because being is intelligible. Now God is the supreme being.

   c) Analogous. Which means that the predicate is somewhat the same but simply different. We want to know what this similarity means.

3. **Reason for this similarity.**

   a) **God is the adequate cause of all creatures.** Hence the perfection of the creature is somehow in Him.

b) **God's perfection is "To Be."** All created perfections are participations of God's perfections. They are actuated in the order of existence by a limited existence which is a participation in the divine "To Be."

4. The nature of this similarity.

It consists in an analogous communication of a form in such a manner that in God the form is identical with the act of existence, while in creatures it is distinct from the "to be." This diversity of ratios establishes what we today term the analogy of proportionality.

5. Analysis of the analogy of proportionality.

a) **This analogy is based on an existential judgment of identity** which is discovered between the terms of the predicate of the prime analogate, e.g., "God is Being," implies that the essence *is* "To Be."

b) **This analogy can be found only between God and creatures.** The reason is that only in God, the prime analogate, can we discover an existential judgment of identity, for only God is pure "To Be."

c) **In all the other analogates the judgment between the terms of the predicate is based on indirect predication.** The reason is that no perfection in an existing creature can be identified with existence.

d) **This analogy manifests causality.** The indirect predication in the judgment between the terms of the predicate of the secondary analogates is not intelligible without an efficient cause of the "to be." This analogy, therefore, is a metaphysical expression of the principle of causality.

6. Doctrine of St. Thomas.

Why does St. Thomas use examples from the analogy of attribution of healthy drug and healthy animal to exemplify the analogy of proportionality between God and creatures? He does this because no other analogy between creatures will express causality which is really what he wants to indicate in that article (article 5, question 13). He warns us, however, in articles 2 and 6 of the same question that a perfection is not predicated of God and creatures as health of drug and animal.

Question II

THE ATTRIBUTES OF GOD

Prologue

The conclusions obtained in the preceding question will be used as principles and guides in our study of the attributes of God. Let us recall, first, that the formal content of our connatural knowledge can never be attributed to God; such content must be denied. God is simply not that. Let us recall, moreover, that in order to arrive at a positive knowledge of the divine essence, we should remove any imperfection, any limitation, which we may discover in our knowledge of created perfection. Only after such removal shall we be able to predicate of God's essence the perfection thus depurated. In this predication we shall identify the perfection with the divine "To Be"; we make it absolute. Finally we shall indicate the nature of the analogy implied in such predication.

How does St. Thomas proceed? As regards the negative attributes,[34] the Angelic Doctor generally begins by considering a

---

[34] These attributes are called negative because our first knowledge is obtained by a negative proposition: God is not what the creature is. The creature is finite, limited, composed. God is not finite, not limited, not composed; that is, God is infinite, pure act, simple. The reason is that any essential perfection of a corporeal being implies an imperfection; it implies essential participation, since it supposes limitation by matter. Now we must begin our search of what the essence of God is by a consideration of the quiddity of corporeal essences. It follows that our first knowledge of the essential attributes of God will be negative knowledge. To affirm, for example, that God is infinite is to deny primarily that He is finite. For this reason these attributes are called negative attributes.

On the contrary, when, in the following chapter, we study the operations of God which, like the negative attributes, are identical with the divine "To Be," we

corporeal creature in which the divine perfection is not essentially exemplified. In dealing, for example, with the simplicity of God, he proposes a body for our observation. Now the nature of a body, because of its imperfection, essentially implies composition. The immediate inference from this observation is that God is not a body. God is not composed of matter and form. This is our negative knowledge regarding the simplicity of God's essence. Hence when we say God is simple, we mean first of all that God is not composed.

The second step is to acquire some sort of positive knowledge of the proposed perfection. To do so, St. Thomas examines those creatures whose essential perfection shares in some manner the absolute perfection of God. These creatures, of course, are the angelic natures, for their essence — not being limited by the potency of matter — does not imply the essential imperfection of corporeal creatures.

Finally, having removed all accidental limitations which are found in any created perfection, St. Thomas then indicates that in God, the supreme cause, this perfection is existence. To do so, he explains that the perfection is predicated of God directly and of creatures indirectly; it is predicated of God as identified with existence, and of creatures as distinct from it. He implies, therefore,

---

shall not begin by a negative knowledge of the essence expressed by a negative proposition. Our mode of procedure will be quite different. Since God is pure immateriality, His only operations are those of an intellectual nature, namely of intellect and will. In order, therefore, to understand what we mean when we say that God knows and loves, we shall have to examine the immanent operations of intellect and will in creatures. It is true, our knowledge of these operations even in creatures is not a connatural knowledge, since these operations are the actions of immaterial beings. But the fact is that these operations are found in creatures and, because of their immanence, imply no imperfection in their definition. Consequently, we shall be able to predicate directly of God's essence what the perfection signifies. We shall rise immediately from our knowledge of created perfections to a positive knowledge of the essential operations of God, operations which are identical with His essence and which could well be called also essential attributes. Regarding these, therefore, we first rise to a knowledge of the divine perfection not by a negative proposition, but by affirming that in God the operation is identical with the divine "To Be."

that the analogy involved in such predication is the one which today we term the analogy of proportionality.

Division: There will be eight articles, each considering a distinct attribute: (1) simplicity, (2) perfection, (3) goodness, (4) infinity, (5) ubiquity, (6) immutability, (7) eternity, (8) unity.

ARTICLE I: God Is Absolutely Simple

What Is Simplicity?: "The concept of simplicity, which we obtain by denying composition, denotes much more, however, than a mere negation of parts. It designates a positive perfection, 'a definite *disposition,* because of which a being need not be made of parts.' Like unity which is not a mere denial of division, but connotes a subject, simplicity establishes the reality of being as a foundation for the negation of parts. It indicates, therefore, a very great perfection; and, as St. Thomas explains, in the same kind or genus of being, the more noble and more perfect a thing is, the more simple it must be."[35]

Negative Knowledge, God Is Not Composed: The object of our connatural knowledge is the material essences. These are essentially composed of matter and form, and that is why they are substantially mutable. Now God is the Unmovable Cause; in Him there is no potency; He is, therefore, pure act. Hence, in God there can be no composition in any order and, clearly, not in the essential order. We conclude: God is not, like a body, composed of matter and form. He is not composed. He is simple.

Positive Knowledge: What is the signification of this phrase, God is simple? Does it mean only that God is not essentially composed of matter and form, that He is not a body? What sort of perfection is latent under the negative expression, God is not composed? What is our concept of the perfection which can be predicated positively of God's essence?

1. God Is His Own Nature: In his search for a created participation of divine simplicity, St. Thomas points out that the specific

---

[35] Cf. *The Philosophy of Man,* p. 24.

nature of bodies is limited and individuated by matter. Consequently, no corporeal individual which is a nature composed of form and matter is identical with its specific nature. That because of which Peter is man is not the same as that because of which Peter is this man. Were it so, only one man, Peter, would be possible; only one could exist. Peter, then, is man because of his form, the soul, which gives him the specific perfection of humanity. He is this man because of the matter which individuates by limiting the form. Now it is just the contrary with beings that are not composed of matter and form. Such are the angels (supposing that such beings exist).[36] They are pure forms and, consequently, each individual is identical with its specific nature. This identity of specific nature and individual manifests a high perfection. It is the perfection of simplicity in the order of essence. Thus we arrive at the positive knowledge of participated simplicity. By removing the limitation of such participation, we shall discover the meaning of divine simplicity. The concept of simplicity which we have now obtained is, therefore, founded on the identity of specific and individual nature. This obviously is not connatural knowledge. It is indirect, imperfect, non-proper knowledge; but it is true, and it allows positive knowledge of God's essence.

2. God Is His Own "To Be": God's simplicity is far more perfect; it is existential simplicity. An angelic form is not its own "to be"; it is really distinct from it. It is, therefore, an imperfect simplicity, for it implies the imperfection of part. God, on the contrary, because He is the cause of created existence, because He is the immovable mover, first uncaused cause, and unparticipated being, is Existence Itself; that is to say, His essence is "To Be." He is, therefore, existentially (absolutely) simple; indeed He is Simplicity Itself.

Predication: Clearly, then, the divine attribute called simplicity can be known to us in a manner not wholly negative. For when we

---

[36] We do not argue from the simplicity of an angelic nature *to prove* the simplicity of God. Such an argument would not be valid, since we do not establish in philosophy the existence of angels but only their possibility. We prove that God is simple from the fact that He is pure act. Here we are merely endeavoring to obtain the concept of a perfection (irrespective of its existence) in order to understand a divine attribute.

predicate simplicity of God by an affirmative proposition, we do not merely mean that God is not composed like a body, but that the perfection of essential simplicity, which signifies the plenitude of a specific perfection, is predicated of Him directly and affirmatively. This, however, must be qualified, for although we may say that we know what God is, and by this we mean that our knowledge is not merely negative, we must immediately add: we know Him imperfectly and by analogy. Indeed this direct predication of the perfection of simplicity, according to what it signifies, entails: first, that we predicate this perfection directly of God who is the *cause* of all created simplicity; second, that we *remove* the imperfection of part which results from the fact that simplicity in a creature can only be essential and, therefore, implies the imperfection of part in the order of existing being; third, that in doing so we identify simplicity with existence so that the perfection is in God in a supereminent manner.

Analogy: It is obvious that this mode of attributing simplicity to God implies an analogy of proportionality in the predication of the same perfection as regards creatures. God is simple: that is to say, God is that being whose "To Be" is identical with its essence. An angel, on the other hand, is simple in this way: it is a pure form whose essence is not identical with, but distinct from its "to be." For this is only essential simplicity, the simplicity of a part and not of the whole.

Conclusions: Several inferences can be deduced from the truth of God's existential simplicity:

1. God Is Not Under a Genus: The logical distinction between genus and specific difference results from the fact of a real composition between distinct parts, of a lack of simplicity in a being. In corporeal entities, for example, the essential composition of matter and form founds and explains the various genera and specific differences.[37] On the other hand, in the pure form which is the

---

[37] Genus is from matter. *"Genus sumitur a materia."* This does not mean that matter is the genus. By no means. Matter is not the genus, but it explains why there is a genus. Cf. *De Ente et Essentia,* c. 3; cf. Boyer, Charles, S.J., *Cursus Philosophicus,* I, p. 344.

angelic essence, the explanation for the different specific perfection is due to the real distinction between the essence and the "to be."[38] Consequently, because to be under a genus supposes some composition and, therefore, a lack of simplicity, we must say that God alone is not under a genus, for He alone is absolutely simple. That is why we cannot ever define God. God has no definition, because He is "To Be."

2. No Accidental Perfections in God: Since God is absolutely simple, His operations are identical with His "To Be." It follows that no accidental actuation is possible. The reason is that not only would such actuation presuppose some potential factor in God, and hence a lack of simplicity, but it would result in further composition. God, however, is absolutely simple.

3. God Is Not the Form of the World: We shall not discuss the statement that God is matter, for that is the apex of all absurdities. Indeed it would be to declare that the first efficient cause of all reality, of all which is in act, is pure potency. Let us rather indicate the error of those who thought that God is the form of the world. That this is an error can easily be established. The substantial form is a participated perfection, for it is limited by the matter. God, however, is absolutely simple, because He is the unparticipated "To Be."

ARTICLE II: The Perfection of God

Is Perfection a Distinct Attribute?: The question of the perfection of God is necessarily connected with every divine attribute. We say that each attribute is absolutely perfect, because it is identified with existence which is the perfection of perfections. The reason is this: act signifies perfection; but existence is the supreme act; therefore, that which is identified with existence is supremely perfect. It follows that every attribute is unqualifiedly perfect. Perfection, therefore, in our knowledge of the essence of God should not be thought a distinct attribute.[39]

---

[38] Cf. *De Ente et Essentia*, c. 6; Boyer, *loc. cit.*

[39] We mean, of course, not distinct in the order of our knowledge. On the

The concept of perfection plays an important role in our effort
to understand what God is. St. Thomas brings up the question of
God's perfection immediately after establishing the simplicity of
God; and in doing so, he connects it not only with simplicity but
with all the other attributes as well.

The kind of simplicity, he explains, which we attribute to
creatures is, even in its highest aspect, an imperfect simplicity, for
it implies the imperfection of part. Take, for example, an existing
pure form. It is simple in the order of quiddities, yet it does not
possess simplicity in its absolute perfection. This we perceive from
the fact that such a form, because it is distinct from existence, is
only a part of an existing angel. In order, then, to understand
more fully the absolute perfection of the simplicity of God as well
as any other attribute, we must consider what the proposition,
"God is perfect," really signifies.

Not a Negative Attribute: It appears from this that the question
of God's perfection will not receive a treatment parallel to that of
a negative attribute. The reason is that the concept of perfection is
not negative. Quite the contrary: act signifies perfection, and in the
order of knowledge, act is prior to potency. We do not say that
our notion of act or perfection as such belongs to our connatural
knowledge. What we know connaturally are material essences which
are essential composites of act and potency. From such knowledge
we abstract the notion of act or perfection. It follows that the notion
of act or perfection which we predicate of God does not belong
to our proper or connatural knowledge. Hence, even though we
cannot arrive at any knowledge of God which is not analogous
and non-proper, still there is no need to begin this question by
showing what God is not. It is true that when we predicate of
God the concept of perfection, we must actually deny any imperfection resulting from limitation; we must, moreover, identify it
with the "To Be." All this makes our knowledge analogous, but
it is positive not negative. We do not claim that we know God

---

other hand, in the order of existence, all the divine attributes are one because
identified with Subsisting Existence.

as He is in Himself; but we know positively, although not connaturally, what it is to be perfect, and we affirm that God is
perfect absolutely. We repeat: It is true that in our endeavor to
understand the meaning of the proposition, "God is perfect," we
must — as was explained in an earlier question — proceed first by
way of causality, since God is the source of all perfection; second,
by removing all limitations; and last, by way of supereminence
in the affirmation of existential perfection. This we must always do
in all affirmative propositions whose subject is the essence of God.
For, although perfection or act is predicated of God according to
what it signifies, still the mode of representation which is that
of the creature necessarily falls short. It fails to represent God as
He is in Himself. But the knowledge obtained is positive.

Analysis of the Concept of Perfection: The concept of perfection
does not include imperfection in its make-up (*ratio*). Perfection
simply signifies act. Now in the order of essences, the form is the
act. In creatures, however, the essential act, the form, is not the
supreme perfection, for its actuation is from the act of existing,
the "to be." The perfections of all beings, therefore, are perfections
precisely because they pertain to existence.[40] The "to be" is the
supreme act, the supreme perfection. " 'To Be,' " says the Angelic
Doctor, "is the most perfect of all things, for it is compared to all
things as that which is act. Indeed, nothing has actuality except
in so far as it exists; therefore, the 'to be' is the actuality of all
things, even of the forms."[41]

Proof: The proof is obvious to those who, like ourselves, have
already established that God is pure act, first efficient cause, and
subsisting "To Be." *To be perfect is to be in act,* and the most
perfect of all acts is "to be." God, however, is the subsisting "To Be."
Therefore God, the pure act of existence, is absolutely perfect.[42]

Analogy: God is a perfect being; and because He is pure act,

---

[40] Cf. *S. Th.,* I, 4, 2, c.

[41] *S. Th.* I, 4, 1, ad 3ᵐ.

[42] God's "To Be" includes all perfections, "because nothing of the perfection of
existing [*essendi*] can be wanting to Him Who is the subsisting 'To Be.' " (*S. Th.,*
I, 4, 2, ad 3ᵐ.)

He is absolutely perfect. All creatures are more or less perfect beings because of the degree of actuation they possess. A being, therefore, is more or less perfect according to the greater or lesser actuation which it receives from its "to be." It follows that God is unqualifiedly perfect because He is His own "To Be." Creatures, on the other hand, are qualifiedly perfect, because they share more or less in the perfection of the divine "To Be."[43] This is another application of the analogy of proportionality.

ARTICLE III: The Goodness of God

Not a Negative Attribute: A being is perfect in accordance with its goodness, for "the good is the formal aspect [*ratio*] of the perfect."[44] Hence, it is logical that, after studying God's perfection, we should reflect upon His goodness. The fact of the matter is that the consideration of the goodness of God is a sequence, an extension, of the question of His perfection. We might add that this question is a direct application of the analogy which we must use in acquiring some positive knowledge of the divine essence. Like the one and the true, the good is a transcendental notion, and, like the other transcendentals, it is predicated directly and analogously of all beings. Consequently, to the problem, what do we mean when we say that God is good, our approach cannot be negative. We do not begin by stating what God is not, namely that He is not evil; but we must affirm that God is good. The point to be made here is, then, that we are endeavoring to obtain a positive understanding of the goodness of God.

Positive Knowledge: In the course of metaphysics,[45] we discovered that a being is good because perfect, and perfect because in act. For since the good is the formal aspect of the perfect, we may

---

[43] In his treatment of the perfection of God (*S. Th.*, I, 4), St. Thomas devotes several articles to showing that the similarity which results from perfection found in God and in creatures is the foundation for the analogy. This similarity enables us to predicate the same perfection of the various analogates. This point has been discussed at length in the preliminary question.

[44] *S. Th.* I, 5, 1, ad 1ᵐ.

[45] Cf. *The Philosophy of Being*, p. 183; *S. Th.* I, 5, 1.

reason thus: A being is good in so far as it is perfect. Now a being is perfect in so far as it is in act. But the act of being is "to be." Therefore, a being is good in so far as it is. Hence, "to be good" is "to be." But God is subsisting "To Be." We may then immediately conclude that God is good, that He is good in the highest degree; in fact, we must say that He alone is essentially good (*bonus per essentiam*), and the reason is that His essence is the pure act of existing; in other words, that He is not merely good, but that *He is Goodness Itself*.

Goodness in Creatures: God's goodness, then, is infinitely more perfect than the goodness of the world of His creation. A creature, no matter how perfect, is good only because it participates in God's goodness. And because the ordinary notion of a perfect creature is in the line of accidental perfection, that is to say, because we speak of a creature as good on account of its accidental perfection, it follows that substantially creatures are designated good only qualifiedly. Being and good are therefore predicated of them with a distinction. We say of a creature that it is a being in an unqualified manner; but we add that it is good only qualifiedly, for its goodness as perceived by us refers to some accidental perfection. On the contrary, we must predicate being and good of the divine essence in the same identical fashion, that is, unqualifiedly, adding, moreover, that God is not only being and good, but He is "To Be" and Goodness.

Analogy: In this way, we conclude that all creatures are good, because they participate somehow in the divine goodness, so that they are like unto God. They are good with participated divine goodness; the goodness of God which is the "To Be" is their first exemplary cause as well as their ultimate end. This, again, is another application of the analogy of proportionality.

ARTICLE IV: The Infinity of God

The infinity of God is obviously a negative attribute. It implies a negation of finitude, of limitation. We must begin our study of infinity by showing what God is not, to wit, that He is not finite.

Negative Knowledge: It is true that finitude, limitation as such, is not a perfection but a lack of it; but it is a necessary adjunct to our connatural knowledge. All human experience is derived from some contact with bodies, and the object which is proper and proportionate to our feeble intellects is the essence of these corporeal beings. The fact that these bodies are finite is obvious. We immediately infer that God is not that; He is not finite.

Mathematical Infinity: The first suggestion of any sort of infinity we meet with is the *potential* infinity which is based on quantitative matter. This we term mathematical infinity. Now, as everyone knows, mathematical infinity is not *actual* infinity; it signifies indefiniteness. It indicates that we can keep on adding another unit *ad infinitum*. Such indefiniteness is in no way actual. At most, it can be called *potential* infinity. Now that is exactly what God is not, for He is the most definite,[46] the most distinct of all beings, because He is the most actual. Consequently, whatever we are able to conceive directly and connaturally, whether it be a limited corporeal entity or — resulting and derived from it — a mathematical infinity, we must absolutely deny of God. He is not finite nor potentially infinite. He is infinite in act. We conclude that our first approach to a knowledge of God's infinity is negative.[47]

Proof: The infinite is opposed to the finite. A body is essentially finite because of the composition of form and matter. The form limits the matter in this way, that it actuates it, specifies it, makes it be this kind of matter, e.g., living matter. The form, moreover, is limited, that is, individuated by matter. Now God is not limited, because He is in no way composed. Hence He is not finite. He is infinite.

Positive Knowledge: In order to obtain some positive knowledge of God's infinity, we shall examine whatever actual participated

---

[46] We do not mean by "definite" here that God can be defined, that He is under a genus and, therefore, limited. "Definite" is used in opposition to the indefiniteness of potential infinity. It means actual perfection.

[47] Let us note in passing that mathematical infinity is, as related to the unit of measurement, a *univocal* but indefinite concept. The same univocal concept of a perfection is multiplied *ad infinitum*.

infinity can be discovered in the world of creatures. Then, by an analogous predication, we shall attribute this perfection to Pure Existence.

Matter, we know, is actuated, made specifically perfect by the form; of itself, it is pure potency. Hence any infinity attributable to matter as such, or by reason of matter, implies a lack of perfection. It can only be a potential infinity; it should never be affirmed of God. On the other hand, the *form* which is the act of a corporeal essence is not made perfect by matter. Quite the contrary: because of matter, it is restricted and limited. Clearly then, if we could discover some sort of participated infinity in a created form, such infinity would necessarily be in the order of the perfect, in the order of act and not of potency. Now we find that the nature of a pure form such as of an angel is not received in matter and, therefore, not limited. Consequently, it is infinite in the order of essence; and because it realizes the plenitude of its specific perfection, it is actually, not potentially infinite. It follows that, after removing the imperfection of the creature, we should be able to predicate directly of God the positive notion of infinity which we have thus acquired from our knowledge of creatures. It must be stated, however, that such predication will be by way of analogy.

Analogy: We must observe that the actual infinity which is attributable to angelic forms is not predicated of them in an absolute manner, or as St. Thomas puts it *unqualifiedly (simpliciter)*, but only *qualifiedly (secundum quid)*. The reason is that these essential forms are not their own "to be." Infinity is said of their essence; it is not existential infinity. God, we know, is His "To Be"; therefore, He is unqualifiedly infinite; indeed, He is Infinity.

N.B.: The infinity of God is not one of indefiniteness but one of actuality and, therefore, of absolute definiteness. It is because of this definiteness that we must state that by His infinity He is distinguished absolutely from all other beings. The notion of existential infinity, therefore, contrary to what is often believed, does away completely with any pantheistic imaginings. We say, "contrary to what is often believed." The reason is that the concept of infinity which is generally proposed is not that of existential infinity which is actual in the highest sense, but potential infinity. Now potential infinity is the indefinite multiplication of an univocal unit; it means univocal indefiniteness. And to accept univocal indefiniteness in God is to take a long step toward pantheism.[48]

ARTICLE V: God Is Omnipresent

Problem: If God is infinite, He must be everywhere and in all beings. We must say, therefore, that the omnipresence of God is really not a negative attribute. Rather, it results from God's infinity as its quasi-property. Hence, what we want to establish here is not only that God is in every being; this is easily shown as we shall see. Rather we want especially to determine, if we can, the mysterious nature of His presence everywhere and in every being. We are not concerned, therefore, with a negative knowledge; we are not concerned with what God is not, but with what He is. In short, we want to know positively the meaning of this statement: God is everywhere and in every being.

What Is To Be in Place?: To understand the profound meaning of St. Thomas' explanation, we should realize that spiritual beings are not in place after the manner of bodies. A body occupies space because of its extension; it is circumscribed by space. A spirit, on the contrary, is not extended; it is simple. Hence, it cannot occupy space. It can only be said to be in place because of its operation upon a body. The reason is that operation requires some sort of

---

[48] Actuation in the order of existence is the most absolute realization of definiteness, because the "to be" is the most perfect of all realities. In creatures, the "to be" is received into and limited by the essence. That is why creatures are so completely "other" than God.

"To be" is the most perfect of all things, for it is compared to all things as act; for nothing has actuality except so far as it is. Hence "to be" is the actuality of all things, even of forms themselves. Therefore, it is not compared to other things as the receiver is to the received, but rather as the received to the receiver. When, therefore, I speak of the "to be" of man, or of a horse, or of anything else, "to be" is considered as a formal principle, and as something received, and not as that to which "to be" belongs. (*S. Th.,* I, 4, 1, ad 3m.)

contact of virtue.[49] The spirit which acts upon a body is present to that body because of its action. It follows that the manner in which God is present to all beings is by an operation which is proper to God, the operation by which God gives each creature its existence. "The essence of God," explains Aquinas, "because independent of every creature, cannot be in a creature except by applying itself through operation."[50] The reason is that "a spiritual substance which is altogether free from site [*situ*] and from quantity has an essence which is in no way circumscribed or limited by place. Hence, it can be in place only by its operation, and in consequence of this operation, its virtue and essence are in place."[51]

Division: Following the order of the *Summa Theologica*, we shall establish the following truths: (1) God is in all things; (2) He is, therefore, everywhere; (3) the nature of God's omnipresence is that He is everywhere by essence, presence, and power; (4) to be everywhere is properly attributable to God alone.

God Is in All Things: Let us state first a fundamental principle. An agent must be joined (*coniungi*) to the patient upon which it immediately acts, for the agent must reach the patient by its virtue. This proposition is evident to us, for it expresses the nature of causality which was discussed on page 18. There, however, this truth was couched in somewhat different terms. It was stated thus: *In the existential order, every effect depends here and now upon its proper cause.* Now since God is His own "To Be," His proper effect is to give participated existence to other beings,[52] for only pure existence can cause participated existence. Moreover, not only does God give existence, but He must preserve it at all times. For an effect ceases to be once the cause ceases to produce it by its virtue. Now in any existent being, the "to be" is that which is most profound, most intimate in a being, since it is that which is

---

[49] Virtue (*virtus*) here does not mean a good habit. It signifies, rather, the perfection, the act, the power of the agent.

[50] "*Essentia autem [Dei], cum sit absoluta ab omni creatura, non est in creatura nisi in quantum applicatur per operationem.*" (*In Sent.*, dist. 37, a. 1, ad 2[m].)

[51] *Ibid.*, q. 2, a. 1.

[52] Cf. *The Philosophy of Being*, p. 134; we shall face this problem from a different point of view in the tract on creation.

most formal.[53] Nothing is in act, nothing *is,* unless it participates in the supreme existence which is God. It follows that by giving and conserving its "to be," God's virtue is intimately in every existing being. But the virtue of God is one with His essence, for God acts by His essence. We conclude that God is intimately present to all creatures, that is, to all existing beings whose essence is not "to be."

N.B.: This intimate presence of God in all creatures does not mean that a composition of creature and God results. Nothing could be farther from the truth. The presence of a cause in the immediate production of the effect demands that cause and effect, although immediately present to each other, be nevertheless absolutely distinct realities.

God Is Everywhere: In the philosophy of nature, it is explained that place is not a being of reason but a reality. Aristotle defines it as *the first immovable term of the container.*[54] Commenting upon this definition, St. Thomas states that the place of a body which is in place is the surface of other bodies which have immediate contact with the first. Place, then, is immovable only in this sense, that although the surrounding bodies may constantly change as, for example, the flowing river in which the stone is placed, nevertheless the surfaces surrounding the stone when considered formally have a determined site (*situs*) and are, therefore, immovable. We should note that place is not to be confused with the "where" (*ubi*) which is intrinsic to the body in place. Now,

> . . . to be in place can be understood in two ways: either after the manner of other things, i.e., as one thing is said to be in another in any way whatever, and thus the accidents of a place are in place; or in a manner proper to place, and thus things placed are in place. Now in both of these senses, in some way God is in every place, which is to be everywhere. First, He is in all things as giving them "to be," power, and operation; so He is in every place as giving it "to be" and locative power. Again, things placed are in

---

[53] *"Esse est quod est magis intimum cuilibet et quod profundius omnibus inest, cum sit formale respectu omnium quae in re sunt. . . ." (S. Th.,* I, 8, 1, c.)
[54] *Physics* IV, 212a, 20.

place inasmuch as they fill place: so, too, God fills every place; not indeed like a body, for a body is said to fill place inasmuch as it does not permit another body to be with it, whereas by the fact that God is in some place, He does not exclude others from being there. Even more, He fills all places through this, that He gives "to be" to the things that fill all places.[55]

N.B.: It should be noted that God is *wholly* present in every place. It will be helpful to recall the principles studied in the philosophy of man[56] regarding the totality of essence and of quantity. There can be, of course, no question of a quantitative whole or part in God, since He is pure existence. Now totality of essence which transcends quantity is not commensurable by place. Hence there is no reason why essential totality could not be in various places simultaneously. The soul of man is wholly in every part of the body, God is wholly everywhere.

God Is Everywhere by Essence, Presence, and Power:[57] Because of various errors, especially those of the Epicureans and of Maimonides, the statement that God is everywhere by essence, presence, and power became necessary. We say that "God is in all things by His *power,* inasmuch as all things are subject to His power; He is by His *presence* in all things, inasmuch as all things are bare and open to His eyes; He is in all things by His *essence,* inasmuch as He is present to all as the cause of their existence."[58]

It belongs therefore to something to be everywhere essentially when it is such that, whatever supposition is made, it follows that it is everywhere; and this properly belongs to God alone. For whatever number of places be supposed, even if an infinite number be supposed besides those which are, it would be necessary for God to be in all of them; for nothing is able to be except through Him. Therefore to be everywhere primarily and essentially belongs to

---

[55] *S. Th.,* I, 8, 2, c; cf. *C.G.,* III, 68, c. 2.

[56] Cf. *The Philosophy of Man,* p. 51.

[57] In theology we discuss the presence of God in the soul by sanctifying grace. St. Thomas remarks that God is present to the soul through sanctifying grace, not merely as an efficient cause is present to the patient, but as the known is in the knower and the beloved in the lover.

[58] *S. Th.,* I, 8, 3, c; cf. *In I Sent.,* dist. 37, a 1, ad 2m.

God and is proper to Him; because whatever number of places
be supposed to exist, God must be in each of them, not according
to a part of Him, but by Himself.[59]

ARTICLE VI: God Is Immutable

The immutability of God was thought by some of the essentialist
philosophers who preceded St. Thomas to be the fundamental
attribute of the essence of God. St. Augustine remarks that "to
exist truly is nothing else but to exist always in the same manner."[60]
Aquinas places immutability in its proper sequence. It is not the
primary attribute, for it implies that God is pure act, that He is
absolutely simple as well as infinitely perfect.

Negative Knowledge: In our first understanding of it, immutability presents itself as a negative attribute; it denies possibility
of change. Now although change supposes imperfection, or at
least lack of perfection — that is to say, it implies some potency
in the subject of change — nevertheless change in itself is not an
imperfection; on the contrary, it is an act, be it only an imperfect
act. It follows that not only does immutability suppose simplicity
and infinite perfection (and could not be, therefore, the most fundamental attribute of God), but — and this is the point we wish to
make here — our first knowledge of God's immutability must
necessarily be a negative knowledge. The reason is simply that our
philosophical concept of changeableness is intimately connected with
knowledge of the proper object of the human intellect, material
essences. For a corporeal being implies mutability in every order
of reality; it can be or not be; it can become another corporeal
substance; it can act and be acted upon. Change to us is a concept
which belongs to our connatural knowledge.[61]

Our first knowledge of God's immutability will consist in a

---

[59] *S. Th.,* I, 8, 4, c.

[60] *"Vere esse est enim semper eodem modo esse."* (*In Joannis Evangelium,* tract.
XXVIII, Cap. 8, no. 8–10; *Pat. Lat.,* Vol. 35, Col. 1678–1679; quoted from Gilson,
Le Thomisme, Vrin, 5th ed., p. 125 ff.) M. Gilson presents an interesting discussion
of the historical development of this problem.

[61] Motion of a corporeal subject is a common sensible.

realization that God cannot change, that He is not mutable. To ascertain this negative knowledge, St. Thomas proposes three arguments, each of which implies a divine perfection which we must know before we can assert that God is not mutable.[62]

Proof: 1. To be mutable, some potency is presupposed; but God is pure act; therefore, God is not mutable.

2. Some sort of intrinsic composition is necessary for any change. God, however, is absolutely simple; consequently, God cannot change. He is immutable.

3. In every change, something new is acquired; but God, because He is infinitely perfect, cannot acquire a new perfection; therefore, God is immutable.

Positive Knowledge: To arrive at a positive concept of immutability which will be directly predicable of God, we must look to the world of creation and inquire whether any creature can be said to share in any manner in the immutability of God. Now change, which we find at least as a possibility in all limited beings, can result from one of two factors. First, it may result from the fact that a certain potency has not been completely actuated and can, therefore, receive a new act. The material element, for example, in a corporeal substance, although actuated by a form, remains in potency to all other material forms. Hence such a substance of its very nature is subject to change; it is mutable. The second factor from which the changeableness of a creature is quite evident is the absolute dependence of any limited being — no matter how perfect it is — upon God for its existence. Were God to withdraw this greatest of all natural gifts, the "to be," a creature would undergo the most radical change possible: it would cease to exist.

It is obvious that all creatures are mutable, at least in this latter sense. All creatures depend at all times on the supreme efficient cause for their "to be." From this point of view, we learn nothing positive of God's immutability. On the contrary, we can only deny that God is mutable, since His "To Be" in no way depends upon another. And the reason, as we all know, is that God is Existence.

---

62 The major premise in all three arguments was firmly established in the *The Philosophy of Being*, p. 17 ff.

On the other hand, if we inquire into the first factor from which mutability results, that is, whether or not in any order of reality there exists a potency which is so completely actuated as to make further change an impossibility in that order, we note a very interesting fact. It is this: spiritual substances which are subsisting forms have their *essential potency fully actuated* in the order of existence. Hence, although mutable in the order of activity by means of accidental determinations, they cannot become anything else substantially; they are incorruptible. Their essence, of its very nature, once it is, cannot not be. The reason for this, as we indicated in the philosophy of man,[63] is that existence which follows the form in no way depends upon matter in the case of spiritual beings. Hence spiritual beings are immutable, not absolutely, not unqualifiedly, that is, not as pure existences; but they are qualifiedly immutable, that is, in the essential order they cannot become something else — they cannot not be. Let us quote Aquinas' profound remark:

> On the other hand, incorporeal substances, because they are subsistent forms which, nevertheless, are to their "to be" as potency to act, do not have the potency for the privation of this act, since "to be" follows upon form, and nothing is corrupted except through this, that it lose its form. Hence, in the form itself there is no potency to non-existence; and so such substances are immutable and invariable as regards their "to be."[64]

Predication: This, then, is the concept of immutability which we are able to obtain from creatures. This we predicate of God analogously by way of causality, negation, and supereminence, that is: first we affirm that God, the supreme cause of all perfection, is the cause of the immutability which we discovered in spiritual substances and, therefore, that immutability is somehow

---

[63] *The Philosophy of Man*, pp. 35, 36.

[64] *S. Th.*, I, 9, 2, c. A parallel text of importance is found in the treatise on the human soul: "It is clear that whatever belongs to a thing according to itself [*secundum se*] is inseparable from it. But 'to be' belongs to a form which is an act by itself. . . . It is impossible, however, that a form could be separated from itself. Hence it is impossible for a subsisting form [of itself] to cease to exist." (*S. Th.*, I, 75, 6, c.) Cf. Gilson, *L'être et l'essence*, p. 99, n. 1.

in Him; second, we deny of the immutability which we predicate of God that it is limited to the order of essence; third, we conclude that this perfection in God is identical with "To Be."

Analogy: We have, therefore, at the end of our search obtained a positive though analogous and imperfect knowledge of divine immutability. The perfection is predicated according to what it signifies, but the mode of representation is that of creature. In other words, when we say:

1. God is immutable, the concept of the perfection which is predicated is obtained from the relative immutability of a spiritual creature regarding its essential perfection.

Having removed the imperfection of a limited immutability, we affirm that:

2. God and only God is absolutely immutable; in other words, we affirm that existential immutability is predicable of God alone.

ARTICLE VII: The Eternity of God

Eternity Follows Immutability: The discussion on the eternity of God logically follows the question on the immutability. The reason is that eternity is first apprehended as a denial of time.[65] Now time measures successive changes, successive becomings, while eternity must deny all successions, all mutations. Hence a true knowledge of eternity supposes some understanding of the attribute of unchangeableness or of immutability. That is why St. Thomas places the tract on eternity immediately after that on immutability.

Negative Knowledge: What do we claim to understand when we say that God is eternal? The human intellect, which depends for its data upon a material phantasm, and whose successive operations are measured by the duration of time, can never completely fathom the mystery of an existential eternity. In its first attempt to grasp a faint understanding of eternity, the intellect is forced to look to that type of duration which is proportioned to its operation and

---

[65] "Just as we attain to the knowledge of simple things by way of composite things, so we must reach to the knowledge of eternity by means of time." (*S. Th.*. I, 10, 1, c.)

which it is able to define; it needs first to consider time. Having
analyzed and defined time, we immediately conclude to the negative knowledge that eternity is not time, and that when we say
that God is eternal, we emphatically declare that God is not in time.

This appears from the Boethian definition of eternity which
Aquinas quotes and analyzes in the very beginning of his treatise.
This definition, we shall show, is nothing but a formal negation
of time. When, therefore, it is attributed to God, this definition of
eternity does not give us any positive knowledge; it only states
that God's eternity is not time.

Analysis of Definition: "Eternity," explains Boethius, "is *the
simultaneous whole and perfect possession of interminable life.*"
To understand the true meaning of these words, we must go to
the philosophical definition of time and indicate precisely how time
affirms what eternity denies.

Aristotle defines time as: *"The number of motion according to
before and after."*[66] This definition presents two essential factors.
Of these, one is formally expressed, the other merely implied. They
are respectively: (1) successive motion; (2) a beginning and an
end. It is obvious that successive motion is the very core of time;
on the other hand, motion, which implies a subject in motion, in
order to be successive needs to have a beginning and an end.

Now the definition of eternity quoted by St. Thomas from
Boethius is precisely a direct negation of the two factors which we
have found in the definition of time. Eternity consists in that which
is not a succession of motion; that is, it consists in that which is
simultaneously whole. This expression, "simultaneous whole," is
therefore first of all a denial of successive motion. For in a thing
in which there is no change, no successive motion, there can be
no before and after of a number of motions. The nature of time
consists in the numbering of before and after of motion. The notion
of eternity which we obtain from a negation of time consists in
a uniformity which results from the denial of successive motions.

Moreover, in order to deny the implied fact that in a subject

---

[66] Cf. Aristotle, *Physics* IV, 11, 220a, 25.

moved successively there is a beginning and an end, the definition of eternity contains the word *interminable.*

It is clear that, in the derivation of the definition of eternity from a denial of time, the phrase "simultaneous whole" is by far the most important. As to the other terms of the definition, namely, *perfect possession of life,* we may say:

1. **Perfect** is used to exclude the "now" of time which, although not a successive duration, is an imperfect act having only transient existence (*esse fluens*).

2. **Possession** implies a denial of change in this way, that it means a firm hold on an object, while motion is a sign of instability. Possession, therefore, designates the immutability and permanence of eternity: it denies instability.

3. **Life.** This is the only term which does not imply a direct negation. Life is the "to be" of living beings. It is the highest aspect of the act of existing.[67]

Negative Definition: St. Thomas insists that this definition of eternity is primarily negative. To the difficulty that the true definition of a perfection cannot be expressed by a negative proposition, he answers by showing that, because of the feebleness of our intellect, definitions of the highest perfections need to be negatively expressed. "Our intellect," he states, "which first apprehends composite things, cannot attain to the knowledge of simple things except by removing the composition."[68] Our first knowledge of eternity, then, is negative.

Proof, God Is Eternal; He Is His Own Eternity: Just as the notion of time flows from an analysis of motion, so our knowledge of eternity follows from the truth that God is immutable, that is, that He is not in time. But God alone, we have seen, is absolutely, unqualifiedly immutable. Consequently, we must conclude that it belongs to God alone to be absolutely eternal; indeed, we may say not only that He is eternal, but that He is His own duration. He is Eternity. The reason for this, explains the Angelic Doctor, is that "whereas no other being is its own duration, since

---

[67] Cf. *The Philosophy of Man,* p. 5.
[68] *S. Th.,* I, 10, 1, ad 1m.

[no other being] is its own 'to be,' God is His own uniform 'To Be.' Hence as He is His own essence, so He is His own Eternity."[69]

Positive Knowledge: In order to obtain a positive knowledge of what eternity is, St. Thomas studies the mode of duration which measures the existence of creatures. He inquires whether any of the more perfect creatures shares eternity in some manner. He then submits that angels participate in this perfection at least in the essential order.[70] He argues that, since immutability is the most fundamental reason for eternity, the degree of immutability which we discover in creatures will be the determining factor in judging in what manner they participate in the divine attribute of eternity. Now we have established in the preceding article that angels possess what is termed "essential immutability." We must, therefore, conclude that angels, because their essential perfection cannot undergo substantial mutations, share in the order of essence in God's eternity. Their duration, therefore, participates somewhat in the eternity of God, since it is the *measure of a permanent "to be."* To be sure, the duration which measures angelic existence is really not eternity, for the angelic form is not "to be" and, consequently, the angelic nature is in potency to successive thoughts and volitions which are changes in the order of action. To distinguish, then, this duration from the existential eternity of God, medievalists called it *aeviternity.* This is the perfection which enables us to obtain a positive knowledge of divine eternity.

Three Types of Duration: There are, therefore, three types of duration: eternity, aeviternity, and time. Each is the measure for a different manner of existence. The fundamental reason for their distinction cannot be anything other than the existence which each duration measures. Consequently, it would not be correct to declare that the difference between these three modes of duration

---

[69] S. Th., I, 10, 2, c.

[70] We say advisedly, "at least in the essential order." St. Thomas, the Christian theologian, goes farther. The angels and blessed in the ever enduring vision of the Word undergo no change, no succession. Hence these creatures share in the eternity of God, not only in the essential order, but in the order of action regarding the beatific vision. This, of course, is not a matter for mere philosophers.

lies in this, that time has a beginning and an end; aeviternity has a beginning and no end; eternity has neither a beginning nor an end. These are only accidental differences which may manifest but not determine the mode of duration. Neither would it suffice to state that eternity, being a simultaneous whole, has no before and after; time has before and after with innovation and veteration (being young and new, and growing old); while aeviternity has before and after but without innovation and veteration. This, as we stated, cannot suffice, since in aeviternity there would have to be some innovation, if not in the measured, at least in the measure itself.

Difference: The true difference is to be sought in *the mode of existence of the measured*. Let us state a principle: Since eternity is the measure of the permanent "to be," we must say that in so far as the mode of existence of any creature recedes from absolute permanence, so must its duration recede from eternity. Applying this principle, we are able to state the true intelligible content of the three types of duration.

Eternity is the measure of permanent existence.

Time is the measure of changeable existence.

Aeviternity is the measure of permanent existence with change annexed to it.

It must be said, therefore, that since eternity is the measure of a permanent "to be," in so far as anything recedes from permanence of existing, it recedes from eternity. Now some things recede from permanence of existing so that their "to be" is subject to change, or consists in change; and these things are measured by time, e.g., all motions and also the "to be" of all things corruptible. But others recede less from permanence of existing, since their "to be" neither consists in change, nor is the subject of change, although they have change annexed to them either actually or potentially. This appears in . . . the angels who have, regarding what pertains to their nature, an unchangeable "to be" with changeableness regarding election, and also with changeableness of knowledge, of affections, and of places in their own manner. Therefore, beings of this sort are measured by aeviternity, which stands between eternity and time.

But the "to be" which eternity measures is neither mutable nor joined to mutability.[71]

Predication: Such, then, is our positive notion of eternity. We obtain it by realizing that, like any other duration, it is the measure of a mode of existence. Second, we deny that the eternal "To Be" is, like that measured by time, a changing "to be." We deny, moreover, that, like the permanent "to be" measured by aeviternity, it has any change annexed to it, but that it is the measure of an unqualifiedly permanent existence. Finally, we predicate it of God, and we say that God is not only eternal, but that He is Eternity, because He is "To Be."

ARTICLE VIII: The Unity of God

Although unity may be termed a negative attribute, since it implies a negation of division in the being which is one, nevertheless, because the notion of "the one" is one of the transcendentals, we do not begin this treatise by seeking a negative knowledge of God's unity; we do not begin by stating that God is one, that is, that He is not many. Rather, we try to discover the true meaning of the transcendental notion, "the one."

Like all the transcendentals, the one is predicable of all subjects, of God as well as of creatures, by means of an analogy of proportionality. We need only discover, then, the intelligible content of this concept and the nature of the ratio necessary for such analogous predication. That is why St. Thomas, in the question devoted to the unity of God, institutes first a brief discussion of the transcendental notion of the one. He asks: what is the meaning of the transcendental one as opposed to the one, the principle of number; what is the intelligible content, that is, what does it add to the concept of being; how does the one differ from the many? Only after this preparatory discussion does the Angelic Doctor face the problem of the unity of God.

---

[71] *S. Th.*, I, 10, 5, c.

Since we have, in the philosophy of being,[72] studied these preliminary questions, it will suffice to recall a few general conclusions before considering the unity of God.

The one implies a negation of division in a subject. Now the division of a being is dependent upon the act of being, the "to be." Consequently, the unity of a being is due principally to the lack of division in its existence. A being such as a house with its many distinctly existing components has a very imperfect unity. As a substance, the house is substantially many units and only accidentally one. The negation of division which "the one" adds to being manifests, therefore, a very great perfection, the perfection, that is, of the unity of the "to be." Hence the more a being is one, the more perfect its "to be," so that "a being guards its unity in the same manner as it guards its 'to be.' "[73] A being, then, will be more or less one according to its aptitude to retain its unifying existence. Consequently, in the last analysis of the transcendental one, the perfection of the unity of a being is discovered in the nature of the relation between the essence and the "to be" of that being.

Obviously, God is perfectly one, since His essence is "To Be." We may quote the argument of St. Thomas which establishes this truth absolutely. He shows that God is not only one, but He is one in a supreme manner.

> Since *one* is undivided being, that something should be supremely one, it is necessary that it should be supremely being and supremely undivided. Now both of these belong to God. For He is supremely being inasmuch as His "To Be" is not determined by any nature to which it is adjoined; but He is subsisting "To Be" Itself, not determined in any manner. Moreover, He is supremely undivided inasmuch as He is divided neither actually nor potentially by any mode of division, since He is simple according to all modes of simplicity, as was shown above. Hence, it is manifest that God is supremely *one*.[74]

---

[72] Cf. *The Philosophy of Being*, p. 172.
[73] *S. Th.*, I, 11, 1, c.
[74] *S. Th.*, I, 11, 4, c.

S U M M A R Y — Question II

THE ATTRIBUTES OF GOD

1. Having established that God is pure act, subsisting "To Be," it is not difficult to infer that God is simple, perfect, infinite, immutable, etc.

2. In this question we are principally interested in understanding what we mean when we say that God is simple, perfect, and the like.

3. Following the principles proposed in the preceding question, we shall establish regarding each attribute:

a) What our *negative* (connatural) knowledge is; that is, what precise aspect of our connatural knowledge of material essence we deny of God regarding each attribute.

b) What our *positive* knowledge is; that is, what particular spiritual perfection (non-proper knowledge) we predicate directly of God in each attribute.

c) How this predication manifests the analogy of proportionality: by way of causality, remotion of imperfection, and supereminence.

ARTICLE I: God Is Absolutely Simple.

1. Because God is pure act, simplicity, which is an immediate inference from this truth, is placed first among the attributes.

2. Negative (connatural) knowledge: Bodies are composed. God is not composed.

3. Positive (non-proper) knowledge: A pure spiritual form is simple in the order of essence because, not being individuated by matter, the individual nature does not differ from the specific nature. This is essential simplicity.

4. In predicating this perfection of God who is the cause of the created perfection, we remove the limitation of mere essential simplicity; we identify it with "To Be" (supereminence). In God, we affirm existential simplicity; in the created pure form we predicate essential simplicity. Analogy of proportionality.

ARTICLE II: God Is Absolutely Perfect.

1. To be perfect belongs to all the attributes. That is why we place it immediately after the first.

2. Perfection is not a negative attribute. Hence no negative knowledge.

3. Positive (non-proper) knowledge: Perfection is act. We obtain the concept of act by abstracting the act from our connatural knowledge of material essences which are composed of act and potency.

4. Predication: To be perfect is to be in act. The act of being is "to be." God is subsisting "To Be." He is absolutely perfect. All the created perfections share in the "To Be." Analogy of proportionality.

ARTICLE III: God Is the Supreme Good.

1. The good is the formal aspect of the perfect. Hence, after perfection we study the good.

2. The good is not a negative attribute because it is a transcendental notion.

3. Positive (non-proper) knowledge: The good signifies being in so far as it is desirable because of its perfection. It signifies being with a relation to the will. Now being is perfect because in act; but the act of being is "to be"; therefore, a being is good in so far as it *is,* that is, in so far as it has a "to be" or is "To Be."

4. Predication: God is subsisting "To Be"; therefore, He is the supreme good. All other beings are good in so far as they participate in His "To Be." Analogy of proportionality.

ARTICLE IV: God Is Absolutely Infinite.

1. Infinity denies limitation. Limitation is based on composition. Hence we place infinity as the second negative attribute after simplicity.

2. Negative (connatural) knowledge: God is not finite, because He is not like a body which is limited because it is composed.

3. Positive (non-proper) knowledge: A pure, spiritual form is not limited by matter. It is infinite in the essential order.

4. Predication: We remove the imperfection of mere essential infinity and identify our concept of the perfection of infinity with the subsisting "To Be." This is existential infinity. The analogy of proportionality is clearly expressed by such predication.

ARTICLE V: God Is Omnipresent (Present in All Beings and Everywhere).

1. Omnipresence is placed here because it is the quasi-property of infinity. It flows from infinity.

2. It is not a negative attribute, since presence is predicable of all subjects. The problem here is to understand the manner of God's omnipresence.

3. Positive (non-proper) knowledge: It is obtained from the manner in which a spirit is present, i.e., by its operation upon a body. Hence, regarding presence in place, we distinguish:

a) Bodies can be only in one place because they are circumscribed by other bodies.

b) Pure forms are in place by their operation upon bodies. A spirit could be simultaneously present in various places, that is, it could act upon several bodies.

c) God is in all beings and in all places (everywhere) because He alone causes the "to be" of all creatures at all times.

4. Predication: Only God can give existence. Hence only God can be present always in all beings existentially. The presence of creatures here or there is only accidental. Analogy of proportionality.

ARTICLE VI: God Is Immutable.

1. The proof of immutability, because it denies change, is based on the fact that God is pure act, absolutely simple, and infinitely perfect. That is why immutability is studied at this point.

2. Negative (connatural) knowledge: Immutability denies change. Now motion, change, or, rather, a moving body, is the object of our sense knowledge. It belongs to our intellectual knowledge which is connatural. Change, although it implies an imperfection in the subject of change, is a perfection; it is an act, but an imperfect act. Because of the implied imperfection we must deny it of God.

3. Positive (non-proper) knowledge: We discover essential immutability in spiritual forms. Such a form is fully actuated by a "to be" which does not depend upon matter. It has no potency to another mode of existence. The only possibility to non-being in such a form is extrinsic and results from its dependence upon the will of God for its existence.

4. Predication: Immutability is raised to the existential order when predicated of God. Hence such predication manifests an analogy of proportionality.

ARTICLE VII: God Is Eternal.

1. Eternity denies time, which is the measure of successive motions. Hence it denies mutation or change. That is why St. Thomas places it after the attribute of immutability.

2. Negative (connatural) knowledge: We deny that God exists in the duration we call time, for time is the number of motion according to before and after; whereas eternity is the simultaneous whole and perfect possession of interminable life.

3. Positive (non-proper) knowledge: Duration is the measure of existence. We rise to the knowledge of a creature whose substantial "to be," because it is not mutable (like that of a corporeal being), shares in some degree in the permanence of divine existence. A duration which is the measure of permanent existence is the perfection which we predicate of God.

4. Predication: Because such a concept, regarding the created angelic nature, implies accidental change, we must remove this imperfection and identify the predicate with the subsisting "To Be." From such predication, we understand that not only is God eternal, but that He is the measure of His own duration. He is Eternity.

Eternity is the measure of an absolutely permanent "To Be."

Aeviternity is the measure of a permanent "to be" with change annexed.

Time is the measure of a non-permanent "to be," i.e., of changeable existence.

ARTICLE VIII: God Is Absolutely One.

It seems proper to close the treatise on the divine attributes by reaffirming in a slightly different manner the foundation for all the divine attributes. We began by stating that, because God is subsisting "To Be," we can easily infer the various attributes. In this final article we explain the perfection of the Pure Act of Existence by a consideration of its oneness. Unity in God does not merely signify (1) that the "To Be" is many, as in a house, (2) or undivided but divisible, as in the lower types of creatures, (3) or undivided and indivisible but distinct from the essence, as in man and angels. Unity in God is absolute. It implies that the "To Be" is identical with the essence; for the Divine Essence is "To Be."

CHAPTER III

THE DIVINE OPERATIONS

Prologue

The Problem: After the treatise on God's existence, after the chapter devoted to the essence of God and to the divine attributes, we come to the difficult problem of the nature of His operations. What do we mean when we say that God understands, that He wills?[1] It should be noted first of all that God's operation is identical with His "To Be," since He is absolutely simple. God is His operation. It follows that the divine act of understanding, or as St. Thomas calls it, the "to understand" (*intelligere*), as well as the act of the will, the "to will" (*velle*), is pure existence. Absolutely speaking then, we may say that the chapter on the divine operations is only a continuation of the treatise on our knowledge of God's essence. That is very true. Yet, in our search for an understanding of the divine operations, in our mode of procedure, and in our approach to a solution, we note an important difference. It is this: in the study of the negative attributes, our primary concern was to obtain a negative knowledge. This consisted in denying that the content of our connatural understanding of material realities could be attributed to God's essence. Having obtained this purely negative knowledge of God's attributes, we then rose

---

[1] We need not establish by a formal proof that all divine actions are of the intellect or the will. These are the only operations which do not necessarily imply imperfection resulting from the limitation by matter; they are the operations of a spiritual substance. Because God is Existence, He is absolute spirituality. Hence, His operations are of His intellect and will. "God," St. Thomas states, "is pure act without any admixture of potentiality. On the other hand, matter is being in potency. Consequently, God must be utterly free from matter. But freedom from matter is the source [*radix*] of intellectuality. . . . Therefore, God is intelligent." (*Comp. Theol.*, I, c. 28.)

to a positive but analogous understanding by considering the divine perfection as participated in a creature endowed with a spiritual nature. Finally, in predicating directly this positive knowledge, we made use of the analogy of proportionality.

Only Positive Knowledge: Now in the study of the divine operations, we do not begin by a negative knowledge. The reason is this: when we speak of intellection, of volition, we mean — even in a creature — the act of a perfect being (*actus perfecti*).[2] Because such an operation does not imply the imperfection which results from limitation by matter, there can be no question of negative knowledge. It is true, nevertheless, that our knowledge of this type of operation is not connatural and proper, for it is obtained not from a consideration of material but of spiritual realities. It is only non-proper and indirect knowledge of a spiritual perfection. Hence, it can be predicated directly of God just as well as of creatures, according to the signification of the perfection. We must declare that God understands, God wills, just as we say that man understands, man wills. The mode of understanding in God, however, is profoundly at variance with that of man. In God, the operation is "To Be"; in creature, it is an accidental determination which, because it is accidental, supposes at least remotely potency, limitation, imperfection, composition in the subject.

Remotion of Imperfection: The point of major importance in this study, then, will consist in showing the profound differences between the divine operation and that of the creature. It is only when we have pointed out the imperfection in the mode of operation of the creature that we can rise to a better realization of the divine act. Hence, it is necessary to remove from the concept which is predicated of God any of the imperfections that may

---

[2] Transient or predicamental action is the perfection of the patient, the act of an imperfect being, of a being in potency; it is motion in the patient from the agent. The patient passes from potency to act. Such an action implies an imperfection, a potency in the patient. On the contrary, an immanent act of understanding or of will does not of its "make-up" (*ratio*) necessitate an imperfection, a passage from potency to act, for it is the perfection of the agent, that is, of a being in act; it is the act of a perfect being.

be implied in the creature's operation. St. Thomas is very insistent on this point. I submit two texts which occur in the first article of the fourteenth question, a question devoted to the divine knowledge.

> Whenever a name taken from any perfection of creatures [such as knowledge, understanding, love] is attributed to God, there must be *removed* from its signification all that which pertains to the imperfect mode which is proper to a creature.[3]
>
> The simple knowledge of God can be named from all these names [wisdom, counsel, intelligence, etc.] in such a way, however, that there must be *removed* from each of them, so far as they are predicated of God, whatever there is of imperfection.[4]

Division: In this chapter there will be two main divisions: (A) the Divine Knowledge and (B) the Divine Will. In connection with the knowledge of God, we shall also examine the problem of the ideas and of truth in God. Then, because "to understand" is the highest aspect of life, we shall present a question on the divine life. Following the treatise on God's will, we shall speak of God's love, of His justice and mercy, of His omnipotence, of divine providence, and of creation and governance of the universe.

Question I

THE DIVINE KNOWLEDGE

Division: There will be six articles: (1) God is the supreme knower. (2) He understands Himself perfectly. (3) Besides Himself, God understands all other things. (4) The relation of God's knowledge to existing creatures. (5) The division of God's knowledge. (6) God's knowledge of free futures.

---

[3] *S. Th.*, I, 14, 1, ad 1m.
[4] *S. Th.*, I, 14, 1, ad 2m.

ARTICLE I: God Is the Supreme Knower

Proof: This assertion is easily established. Let us recall the fundamental law of all knowledge: Immateriality is the root of knowledge.[5] The reason is this: Knowledge consists in an intentional union between knower and known. This union takes place in the knower, for "to know" is the operation, the act of the knower. Now the intentional union which is knowledge demands that the knower be free from matter. Let us explain. "To know" is to possess the form of another intentionally; it is an extension. Matter, on the other hand, limits and restricts.[6] Consequently, the greater the freedom from matter, the more perfect the knowledge. Now God, because He is pure existence, is not only immaterial; He is Immateriality. He is, therefore, the supreme knower.

Predication: Our understanding of this perfection, *knowing being,* we have obtained from creatures. We predicate it directly of God: God is a knowing being. In order to do this without error, we must first predicate this perfection of God, the *cause* of the knowing creature. Second, we must *remove* whatever imperfection we find in the mode of created knower.[7] Finally, we affirm the *supereminence* of the supreme knower, God, who is pure existence.

From this, we may draw the following inferences:

1. Knowledge in God is not, as in creatures, an accident of the genus quality; it is substance which is pure act.

2. Hence, the knowledge which in us is obtained piecemeal and successively is simple and one in God. For while we speak of concepts, reasonings and conclusions, wisdom, counsel, and prudence, we must understand that all this is one in God.

3. Consequently, the mode of knowing which depends on the nature of the knower is imperfect in creatures but perfect in God.

---

[5] Cf. *The Philosophy of Man,* p. 70.

[6] Cf. *S. Th.,* I, 14, 1, c.

[7] This we hope to accomplish in the following articles in which we shall study the object of divine Knowledge and the way God understands.

We do not speak, therefore, of habitual and potential knowledge in God; it is all actual, for God's knowledge is "To Be."

ARTICLE II: God Understands Himself Perfectly

Problem: In establishing that God is the supreme knower, we have implicitly suggested that He knows all beings. In order, however, to understand better what divine knowledge really is, we intend to consider the various objects of God's knowledge together with the manner of understanding these objects. In doing so, we shall the better grasp the perfection of the divine operation, and we shall thus attain the goal of our search which is to have a profound realization of what God is.

Division: Naturally, the first object of God's intellect is Himself. We shall posit first that God knows Himself absolutely, that is, that He comprehends Himself, and then we shall probe into the nature of divine intellection.

God Knows Himself Perfectly: This proposition is easily established. God is supremely intelligent; He is the supreme knower, for He is absolutely immaterial. He is also supremely intelligible; indeed we must say that He is Intelligibility Itself, for He is "To Be." Moreover, He is present to Himself, and the unity between the supreme knower and the supremely intelligible is a unity of identity.[8] God, therefore, knows Himself perfectly; He comprehends Himself.

> God comprehends Himself perfectly, as can be thus proved. A thing is said to be comprehended when the end of the knowledge of it is attained, and this is when a thing is known as perfectly as it is knowable. Thus, a demonstrable proposition is comprehended when known by demonstration, not, however, when it is known by some probable argument. Now it is manifest that God knows Himself as perfectly as He is perfectly knowable. For everything is knowable according to the mode of its act, since a thing is not known in so far as it is in potency, but in so far as it is in act. . . .

---

[8] This identity will appear fully in the following discussion on the reason for the perfection of God's knowledge.

Now the power of God in knowing is as great as His actuality in existing because through this, that He is in act and free from all matter and potency, God is knowing as was shown above. Whence it is manifest that He knows Himself as much as He is knowable; and because of this, He perfectly comprehends Himself.[9]

Nature of Divine Intellection: To the question, how does God know Himself, we answer immediately: God knows Himself by (*per*) Himself, by His essence (*per essentiam*). In order to understand the profound meaning of the question proposed, "How does God know Himself?" as well as the answer, "by Himself," it will be helpful to review some principles studied in the philosophy of man.[10]

Perfection of the Operation of Knowledge: The operation which terminates in knowledge is the most perfect action of any living being. It is an immanent act and is termed the act of a perfect being. A transient act, on the other hand, is the act of an imperfect being, for it is the perfection of the patient. The transient action is a motion from the agent in the patient and implies that the patient is imperfect, since it passes from potency to act. On the contrary, an immanent operation of understanding is the perfection of the agent; it is the act of a being which is in act; it is, as St. Thomas calls it, the act of a perfect being.

In the immanent act of knowledge, there are two stages to be considered: (1) the union of intellect with intelligible species; (2) the act of understanding. Now in man, the first step in the process of intellectual knowledge, which is the eduction of the intelligible species from the potency of the possible intellect, is really not the act of a perfect being. Only in the second stage, only in the act of understanding, can we speak of such an operation. And even there, we perceive that the union of intellect and concept which results from the act of understanding is not absolutely perfect, for this unit is made up of distinct parts. In God, on the contrary, we shall show that both stages are really one act, and that this is the act of a perfect being in the highest sense.

---

[9] *S. Th.*, I, 14, 3, c.
[10] Cf. *The Philosophy of Man*, p. 69 ff.

Let us now analyze these two stages of intellection in God and in man and, in doing so, indicate their profound diversity.

FIRST STAGE: The Union of Intelligible Species With Intellect

In Man: Creatures, because they are not their own "to be," are in potency to action.[11] Their operative potencies — in the present problem, the intellect — need some actuation before they can proceed to the operations of life. The intellect of man, then, to be capable of giving forth the act of understanding, needs to be actuated by a distinct representative form of the object, the intelligible species. Such a reception is really the act of an imperfect being: a potency (the possible intellect) is actuated by the action of a distinct agent (agent intellect with phantasm). This reception is not the act of understanding, the "to understand"; but it is a preparation, a beginning which is so intimately connected with the operation that the act of knowledge must necessarily and immediately follow. It is true, the union which takes place at this reception of the intelligible species is indeed of a very high order, so much so that we must affirm that *the intelligible in act is the intellect in act.* Yet, as we pointed out, this unity is not absolute, for it is made of distinct parts, to wit: the operative potency and the intelligible species.

In God: This is not the case with God's knowledge. God is pure act. His intellect, therefore, is not a distinct potency; it is Existence Itself and, consequently, it cannot be actuated. In God, therefore, by no means can the union which is knowledge result from distinct parts. It must be a unity of identity. The reason is that the object of knowledge is God's essence which is not only intelligible in act but pure intelligibility. Moreover, the divine essence is identical with the divine intellect. As applied to God's knowledge, therefore, the phrase *"intelligibile in actu est intellectus in actu"* is absolute. The unity is perfect.

By Himself: It is not to be thought, however, that God under-

---

[11] Cf. *S. Th.,* I, 54, 1.

stands without an intelligible species; rather, we must say that the intelligible species in God's knowledge is the essence of God. Hence, the intelligible species is absolutely one with the intellect; it *is* the intellect.[12] Consequently, and this is the point to be emphasized, God understands Himself *by Himself, by His essence,* and not by means of a distinct representative species.[13]

Summary: By way of summary, we may conclude: (1) Man, whose intellect is pure potency in the order of knowledge, does not know himself by himself, but by something else, that is, by means of a *distinct* intelligible species which actuates the intellect and enables it to break forth into the act of understanding. (2) God, whose essence is pure act in the order of existence as well as in the order of intelligibility, knows Himself by Himself; that is, the intelligible species by which God understands is His own essence which is not distinct but identical with His intellect. God, therefore, understands Himself by Himself.

Difficulty: Against this solution which Aquinas proposes regarding the first stage of intellection in God, it may be argued in

---

[12] *"Ipsa species intelligibilis est ipse intellectus divinus."* (*S. Th.,* I, 14, 2, c.)

[13] An interesting point regarding knowledge of self is brought out in a difficulty proposed against the statement that God knows Himself by Himself. The point at issue is simply that knowledge of self demands a spiritual nature or form. The difficulty is found in a quotation from the *Book of Causes* which reads: "Every knower who knows his own essence returns completely [*est rediens reditione perfecta*] to his own essence." The question is, what does this "complete return to one's own essence" signify? St. Thomas, who has used this assertion repeatedly, gives a very simple meaning to this technical phrase. He points out that self "redition" merely means self-knowledge and postulates a subsisting form. Accordingly, any material form which depends upon matter for its "to be" is not capable of returning upon itself, of knowing itself. The reason for such a statement is that being as it were submerged by matter which is the one obstacle to knowledge, a material form — although it might be capable of knowing another — can in no way, by returning upon itself, know itself. Such are the sense faculties. The soul of man, however, since it is subsistent, can return to self (*"forma . . . in quantum in seipsa habet esse, in seipsa redit"*); it can know itself but not by itself and, therefore, not by a perfect "redition." For the proper object of the human intellect is not itself. It knows itself indirectly by knowing another. Finally, God who is pure subsistence knows Himself by Himself. He returns perfectly to His essence. (Cf. *S. Th.,* I, 14, 2, ad 1m.)

this wise: "To know is in a certain manner to be moved."[14] This Aristotelian dictum which St. Thomas adopts and quotes seems contrary to our solution. Motion from another implies change from potency to act. Knowledge which implies such change cannot be the act of a perfect being.

Solution: This difficulty can be easily solved. The dictum quoted obviously refers in general to the imperfect mode of knowledge of the human intellect; it refers more particularly to the initial stage of that knowledge, namely, to the reception of the intelligible species. This reception, as we have remarked, is not the act of a perfect but of an imperfect being, of a being in potency. For the possible intellect of man before its actuation by the intelligible species is a being in potency.

It appears, then, that the difficulty loses its force regarding the intellect of God which is Act. While we are in agreement with the necessity in the human intellect of an initial change preliminary to the act of understanding, we must simply deny that such is the case regarding divine knowledge, for the intellect of God is Act: it is the "To Be."

We may add with St. Thomas that the act of understanding, the "to understand" by which the union of actual knowledge is attained, is in no way — even in man — a certain "to be moved," *"quoddam pati et moveri."* It is for the human intellect the act of a perfect being. This point we shall immediately examine.

SECOND STAGE: The Act of Understanding

Finally, in God, the absolute perfection of the operation of knowledge is completely expressed by this, that the act of understanding, the "to understand," is the "To Be."[15]

In Man: It will be remembered that the act of understanding of a created intellect is a quality which is distinct from the intellect

---

[14] *"Intelligere est quoddam pati et moveri."* (*Loc. cit.*)

[15] *"Ex necessitate sequitur quod eius intelligere sit . . . eius esse."* (*S. Th.,* I, 14, 4, c.*)

as well as from the intelligible species. Such an operation, we pointed out, is the act of a perfect being, even in a creature. For the created intellect which has been informed by the intelligible species is no longer in potency to the act of understanding which flows from it by a "certain resultance." The actuated intellect must cause its "to understand," since it is now in act to act. Yet the fact that this act of understanding is identical with neither the operative potency nor the intelligible species indicates some radical limitation, some fundamental imperfection, in the mode of created knowledge. What can the reason be for this imperfection?

The Reason for the Distinction Between the Act of Understanding and the Intelligible Species: The answer is not far to seek. When we consider the nature of the *existing* creature, we have to concede that such a nature is not its "to be"; it is distinct from it. The reason is that this nature is a limited essence, limited by reason of its intelligibility to be of this species and to be this individual.[16] That is why, of course, such a nature or essence limits its mode of existence to a determined and restricted "to be." Now a nature is a dynamic principle of action which by its natural appetite, that is, by its finality, tends to perfect itself. A created nature, however, being limited to a definite and restricted mode of existence, cannot acquire a more perfect "to be." It can only grow in the direction of action; it can only tend to perfect itself by acquiring in that order new modes of existence which are accidental actuations of its remote potencies. We may say, therefore, that even though the act of understanding, the act of a perfect being, unlike the intelligible species does not strictly actuate the operative potency, nevertheless in a more profound sense, that is, considering the limitation of the first principle of action which is the nature, we must affirm that this operation is a true actuation. That is why St. Thomas explains that, just as the "to be" is the perfection

---

[16] Potency limits itself. Cf. *The Philosophy of Being,* p. 37.

of the one existing, so the "to understand" is the act and perfection
of the subject of operation.[17]

In God: Accordingly, the act of understanding in God must be
identical with His "To Be." "For," explains the Angelic Doctor,
"if the 'to understand' were other than His substance, then something else would be the act and perfection of the divine substance
to which the divine substance would be related as potency to act,
which is altogether impossible, for [these words are significant]
the 'to understand' is the act and perfection of the one understanding."[18] In other words, an act of understanding, because it is the
act and perfection of the one understanding, must be proportioned
to the subject of intellection. Hence, if the divine "to understand"
were not "To Be," the essence of God would have to be distinct
from His "To Be," and that would be to say that God is not God.

Conclusion: Because the form (essence) of a creature is not
"to be" but has existence, its act of understanding must necessarily
be distinct from the intelligible species.[19] "In God, however, there
is no form [essence] which is not 'To Be.' Hence, since His essence
is also the intelligible species, it necessarily follows that His 'to
understand' is His essence and His 'To Be.' "[20]

It is the supreme perfection of the act of understanding that it
be identified with existence as well as with the essence. The imperfection of human understanding is radically founded on this
fact, that the essence of man is not his existential act. In God,
therefore, the absolute identity established above manifests the
analogy which true predication requires. Knowledge, which is an
intentional union, is predicated correctly of God and of man if
we understand that in God such a predication implies the unity
of absolute identity of the factors which must enter into such union;
in man, on the other hand, we discover a union of distinct parts.

---

[17] *"Intelligere . . . manet in operante sicut actus et perfectio eius, prout esse
est perfectio existentis." (S. Th.,* I, 14, 4, c.)

[18] *Loc. cit.*

[19] *"Sicut enim esse consequitur forma, ita intelligere sequitur speciem intelligi-
bilem." (Loc. cit.)*

[20] *Loc. cit.*

"Thus it follows that in God the intellect, the object understood, the intelligible species, and His 'to understand' are entirely one and the same. Hence, the fact that God understands in no way implies multiplicity in His substance."[21]

ARTICLE III:

A. **Besides Knowing Himself, God Knows All Other Existing Beings;**

B. **He Knows Them in Himself, Not in Themselves, That Is, He Knows Them in His Essence and Not by a Distinct Species Representative of the Object Known;**

C. **Consequently, He Knows Them Perfectly and by a Proper Knowledge.**

We have established that God knows Himself, that He knows Himself perfectly, that is to say, that He comprehends Himself. The reason is that God is pure immateriality and absolute simplicity. Hence the object known, the intellect, the intelligible species, and the act of understanding are one. The union of knowledge, therefore, is absolute; God's knowledge of Himself is perfect.

The Problem: Now we ask: Does God know creatures; how does He know them; and is this knowledge perfect?

A. God Knows All Things

The first and most immediate reason why God knows all things is that He is the cause of all reality besides Himself. Now God knows Himself perfectly. Obviously, such perfect knowledge will include the things to which His virtue and power extend as the first efficient cause of all existing creatures. Hence, knowing Himself perfectly, He knows all other beings.

Another and perhaps a more profound explanation looks more to exemplarity than to efficiency. It is this: the "To Be" of God, the first efficient cause, is also His act of understanding. Hence, any effect which pre-exists in the First Cause is in Him in a

----

[21] *Loc. cit.*

manner most intelligible, that is to say, as identified with His "to understand." This appears evident from the fact that whatever exists in another must exist in accordance with the mode of existence of that other being. Now God's mode of existence, the *Ipsum Esse,* is, we know, Intelligibility Itself. God, therefore, knows all things, because He knows His existence.[22]

B. How God Knows All Things

We must now examine the more difficult problem of the *how.* How does God know all creatures? In order to give an adequate answer to this question, we should first state a fundamental distinction. There are two ways of knowing an object, or rather, two ways by which we arrive at the knowledge of an object. The object is known *in itself,* or it is known *in another.* Let us explain.

1. We know an object *in the object itself* when we obtain our knowledge of the object by means of an intelligible species which is proper and adequate to the object known, a species which is either the object itself, or an intelligible form directly derived from and representing just the object. An example will clarify our statement. I see Peter. In my external sense of sight, the sensible species representing Peter is proper and adequate. It is a formal representation of Peter. I know Peter *in himself.*

2. On the other hand, we know an object *in another* when we obtain our knowledge by the species of another being. Were I to see Peter, for example, by looking into a mirror which reflects Peter's image, the sensible species received would be the mirror's, not Peter's. And yet, by means of this species, I really know Peter; but I know him in another, not in himself.

Applying this distinction to the knowledge which God has of creatures, we must declare that God knows them *not in the objects themselves* but *in Himself.* First, He does not know them in themselves, that is to say, by means of a distinct intelligible species proportioned to the object, because such a mode of knowledge would necessitate a determination, a specification, of God's intellect

---

[22] *S. Th.,* I, 14, 5; cf. *C.G.,* I, 48, 58.

by creature.[23] Second, He knows them in another, that is, in Himself. In other words, God knows creatures by an intelligible species which is His own essence.

N.B.: We should not confuse this clear-cut distinction, "an object is known in itself or in another," with another somewhat similar phrase which was used earlier, namely, "we do not know God as He is in Himself." The first is applicable to the knowledge of an object by anyone. The second we limit to our knowledge of the essence of God and of immaterial essences.

Moreover, the meaning of these two phrases is completely different. When, at the beginning of the tract on our knowledge of God's essence, we stated that "we do not know God as He *is* in Himself," we meant that we can have no connatural, proportionate, proper knowledge of God as He exists. Whatever knowledge we can have of Him is not connatural, but only indirect and non-proper, a knowledge which can be attained only by way of negation and analogy. Such knowledge is, therefore, quite imperfect.

In the present discussion of God's knowledge of creatures, the phrase, "a thing is known in itself or in another" signifies something else. When I see Peter by means of a species of the mirror, I see him as he *is* in himself, but I know him in another, that is, by means of the species of another. We may say, then, that the present distinction is directly concerned with the means, the species by which one knows. On the other hand, the phrase, "not to know the object as it *is* in itself," refers immediately to the perfection of the knowledge. It implies that the mode of existence of the object is more perfect than the mode of knowledge of the subject. Such knowledge, then, is necessarily imperfect.

Now when an object is known in another and not in itself, it does not necessarily follow that such knowledge is less perfect than if the object were known in itself. When I know Peter in a mirror, my knowledge of Peter is proper and could be just as perfect as if I saw him by means of a sensible species caused directly

---

[23] We need not give a formal proof of the impossibility of such determination, since God is pure act.

by Peter. Hence, to know an object in the species of another does not imply any imperfection. Indeed such species may result in more perfect knowledge than that caused by the object when the mode of existence of the other is more perfect.

Applying these reflections to God's knowledge, we may conclude: God knows Himself in Himself. He knows all creatures not in themselves but in another; He knows them in Himself. In other words, the intelligible species by which God knows Himself and creatures as well is His own essence.

C. Perfection of God's Knowledge of Creatures

The question of the perfection of God's knowledge of creatures is really a continuation of the problem of the *how*. We have established that God knows all creatures by means of the intelligible species which is His essence. The further question is: How is it possible for this infinitely perfect essence which is pure existence to represent finite creatures and to represent them as they are in themselves, so that God's knowledge of creatures may be proper and proportionate to them? Such a proper knowledge would demand that God know them with their limitations, their distinctions, their imperfections. Yet the intelligible species by which God knows them is absolutely simple and infinitely perfect.

God the Efficient Cause: It would not be sufficient to say that God knows all creatures in general (*in communi*), that is, only as beings, in so far as God is the universal cause of their existence. Such knowledge would be extremely imperfect, since it would not manifest the limitation, distinction, and multiplicity of the various created natures.

God the Exemplary Cause: The solution to this problem will demand a serious reflection upon a profound truth. God's essence is not merely the efficient cause of all that is; He is also the first exemplary cause of the various grades of perfections which make up the world of creatures. To assert, as some have done, that in the perfection or virtue of an efficient cause, we can infer the distinctions of the various effects, is to deny, implicitly at least, the principle of limitation which declares that an act must be limited by potency. In the course of metaphysics, it was shown that an efficient cause, no matter how perfect, cannot account for the intrinsic limitation of a limited being, unless the act be limitable by reason of a limiting potency.[24]

Accordingly, God, knowing Himself merely as efficient principle of all created reality, could not know the distinctions and limitations of the various created individuals unless He saw in the imitability of His essence the ultimate reason for their limitations. For, as St. Thomas points out, a universal efficient principle cannot, merely because it is efficient, cause multitude and diversity, limitation and distinction. It can only cause that in which the effects are alike: it can cause existence.

To the question, therefore, how can God — knowing creatures by means of an intelligible species which is His essence — know them by a proper and perfect knowledge, that is, according to their multiplicity and diversity, we answer:

1. In so far as He is their efficient cause, God knows what they have in common, that is, that they have existence, that they are.

2. In so far as He is their exemplary cause, He knows the various modes of participability of His essence; for "the nature proper to each [creature] consists in this, that in some manner it participates in the divine perfection."[25]

Conclusion: God, therefore, knowing Himself perfectly, that is, not merely as an effective cause but as the supreme exemplar knows all creatures by a perfect and proper knowledge.

Difficulties: It will help us greatly to understand this profoundly satisfying conclusion if we answer some difficulties.

First Objection: The first is simply this: How can the all-perfect, the all-simple essence of God contain the imperfections which result from limitation and from multiplicity?

Second Objection: The second is more formidable: How can matter, pure potency, matter which is not intelligible, be understood in an intelligible species which is pure act and absolute in-

---

[24] Cf. *The Philosophy of Being,* p. 30.
[25] *S. Th.,* I, 14, 7, c.

telligibility? And yet, a complete, a perfect understanding of the many material individuals demands that matter, the principle of individuation, be fully cognized. Or to put this difficulty briefly: How can God know material individuals?

Third Objection: The third objection seems really the most difficult: How can God, contemplating His essence which is Reality and Goodness, know evil, which is a lack of reality, a privation of goodness?

Reply to the First Objection: The first difficulty really has been partially solved. We must consider that in God, all possible perfections are found in a supereminent manner and, therefore, not only the perfection of existence in which all beings are similar, but also the perfections of the various forms which distinguish them; for the perfection of living differs from non-living because of the degree of perfection, of intelligibility of the essence which limits the perfection of "to be." These essences which manifest various degrees of intelligibility are in God in a supereminent manner. God, knowing His essence, knows them just as anyone knowing a more perfect act, for example, knowing the essence of man, knows the less perfect, animal. This type of knowledge is not knowledge of the essence of God considered merely as an efficient principle; but, rather, it envisages the essence of God as the exemplary cause of all.

God, therefore, knows the limiting factors of the various natures of creatures, because these factors are intelligible and, therefore, are contained in the essence of God as participable, as the supreme exemplar. He does not know them because He, the efficient principle, wills these various limitations to exist. The will of God looks to the *esse,* to the actuation of a nature. But this nature must be conceivable to be actuated. Hence, it is the intellect of God which — contemplating the beauty of His essence — understands the various participabilities of that essence, precisely because they are intelligible. These participabilities are the limiting factors of the various created or creatable natures.

Reply to the Second Objection: The second difficulty looks to God's knowledge of the material individual. If matter is not intelligible, it cannot be fundamentally rooted in the essence of God. Indeed, we must always deny of God whatever is material. This difficulty is very great in a philosophical system which takes so much from Aristotelian doctrine. A slavish follower of the Stagirite would have granted the impossibility of ever obtaining true intellectual knowledge of the material individual. He would have simply stated that the material individual is not intelligible. The answer to our difficulty is that matter is intelligible, not in itself, but mediately, by reason of its relation to form. Matter, or rather, the material individual, is known in the essence of God as its exemplary cause because of the intelligibility of the forms to which matter is related. Besides this, and as complementary to this knowledge, we may say that the material individual is known in the essence of God as in its efficient cause in so far as God wills to actuate this individual nature in the order of existence.

But St. Thomas goes even farther. He not only states that, because of the form, matter has a relation to existence; he affirms that matter itself, in so far as it has a "to be," retains a certain likeness (*similitudinem quandam*) to the divine "To Be."[26]

Reply to the Third Objection: Although the third difficulty seems the most formidable, it really is not, for we have already established the necessary preliminary principles for a succinct and complete solution. By knowing all the good things, God knows all evil, for evil is merely the lack of good; and, consequently, as He knows the good things perfectly, He sees what is lacking in their goodness and perfection.[27]

To conclude: God knows all creatures in His essence. He understands them in a knowledge that is perfect and proper.

ARTICLE IV: What Is the Relation of God's Knowledge to the World of Creatures, or Is the Knowledge of God the Cause of Things?

---

[26] *S. Th.*, I, 14, 11, ad 3[m].

[27] Cf. *S. Th.*, I, 14, 10. The problem of the relation of the will of God to evil is much more difficult. We shall speak of it at length later.

Problem: At this point, St. Thomas brings up the pivotal question of the treatise on God's knowledge. It is this: Can the knowledge which God has of creatures be termed in any manner the cause of the world of creatures? The answer which Aquinas gives to this is clear and definite. Yet, it has often been misunderstood and misinterpreted. Yes, affirms the Angelic Doctor, yes, God's knowledge is the cause of creatures, not however in the order of efficient causality, but in the order of specification.

Knowledge Is an Exemplary Cause: This distinction, which is of the highest importance, occurs in the various tracts of philosophy. In the course of metaphysics, a clear-cut distinction was made between formal and efficient causality. It was explained, moreover, that the exemplar belongs to the genus of formal causality; that it is an extrinsic formal cause; that it does not, like an efficient cause, produce an effect by the exercise of action, but communicates its perfection through the action of the efficient cause. It specifies.[28] As an application of this fundamental doctrine, it was explained in the philosophy of man[29] that the intellect cannot move the will in the order of exercise, that is, as an efficient cause, but that it does move the will in the order of specification, that is, in the order of formal and final causality, the order of the object and of the end. The term of the act of understanding is knowledge; this term is in the agent. In its highest aspect, this act consists in the contemplation of truth which is in the intellect. Evidently, such an operation can never terminate outside the intellect; and, consequently, by an act of knowledge, the intellect can never move another in the order of exercise. In other words, the intellect as such cannot be an efficient cause.

Knowledge Specifies the Will: The influx, then, which the intellect may have upon another, the will, can only be in the order of specification, that is, in the order of the object and of the end. Its causality is limited to that of an extrinsic cause, either formal or final. Hence, in the production of an effect outside the agent, the act of the intellect which is knowledge can never be the efficient

---

[28] Cf. *The Philosophy of Being,* p. 161.
[29] Cf. *The Philosophy of Man,* p. 185.

cause, for "an intelligible form, according to its nature, is not a principle of action."[30] Nevertheless, the act of understanding should be considered regarding such an effect, but only in so far as we restrict its causality to the order of specification. Let us explain. A spiritual agent acts by intellect and will. The will is the supreme mover in the order of exercise; that is, it is the supreme efficient cause. In the order of object and end, however, the will needs to be specified. This specification is from the intellect. Consequently, any effect produced by a spiritual agent must depend upon his will, the efficient cause, and upon the intellect, the specificative cause.

The Will of God Is the Efficient Cause of the Existing Creature: The point to be settled here is in what, precisely, consists the efficiency of the divine will regarding an existing creature. All Christian philosophers, indeed all philosophers who are worthy of the name, proclaim that whatever exists exists precisely because God wills it to exist. We depend at all times upon the will of God for existence; so much so that, should God ever will it, the world of creatures would cease to be.

Foundation for God's Knowledge of Possible Essences: When St. Thomas insists, and he does so in many of his works, that the knowledge of God is the specificative cause of all created reality, he indicates that it is not the will as will which determines the intelligibility of the various existing natures. As we have explained in the preceding article, it is the intellect contemplating the divine essence which sees the infinite participabilities of that essence. These are the various possible natures, the natures which could be actuated in the order of existence. But the intellect as intellect cannot actuate them; it cannot be the efficient cause of the existing natures. It is by the operation of His divine will that God efficiently causes certain of the understood natures to be actuated, to exist. The existing creature exists because of the will of God; it depends upon the will as its efficient cause. On the other hand, the determination, the specification, of the various natures depends upon God's knowledge of His essence.

---

[30] *"Forma intelligibilis non nominat principium actionis."* (*S. Th.,* I, 14, 8. c.)

Conclusion: Hence, to the question, what is the relation of the divine knowledge to the world of existing creatures, St. Thomas answers definitely: *God's knowledge is the specificative, the exemplary cause.* The essence of God as known by His intellect is the specificative, the exemplary cause of the form, of the nature of the creature. If, moreover, we ask what is the efficient cause of the *existing* creature in so far as it exists, we answer, "the will of God." If, finally, we propose to give a complete answer to the question, what is the adequate extrinsic cause of an existing creature, we reply with St. Thomas: not knowledge alone, nor the will alone, but knowledge to which is annexed the act of the will.[31] For the knowledge determines the nature of the effect; it specifies. The knowledge is the *formal extrinsic cause.* The will, on the other hand, is the efficient cause which by its action gives the "to be."

Because of the importance of St. Thomas' article we quote the body of article eight. It should be read and meditated upon. It is the fundamental solution, not only for the problem of God's knowledge, but for the problem of the will as well.

The knowledge of God is the cause of things. For the knowledge of God is related to all created things as the knowledge of the artificer is related to things made by his art. Now the knowledge of the artificer is the cause of the things made by his art, because the artificer works through his intellect. Hence the form in the intellect must be the principle of operation, as heat is the principle of heating. Nevertheless, we must consider that a natural form does not denote a principle of action in so far as it is a form remaining in that to which it gives "to be" but in so far as it has an inclination to an effect; and likewise, an intelligible form does not denote a principle of action in so far as it is only in the one understanding unless there is adjoined to it the inclination to an effect, which inclination is through the will. For since an intelligible form has a relation to opposites (inasmuch as the same knowledge relates to opposites), it would not produce a determined effect unless it were determined to one through the appetite, as the Philosopher says. Now it is manifest that God causes things by His intellect, since His "To Be" is His "to understand"; and hence His knowledge must be the cause of things, in so far as His will is joined to it.[32]

---

[31] *"Scientiam secundum quod habet voluntatem adiunctam."* (*Loc. cit.*)
[32] *S. Th.,* I, 14, 8, c.

ARTICLE V: Division of God's Knowledge

Following the solution established in the preceding article, a solution based on the distinction between God's knowledge as specificative cause of the various created individual natures, and God's will as the effective cause of their actuation in the order of existence, St. Thomas proposes a division which looks to the existential act of the object itself. This distinction results from the fact that some of the objects of God's knowledge are, were, or will be actuated in the order of existence, while the others — although actuable because possible essences — nevertheless will never exist. As regards, then, the object of knowledge, we may divide the knowledge of God into two general classes. The first is the *knowledge of vision* which comprises all existing realities; the second is the *knowledge of simple intelligence* which embraces the infinite multitude of possible essences.

Knowledge of Vision: The term "vision" is used to indicate that God sees these various objects actually existing.[33] "For though some of them may not be in act now, still they have been or they will be. . . . For, since God's act of understanding, which is His 'To Be,' is measured by eternity, and since eternity is without succession, comprehending all time, the present glance of God extends over all time and to all things which exist in any time, as to objects present to Him."[34]

Knowledge of Simple Intelligence: "There are other things in God's power, or the creature's, which nevertheless are not, nor will be, nor have been. As regards these, God is said to have knowledge of simple intelligence."[35] These things are the possible natures which God, contemplating His own essence, understands as actuable. The reason why God understands them is that these natures are intelligible and are, therefore, contained in the essence of God, the infinite exemplar of all that is intelligible. These possible natures do

---

[33] We use the word "vision" in the same manner, "because the things we see around us have a distinct 'to be' outside the seer." (*S. Th.*, I, 14, 9.)

[34] *Loc. cit.*

[35] *Loc. cit.*

not exist, because, as St. Thomas points out, God, the efficient cause of all existence, does not will to give them a "to be."

Scientia Media: To the division of knowledge proposed by St. Thomas it is customary to add a third class of objects and, therefore, a third class of knowledge. These objects are the free acts of any intellectual creature which would have been elicited had the creature been placed in certain definite circumstances. These acts are called the free futurables. The classification proposed for the sake of clarification is that God knows the free futurables in the type of knowledge called *middle science.*

Father Remer, S.J., points out that this last classification is really only a subdivision of the type of knowledge which St. Thomas designates as knowledge of simple intelligence.[36] The reason is that these futurables, although they will never be actuated in the order of existence, are intelligible and therefore true. Wherefore, they are contained fundamentally in the intelligibility of the divine essence. God, contemplating His essence, understands them. There can be no question in their case of a determination on the part of the divine will, since there is no actuation in the order of existence.

Let us note in passing that any operation of a free nature has a measure of intelligibility and, consequently, is known by God's intellect as one of the actuable beings which are contained in the exemplarity of the divine essence. Regarding these operations, there can be no question of a determination from God's will. A spiritual substance acts efficiently by the will, and the causality from the will of God pertains to the actuation in the order of existence. The will of God does not determine the intelligibility of a nature or of an operation. God knows a free operation not because He wills to predetermine the operation, but because such an operation is intelligible in itself; it is an essence. The act of the divine will is not in the order of exemplarity or of specification; it is purely in the order of exercise, of efficient causality, of the actuation of the "to be." A great deal of paper and ink would not have been

---

[36] "*Addi potest iure scientia media, si scientia simplicis intelligentiae inadequate accipiatur.*" Remer, *Theologia Naturalis,* V Edit. (Romae: Univ. Gregorianae), p. 140.

wasted had philosophers been mindful of this capital distinction of the Angelic Doctor. "Hence, it is not necessary that whatever God knows is, or has been, or will be; but only as regards what He *wills to be* or *permits to be.*"[37]

N.B.: The following should be carefully noted. The classification of the three types of knowledge does not indicate that there are various media of the divine knowledge. It was established definitely in the third article of this question that God knows all things *in Himself.* God's essence is the unique medium of divine knowledge. The three classes proposed in our present discussion look primarily to the objects themselves and are determined in accordance with the nature of their relation to actuation in the order of existence. They look, secondarily, to the knowledge of God upon which these objects must in some manner depend. If, then, we reflect upon the relation of dependence of the various objects of God's knowledge upon the divine essence, we must, in accordance with the principles inferred in the fourth article regarding the relation of God's knowledge to the objects, state the following conclusions:

Conclusions: 1. In the knowledge of simple intelligence taken adequately and, therefore, as including the *scientia media,* the object of knowledge in no way depends upon an act of the divine will.

2. In the knowledge of vision, (*a*) the existing object depends *for its intelligibility* (*secundum veritatem*) upon the exemplarity of the divine essence as known by the divine intellect; (*b*) the existing object depends *for its actuation* in the order of existence upon the efficiency of the divine will.

These conclusions should be kept in mind as we face the problem of God's knowledge of those free acts of a creature which will be placed in time, namely, the problem of the *free futures.*

ARTICLE VI: Knowledge of Free Futures

Problem: How does God know the free futures? This problem has been a source of unnecessary dissension among philosophers

[37] *S. Th.,* I, 14, ad 3[m].

and theologians. For us who have studiously established the fundamental principles of God's knowledge as proposed by the Angelic
Doctor, a general solution — at least in its inception — should not
be too difficult to formulate. Indeed, such a solution has been
virtually suggested in the discussion on the relation between God's
knowledge and its various objects. Let us then boldly state the
problem: How does God from all eternity know with absolute
certitude which free acts will be elicited in time by the various intellectual natures?

Many solutions have been offered. We briefly present only three
of the more influential and widespread theories.

Knowledge of the Created Will: Some theologians thought that
God, possessing as He does a perfect knowledge of the human will,
can know with certitude which actions the various free individuals
would elicit under any set of circumstances. This certitude, they
claim, should result from God's exhaustive knowledge of the cause
of these free operations, that is, from a knowledge of the created
will.

This doctrine is erroneous. Now no one has ever defended the
freedom of the will in a more comprehensive and absolute
manner than Aquinas. For in the doctrine of St. Thomas, until
the free act is elicited, if one were to consider the cause of this act,
that is, the will of man, no certain knowledge can be had as to
what the act will be. Indeed, no matter how perfectly he may
understand the nature of the cause of the free act, which cause
is the will of the creature, no one — not even God — is able to
know with absolute certitude what the free operation will be. At
best, he can guess with greater or less accuracy; he can conjecture
with greater or less probability. He simply cannot be absolutely
certain. For the freedom of the will means precisely that until the
act has been elicited, the will is capable of not placing it or of
eliciting another operation. Hence, concludes the Angelic Doctor,
a future free act "considered as contingent is not yet determined to
one, for a contingent cause [the free will] has a relation to opposites [*se habet ad opposita*], and in this sense a contingent thing
is not subject to *any certain* knowledge. Hence *whoever* [even God]

knows a contingent effect, in its cause only, has merely a con-
jectural knowledge of it."[38] To say, then, that God knows the free
futures in His knowledge of their cause, namely, in the created
will, is to deny implicitly that the will is free.

Predeterminists: Another school of theologians has suggested
that God's knowledge of the free futures is founded upon a divine
motion predetermining the will of the creature to a definite act.
God, they say, knows the free futures in the decree of His will by
which He wills to actuate this predetermining motion. In other
words, God knows the free futures because He predetermines the
will of the creature by a divine motion which precludes any other
action on the part of the creature except that which is predetermined
by God.

This opinion has been refuted at length in the treatise on the
human will.[39] It implies a denial of the very nature of freedom
which is opposed to necessity. Moreover, as we already established
in the same tract, it is obviously against the principles and the texts
of St. Thomas. We shall not at this juncture go into a formal
refutation of this opinion, as the matter has been sufficiently discussed in the philosophy of man.

N.B.: We do not deny that God moves the will of man either
by a natural motion or by His grace. What we deny is, first, that
because of this motion the will is necessarily determined and, second,
that this determination of the will of man by the divine motion is
the reason why God knows the free futures.[40]

Doctrine of St. Thomas: We need only repeat the conclusions
proposed in the preceding article.

1. The intelligibility of any reality, and hence the intelligibility
of the free futures, is seen by the divine intellect in the *exemplarity*
of the divine essence. It is neither because of a predetermining
motion, nor is it because of His perfect knowledge of the nature
of the created will that God understands what the action will be.

---

[38] *S. Th.,* I, 14, 13, c.

[39] Cf. *The Philosophy of Man,* p. 195.

[40] The question of the divine motion is treated in the very last question of this
book, the tract on the governance of the world.

It is because the operation is intelligible, because it has truth and, therefore, is known in the exemplarity of the divine essence.

2. The actuation in the order of existence by the "to be" depends, of course, upon the efficiency of the divine will. God, therefore, knowing in the exemplarity of His essence the intelligibility of the free act of the creature, freely wills its actuation in the order of existence. Consequently, in the knowledge of vision, God actually sees, from all eternity, the creature placing his free act in time. This knowledge of vision is expressed by the following text, a text which has too often been misunderstood and misinterpreted.

> Now God knows all contingent things not only as they are in their causes, but also as each one of them *is* actually in itself. And although contingent things become actual successively, nevertheless God knows contingent things not successively, as they are in their own "to be," as we do, but simultaneously. The reason is that His knowledge is measured by eternity, as is also His "To Be"; and eternity, existing simultaneously whole, embraces all time, as was said above. Hence, all things that are in time are present to God from eternity, not only because *He has the essences of things present within Him,* as some say, but because His glance is carried from eternity over all things as they are in their presentiality. Hence it is manifest that contingent things are infallibly known by God, inasmuch as they are subject to the divine vision in their presentiality; and yet they are future contingent things compared to their own causes.[41]

S U M M A R Y — THE DIVINE OPERATIONS

Prologue

1. Our knowledge of the divine operations is not negative; it is positive and non-proper.

---

[41] *S. Th.,* I, 14, 13, c.

2. The concept which we predicate is obtained from a consideration of the operations of spiritual creatures.
3. We must remove the imperfection which we find in the operations of these creatures.
4. In the predication, we affirm that the operation of God is "To Be."

Question I

DIVINE KNOWLEDGE

1. **Problem:** What do we mean when we declare that God understands?
2. **Division:** To solve this problem, we need to consider:
   a) The various objects of God's knowledge;
   b) His mode of understanding;
   c) The relation of God's knowledge to other beings.

ARTICLE I: God Is the Supreme Knower, Because He Is Pure Immateriality.

ARTICLE II: The First Object of God's Knowledge Is God Himself.

1. God knows Himself perfectly because:
   a) He is the supreme knower;
   b) He is supremely intelligible;
   c) The union between knower and known is perfect: it is a union of identity.
2. The nature of divine intellection: *He Understands Himself by Himself.*
   Two stages in the process of intellection:
   a) **Union of intellect and intelligible species.**
      In man: There is a passage from potency to act; the act of an imperfect being.

In God: The species is the divine essence and is identical with the intellect; it is the act of a perfect being. God, therefore, understands Himself *by Himself,* that is, by His essence.

b) **Act of understanding.**

In man: Although it is the act of a perfect being, nevertheless, because it is distinct from the intelligible species and from the intellect, the act of understanding supposes a remote potency in the subject, namely, that the creature is not its "to be."

In God: The act of understanding is "To Be."

ARTICLE III: God's Knowledge of Creatures

1. **God knows all other things,** because He, the supreme intellect, is their efficient cause.
2. **How does He know them?**
   a) God does not know created things in themselves, that is, not from a species derived from and proportioned to the object,
   b) But *in Himself,* that is, in the divine essence.
3. **Perfection of this knowledge:** The essence of God is not only the efficient but also the exemplary cause of all creatures. God knows all things according to their limitation and multiplicity, because all the various degrees of intelligibility are contained in the divine essence. Hence, contemplating His own essence, God understands all the possible imitations and participations of that essence which may be actuated if He wills to give them existence.

ARTICLE IV: The Relation of God's Knowledge to Existing Creatures.

1. **Problem:** Is God's knowledge the cause of existing creatures?
2. **Solution:** We distinguish between exemplary or specificative causes and efficient causes.
   a) God's knowledge is the exemplary cause.
   b) God's will is the efficient cause.
   c) God's knowledge with the will is the adequate extrinsic cause.

ARTICLE V: Division of God's Knowledge According to the Mode of Existence of the Object.

1. **Knowledge of Vision:** All existing beings, i.e., those which were, are, or will be. This knowledge implies not merely knowledge of intellect but the act of the divine will giving existence.
2. **Knowledge of Simple Intelligence:** All pure possibles. This knowledge does not imply the act of the will. It belongs only to the intellect.
3. **Middle Science:** All free futurables. This knowledge embraces the free acts of any intellectual nature which would have been elicited had the creature been placed in certain definite circumstances. Because they have a degree of intelligibility, they are contained in the divine essence as known, not as willed.

ARTICLE VI: Knowledge of Free Futures.

1. **Problem:** How does God know the free acts of any creature which will be elicited in time?
2. **Principle:** The free futures are intelligible in themselves, regardless of their "to be." Because of this intelligibility, they are rooted in the divine essence and known by the divine intellect. The fact that God wills to actuate them by giving them "to be" is beyond His knowledge of their intelligibility as actuable essences.
3. Hence, **God knows the free futures:**
    a) In the knowledge of *simple intelligence* together with their contradictories as possible;
    b) In the knowledge of *middle science,* in so far as one would be, if the creature were placed in certain circumstances and the "to be" given;
    c) In the knowledge of *vision;* because He wills to give existence, God sees them actually taking place.

Question II

CONSEQUENTS OF KNOWLEDGE:

DIVINE IDEAS, TRUTH, LIFE

There will be three articles in this question: (1) The Ideas in God; (2) God Is Truth; (3) God Is Life.

ARTICLE I: The Ideas in God

St. Thomas and Platonism: St. Thomas owes a great deal to Platonism. The tract on ideas is an evident indication of Plato's profound influence upon his thought. We must add, however, that although accepting certain of Plato's fundamental notions, the Angelic Doctor transforms them so completely that the very use of these notions implies a refutation of Plato's most cherished tenets.

Such is the Thomistic doctrine of ideas[42] and the subsequent notion of participation. The theory of participation which is so essential in the natural theology of Aquinas is undoubtedly Platonic in its origin. In Thomism it undergoes a complete transformation.

The Ideas of Plato: Plato[43] posits distinct subsisting ideas. These are the various specific and generic perfections which exist as distinct realities in the world of ideas. Each of these is universal, infinite in the order of essence. Because of their infinite perfection, these ideas are participable and are participated by other limited beings in two distinct ways. (1) The corporeal individual is a limited, imperfect participation in the subsisting idea. (2) The intelligible species in the human intellect, by means of which we understand,

---

[42] The word "idea" in St. Thomas' writings refers generally to a exemplary cause. It is not synonymous with the concept *"verbum"* in which we understand the object of knowledge. The terms generally used by St. Thomas for such a concept is *conceptus, verbum, intellectus indivisibilium;* never "idea."

[43] We do not pretend to state definitely what Plato really thought. Rather we wish to express what Thomas believed to be Plato's views, and why he differed from the Greek philosopher. (Cf. *S. Th.,* I, 15; I, 84, 1.)

does not result — according to Plato's theory — from sense knowledge which is caused by the existing individual. Rather it is a
direct participation in the subsisting idea. That is the Platonic
explanation for the fact that our concepts are of a universal essence
and not of individuals. Individuals are not known, because they
are not intelligible.

It is obvious that such a theory could not be acceptable to a
Christian philosopher, for the immediate term of the creative act
of God is the individual. The individual, therefore, is a participation in the perfection of God who creates it. Consequently, the
individual is intelligible.

Doctrine of St. Thomas: Hence, although Aquinas adopts the
notion of participation, with him such a notion signifies always the
direct dependence of an existing individual upon God's knowledge
and in no way upon distinct subsisting ideas. For this reason,
following St. Augustine, the Angelic Doctor points out the following: (1) There are no distinct subsisting ideas: the ideas are in
God. (2) These ideas are nothing else but the knowledge that God
has of His essence, in so far as it is imitable or participable. (3)
The ideas in God are, therefore, the exemplary cause of all creatures.
(4) Consequently, they (the ideas) are *not universal,* specific, subsisting realities; they are *individual* exemplars in the intellect of
God and, hence, are not distinct from God's essence, the subsisting "To Be."

Conclusion: Contrary to Plato's view, we conclude:

1. The existing individual participates of God's perfection, not of
a distinct subsisting idea.

2. The intelligible species by which we understand is not caused
directly by the idea; it results, rather, from sense knowledge of
an existing individual. It is a universal, representative form and
not the image of the individual; and its universality results from the
abstractive process of intellectual knowledge in man.[44]

3. The ideas in God are the exemplary cause of created reality.
Together with God's will, they are the adequate cause of all existing

---

[44] Cf. *The Philosophy of Man,* p. 119 ff.

individuals. The ideas in God are, therefore, not universal but individual exemplars.

Inferences From This Doctrine: St. Thomas proposes several illuminating inferences. Some of these require no comment.

1. The ideas in God are not distinct from His essence.[45]

2. There are innumerable ideas in God. This multiplicity is not opposed to the divine simplicity, for the intelligible species by which God understands these various creatable essences is one: it is the divine essence. Certainly, it is not contrary to the simplicity of the divine intellect to know many things. But it would indeed be the denial of divine simplicity, and in truth the denial of God, if the divine intellect were informed by a multitude of distinct intelligible species.[46]

3. We should distinguish between God's knowledge of the pure possibles which will never be actuated in the order of existence and His knowledge of the essences which will exist. We may recall that such a distinction was instituted in the fifth article of the preceding question. There, we spoke of knowledge of simple intelligence and knowledge of vision. This classification has to do largely with the mode of existence of the object. At this juncture, however, the distinction proposed, although based fundamentally on the same consideration of the mode of existence of the object, looks more to the knowledge of God as divided into speculative and practical. The pure possibles are in the order of *speculative knowledge;* the essences which will be created are in the order of *practical knowledge.* To make this clear, St. Thomas uses two distinct terms: *"ratio"* (knowledge of a possible essence) and *exemplar.* The word "exemplar" signifies exemplary cause; it looks to the actuation in the order of existence by the will; it is in the order of practical knowledge. On the other hand, *ratio* indicates the pure consideration of an essence; it does not look to the will for existential actuation. Such knowledge may be purely speculative.

As ideas, according to Plato, were the principles of the knowledge of things and of their generation, an idea, as existing in the mind

---

[45] Cf. *S. Th.*, I, 15, 1, ad 3ᵐ.
[46] Cf. *S. Th.*, I, 15, 2, c.

of God, has a relation to both. So far as the idea is the principle of the making of things, it may be called an *exemplar,* and pertains to practical knowledge. But so far as it is a principle of knowledge, it is properly called a *ratio,* and may pertain to speculative knowledge also. As an *exemplar,* therefore, it is related to everything made by God in any period of time; whereas as a principle of knowledge it is related to all things known by God, even though they never come to be in time; and to all things that He knows according to their proper *rationes,* in so far as they are known by Him in a speculative manner.[47]

ARTICLE II: God Is Truth

Reasons for Placing This Question Here: It is customary in textbooks of philosophy to incorporate the transcendentals — the one, the true, and the good — into one comprehensive treatise. In the *Summa Theologica,* however, St. Thomas studies each one separately, and only occasionally does he show their interrelations. His general treatise on the transcendentals is found on the very first page of his *De Veritate.* In the first part of the *Summa Theologica,* we find a complete treatment of his natural theology, in which the one, the true, and the good are studied as predicated of God. Here, Aquinas proposes the various transcendentals separately and always in connection with some previous question which seems to be the occasion for bringing up the problem of this or that transcendental. The good, for example, is studied in connection with the question of perfection; for the good is the very marrow of that which is perfect (*bonum est ratio perfecti*). The good, therefore, is a fundamental, direct, and positive predicate of God. On the other hand, the problem of the one has to be solved in order to arrive at an understanding of the unity of God. Now unity is an attribute which integrates all the other attributes by denying absolutely the divisibility of the divine "To Be." Hence, the nature of divine unity is sought, discovered, and understood only after the existential simplicity, the infinite perfection, and the eternal immutability of the divine essence have been explained.

---

[47] *S. Th.,* I, 15, 3, c.

For these reasons, although the goodness of God is presented in the sixth question, the treatise on the one occurs only after simplicity, infinity, and all the other negative attributes have been studied. Divine unity is the last of these attributes.

Unlike the one and the good, the problem of the true does not occur in the treatise on the essential attributes of God, but in the chapter on the divine operations. For truth is primarily in the intellect and only secondarily can it be predicated of a thing. Because of this connection with the intellectual operation, St. Thomas, immediately after treating of knowledge, inquires into the natural resultance of knowledge: truth.

We need not discuss here the profound metaphysics of the transcendental true, for this has been studied in the philosophy of being. Nor do we intend to solve the arduous and complicated problem of formal truth, for that would take us too far afield into the epistemological problem. We shall rather limit ourselves to the true as predicated of God. God, we shall explain, is not only the true, but He is Truth Itself — both transcendental and formal.

Formal and Transcendental Truth in God: *Formal truth* is in the intellect. It consists in the conformity of the intellect with its object, in so far as the intellect knows what the object is. *Transcendental truth,* on the other hand, is the conformity of the object to its intellectual exemplar. Clearly, transcendental as well as formal truth is attributable to God, for His essence, which is "To Be," is not only conformed to His intellect; it is one with the intellect. Hence, the true which founds a relation, as well as truth which is the relation itself, are in God by a conformity of identity, for the essence, the intellect, and the "to understand" are the "To Be." Hence not only should we attribute *the true* to God, but we must add that He is Truth Itself.

> As was said above, truth is found in the intellect according as it apprehends a thing as it is; and in things according as they have "to be" conformable to an intellect. This is to the greatest degree found in God, for His "To Be" is not only conformed to His intellect, but it is the "to understand"; and His act of understanding is the measure and cause of every other "to be" and of every other in-

tellect; and He Himself is His own "To Be" and "To Understand." Whence it follows not only that truth is in Him, but that He is the highest and first truth itself.[48]

All Created Truth Participates in the Divine Truth: To supplement this realization of divine truth, and the better to understand the connection between the true (transcendental) as predicated of creatures with their exemplars in the divine intellect (formal truth), we quote the following passage.

> Now we have said that truth is primarily in the intellect, and secondarily in things, according as they are ordered to the divine intellect. . . . If we speak of truth as it is in things, then all things are true by one first truth, to which each one is made similar according to its own entity. And thus, although the essences or forms of things are many, yet the truth of the divine intellect is one, in relation to which all things are said to be true.[49]

ARTICLE III: God Is Life

Why Discuss Life at This Point?: We may wonder why the problem of life is brought in at this point. The answer is simply this. The highest operation of life, the act of a perfect being *par excellence,* is the act of understanding. Moreover, in God the act of understanding is "To Be"; it is "To Live." Hence after the question of God's knowledge and its consequents, namely, the ideas and truth, we naturally inquire into the signification of the operation of life in God.

What Is Life?: It will not be necessary to discuss what life is in itself. In the philosophy of man,[50] we gave a long metaphysical disquisition on the definition and the predication of life, not merely in so far as life is an operation of a living being, but in itself. As a result of this inquiry, we came to realize that life in itself, and not as an operation, is the abstract of "to live." Now "to live," explains St. Thomas, is the "to be" of living beings. Life, therefore, is the "to be" of a living being conceived abstractly.

---

[48] *S. Th.,* I, 16, 5, c.
[49] *S. Th.,* I, 16, 6, c.
[50] Cf. *The Philosophy of Man,* p. 5 ff.

Perfection of the Operation of Life in God: Here, then, we are concerned only with life as an operation. Now as we have pointed out, every divine operation is necessarily identical with existence, and consequently, we must understand that in God the operation of life is "To Be." Not so in creatures; the immanent actions of these limited beings, no matter how perfect they be, are distinct accidents under the genus of quality. This fact helps us to understand the perfection of life in God; it helps us to understand the content of our thought when life as an operation is predicated of God, the supreme living being, and of creatures. It is a predication which obviously implies an analogy of proportionality. For the operation of life in God is "To Be"; in creatures it is a reality distinct and proportioned to the existential principle of life which is "to be," as well as to the essential principle which is the living form, the soul. God is His own operation of life; creatures have these operations distinct from and superadded to their substantial make-up.

Relative Perfection of Life in Creatures: This is why, after a long exposition of the three elements which enter into the perfection of a living operation, namely efficiency, exemplarity, and finality, St. Thomas first indicates the relative perfection of the intellectual act in man.[51] Rising thence to God's action, he thus points out the profound difference between the operation of life in God and man.

> But although our intellect moves itself to some things, yet others are given it by nature, as are first principles, which it must accept, and the last end, which it cannot but will. Hence, although with respect to some things it moves itself, yet with regard to other things it must be moved by another. Hence, that being whose nature is His "to understand," and which, in what it naturally possesses, is not determined by another, must have life in the most perfect degree. Such is God; and hence life is in Him absolutely.[52]

"All Things in God Are the Divine Life": Indeed, so perfect is the supreme operation of life in God, that is, the act of the intellect

---

[51] Cf. *S. Th.*, I, 18, 3. This article was analyzed in *The Philosophy of Man*, p. 18 ff.

[52] *S. Th.*, I, 18, 3, c.

in which God knows all things, that we can truly say that all things as understood in Him are the divine Life Itself.

> In God "to live" is "to understand," as was said before. But in God intellect, the thing understood, and the act of understanding are one and the same. Hence whatever is in God as understood is His very "to live" or life. Now, therefore, since all things that have been made by God are in Him as things understood, it follows that all things in Him are the divine life itself.[53]

S U M M A R Y — Question II

CONSEQUENTS OF KNOWLEDGE:

DIVINE IDEAS, TRUTH, LIFE

The *ideas, truth,* and *life* are the consequents of divine knowledge in this way:

1. **The ideas belong to divine knowledge, because they are the exemplars** of all creatures seen in the divine essence by the divine intellect. They are the divine essence itself as imitable and known by the divine intellect. This is not Platonism.

2. **Truth flows from knowledge;** it is the relation of knower to known, and of known to knower, that is, either formal or transcendental. God is absolute Truth, both formal and transcendental, because the relation between His intellect and His essence is one of identity.

3. **The highest operation of life is the act of understanding.** That is why life is considered here as a consequent of knowledge. In itself, life is the "to be" of a living being conceived abstractly. As an operation, life in a creature is a distinct, an accidental form. In God, life is identical with the operation of life. Hence while we speak of a creature which *has* life, we must affirm that God *is* Life.

---

[53] *S. Th.,* I, 18, 4, c.

Question III

THE WILL OF GOD

Prologue

Problem: The problem of the will of God is undoubtedly one of the most profound in the science of philosophy. It is not only a difficult question, but one whose solution is far-reaching in its consequences. There are indeed many aspects of the problem of the will of God; or to put it more exactly, there are various distinct problems. Not all of them need be treated at this point; indeed not all of them belong to a course in natural theology. We are not concerned in this treatise with the ascetical point of view, that is, with the conformity of our will with the will of God. Such a consideration consists largely in a practical application of principles studied here and in revealed theology. We may, however, briefly point out that a treatise on conformity with the will of God does not pretend to make a study of the will of God as it is in itself. It is concerned, rather, with the manifestations, or as theologians express it, with the "signs," of God's will. For example, when we say, "Thy will be done," we refer not to the will itself but to the precepts given us by God.

Moreover, we do not intend to discuss the already established truth that God, like all spiritual beings, acts efficiently by His will; so that although the intelligibility of all creatable essences is discovered by the divine intellect, the production of these essences in the order of existence depends upon the will as the efficient cause of their "to be."[54]

The central question in this tract is concerned with the necessity and freedom of God's will as regards its object. After establishing that God does not act as regards the production and governance of the world by a necessity of nature, but by intellect and will, we shall study the problem of the will of God from two distinct

---

[54] "*Ex voluntate Dei dependet quod res in esse producat.*" (*S. Th.,* I, 9, 2, c.)

angles: If God's will as well as its operation, namely the "to will," be identical with "To Be," (1) how can God will anything freely; (2) how can some of the effects, willed as they are by a will that is a necessary being, a will that is always in act and therefore immutable, be termed contingent? We may express this last problem more realistically thus: How can the human acts, which depend for their existence upon the will of God in so far as He wills them to exist, be contingent, that is, free and not necessary? This problem appears even more insoluble when we reflect that the will of God, because identical with pure existence, cannot be determined. It cannot change; it cannot be actuated; it has no cause but is the cause of all existence. In short, our difficulty is this: Because the divine will is its own "To Be," anything that God wills is necessitated; it cannot be free.

These enormous difficulties are responsible no doubt for the error of the Neo-Platonists and the long line of pantheistic idealists down to our own age who, while not always expressing this problem in the metaphysical manner of St. Thomas, seem implicitly at least to have sensed it.

Two Extreme Positions: There really are two extreme positions regarding the necessity and freedom of God. The first, the position of the Neo-Platonists, belongs to those who teach that God acts by a necessity of nature. The other position, that of the voluntarists, takes the stand that the will of God is supreme and free, not only as regards the production and governance of the world, but also in determining the intelligibility of being. For in this theory it is the will itself rather than the divine essence as known by the intellect of God which determines the possibility and intelligibility of the world.

Neo-Platonist-Pantheists: Plotinus (205?–270?), the leader of this school, proposes a First Principle who by a necessity of nature produces an intelligible world by means of a necessary illumination.[55] This necessity, based on an immutability which is not at all the dynamic immutability explained by the Angelic Doctor but is

---

[55] Cf. *Enneades*, III, 2, 1.

really a lack of power and virtue, is presented by Giordano Bruno (1548–1600) and the pantheists of the Renaissance as an unanswerable argument against freedom in God. Later, Spinoza (1632–1677) was to explain that all things are really determined by the necessity of the divine nature. It follows, then, that whatever contingency and freedom is perceived by us is due solely to the weakness of our intellect.

God Does Not Produce the World by a Necessity of Nature: St. Thomas has vigorously refuted this error. In the *Summa Theologica,* I, 19, 4, he offers three conclusive arguments which are based immediately upon evident metaphysical principles. These arguments establish that God does not act by a necessity of nature but by intellect and will. It will suffice to mention one of these.

Any agent which acts by necessity of nature must depend upon a superior, an intellectual cause. The reason is that such necessity can only mean a natural appetite, that is, an inclination to an end that is necessarily sought. Now, as everyone knows, such necessary finality always presupposes a superior intellectual cause.[56] God, however, is the first cause; hence He cannot act by mere natural necessity; He must act by intellect and will.

Voluntarists: Completely opposed to this denial of willful operation is the doctrine of Ockham, Descartes, and the voluntarists of all time. According to these, the will of God is not only free regarding the bringing of the world into existence, but it is the determining cause of its intelligibility; indeed, it is the cause of the intelligibility of being.

Criticism: This doctrine is an implicit denial that being itself is intelligible, since in point of fact, according to these philosophers, the will of God is wholly responsible for such intelligibility. The result of the denial of the intelligibility of being is, of course, the

---

[56] The end is in the intentional order, for the end is the effect *as desired.* Consequently a being which acts because it is necessitated by its nature does not determine the end, which it seeks necessarily. This end therefore needs to be determined by a superior agent which is intellectual. Otherwise the necessary action of a nature would not be intelligible.

denial of truth, for there can be no absolute truth, no necessary morality, when the foundation of truth is no longer the necessary intelligibility of the essence of God but the act of His will which is free and not necessitated. That which is true today may be false tomorrow if God so wills it. We are now immersed in a relativism which must terminate as it did historically in the skepticism of Hume.

Doctrine of St. Thomas: St. Thomas, the moderate intellectualist who never lost sight of reality, rejects both errors. Against the doctrine of the voluntarists (a doctrine which was to develop fully only after his day) the Angelic Doctor repeats again and again that the will of God is supreme in the order of existence, but that its specification is from the intellect which contemplates the absolute intelligibility of the creatable natures, founded as they are in the divine essence. On the other hand, the pantheistic tenets of the Neo-Platonists always appeared fantastic to Aquinas. To him, the great existentialist, such a doctrine showed a complete misunderstanding of the supreme existential reality, the subsisting "To Be." It seemed to him the height of contradiction to declare that Pure Existence could be necessarily inclined, and by a necessity of nature, to the limited "to be" of a creature; that the Uncaused Cause could be necessarily determined by the world of creatures whose "to be" is from God.

St. Thomas, therefore, while admitting the absolute necessity of the "to will" regarding the divine goodness, insists that God freely creates the world, a world already intelligible in His essence and conceived by His intellect. This intelligibility is independent of the divine "to will," and therefore the freedom and contingency of the human acts are fully vindicated. For the divine "to will" is in no way necessitated by the intelligibility of the creatable essences; nor, in its turn, does it necessitate the human act whose intelligibility established its freedom. The will of God merely wills or does not will the "to be" of an action whose determination is from the free will of the creature.

The will of God is both free and necessitated, but regarding distinct objects. Some of these objects, once they are freely willed by

God, will be necessitated by reason of their nature; others are free by reason of their nature which is free.

Division: There will be three articles: (1) there is will in God; (2) God wills freely all other things besides Himself; (3) the will of God does not impose necessity on all the things willed. We shall close this question with a short appendix about the relation between God's will and evil.

ARTICLE I: There Is Will in God

Difficulty: At first, one might wonder what is meant by this expression, "There is will in God." The will in man we know is an operative potency, an accidental form which, being actuated in the order of exercise by God and being specified by the human intellect, gives forth freely the act of choice. In God, certainly, there is no operative potency, for He is pure act; there is no distinct accidental form, since God is absolutely simple. Indeed there is no action, no operation, which is not the "To Be." How, then, can there be will in God?

Solution: We answer that when we speak of will in God, we do not mean precisely that God has a distinct faculty called the will. We may recall the parallel problem of intellect in God. When we discussed God's knowledge we explained that, since God is absolutely immaterial, He understands and, therefore, in Him there is intellect. This intellect, we showed, is not a distinct faculty but the "To Be," so that we must not say that God *has* an intellect, as we affirm of man, but rather that God *is* intellect.

In the same manner, because God is unqualifiedly spiritual, He not only knows but He loves; and because He loves, He wills to communicate His goodness. This free communication of perfection which presupposes an operation which terminates outside of Himself, this "to will," this "to love," is in God identical with the "To Be," for the will of God is pure existence. In no way, therefore, do we postulate in God the kind of a will which we discover in rational creatures, one which first wills the end and then the means. The "to will" in God is one, because it is "To Be."

In order to understand better the function of the will in God, we need to recall certain principles of metaphysics and rational psychology.

What Is the Will?: The will, we saw in the philosophy of man,[57] is an intellectual inclination, an appetite of a rational being to the absolute good. It flows from an intellectual nature and necessarily accompanies it. This truth can be established thus. Every nature has an inclination for the form which is its act, so that if it lacks this perfection it must necessarily tend toward it; and if it possesses it, it must rest in its possession. This is true of the good of nature which is the end of every being; and in things lacking knowledge, or in a nature considered as such, this inclination is not distinct from the nature itself. It is the nature seeking its end. St. Thomas calls this inclination the natural appetite or the appetite of nature — a phrase which has often been totally misunderstood.[58] In like manner, we argue that an intellectual nature has, as a result of its intellectual knowledge, a similar inclination, not this time to the good of nature, but to the known good. This new inclination, then, demands a new subject which we term "will." Like the good of nature, the known good when lacking is sought; when possessed, it is enjoyed.

There Is Will in God: Every intellectual being, then, must have will. In God, however, the intellect as well as the will are one with

---

[57] Cf. *The Philosophy of Man*, p. 156.

[58] This phrase of the Angelic Doctor has sometimes been misinterpreted by Christian philosophers when discussing the problem of man's desire for his supernatural end, the vision of God. While relinquishing this problem to the theologians to whom it properly belongs, we should like to state that when St. Thomas speaks of a natural desire or appetite for the vision of God, he means a necessary exigency, whether known or not, in the nature of man — as found in the present order of Redemption — to his supernatural end, for man is not in the order of pure nature. Now in his present situation in the order of Redemption, a man who has reached the age of reason, whether he be in the state of grace or in the state of sin, possesses a nature which is now related to the vision of God as to its last end. Hence, St. Thomas speaks of an appetite of nature (understanding the nature of man as related to its present supernatural end) for the vision of God. Let us repeat once more that a *natural* appetite, a natural desire, need not result from the *known* good. It is merely the inclination of a nature to its end. (Cf. *De Malo*, V, 3; *S. Th.*, I, 62, 2; *In II Sent.*, dist. 33, q. 2, a. 2.)

His essence. God's will, therefore, is "To Be." Hence, when we explained in a previous question that God acts by His essence (*per essentiam*), we meant that He acts after the mode of intellect and will.[59] We conclude: there is will in God. The will of God as well as the act of willing are, in God, identified with "To Be."

ARTICLE II: God Wills Freely All Things Other Than Himself

Freedom of God's Will: The will of God is "To Be." We may immediately infer from this identity of will and "To Be" that the will of God is necessitated by the divine goodness which is identical with the will. For the divine goodness is "To Be." We may infer from this that, regarding all other good distinct from the divine goodness, the will of God is not necessitated; it is free. Freedom implies a lack of determination of an inclination. Now matter, we know, is that which determines by limiting. That is why the sense appetite, which results from knowledge which is limited by the conditions of matter, is necessitated and not free. God, however, is absolute spirituality. Hence, regarding any known good which is not His own goodness but is distinct from Him, the will of God is in no way necessitated; it is free.

Difficulty, Freedom as Opposed to Immutability of the Will of God: In opposition to the doctrine of the freedom of God's will, some obvious difficulties are often brought up. Precisely because the will of God is the unchangeable eternal substance of God, it would seem to follow that the will is immutable and, therefore, not free; for freedom demands the possibility of willing or not willing: it imports necessarily the possibility of change. Now God's will is immutable and therefore necessitated, not free.

Distinction: In order to offer a complete solution to this difficulty, we shall first propose an important distinction. When we speak of necessity, we may explain that something is necessary either *absolutely* or *by supposition*. It is necessary *absolutely* when the

---

[59] "Because the essence of God is His intellect and will, from the fact of His acting by His essence, it follows that He acts after the mode of intellect and will." (*S. Th.*, I, 19, 4, ad 2ᵐ.)

predicate of what is affirmed pertains to the essence of the subject. Man, for example, is an animal with absolute necessity, since the predicate belongs to the definition of the subject. On the other hand, a thing is necessary only *by supposition* when the necessity depends on the supposition of its being true, as, for example, supposing that John is sitting, we may state that John necessarily sits *by necessity of supposition.*

Solution: Applying this distinction to the will of God, we may declare:

1. God wills His own goodness with *absolute necessity,* for the divine will has a necessary relation of identity with the divine goodness.

2. God does not will other things with absolute necessity, since these other things are not identical with, neither have they a necessary relation to, the divine goodness. He wills them freely.

3. Supposing, however, that God has freely willed from all eternity to create this world and to govern it in accordance with a definite plan, we may say, since the will of God is immutable and efficacious, that He wills this actual order of the world *by necessity of supposition.* "Hence," explains Aquinas, "since the goodness of God is perfect and can exist without other things, inasmuch as no perfection can accrue to Him from them, it follows that for Him to will things other than Himself is not absolutely necessary. Yet it can be necessary by supposition, for supposing that He wills a thing, then He is unable not to will it, as His will cannot change."[60]

Conclusion: The important point in this solution which should be remembered is that *the divine act of willing a creature has no necessary order to divine goodness.* That is why the divine will is free to create or not to create this or that world. This point is well brought out by the Angelic Doctor. To the query that because God knows all things necessarily, He must therefore will them necessarily, since the divine knowledge as well as the divine will are one with His essence, he answers:

---

[60] *S. Th.,* I, 19, 3, c.

Just as the divine "To Be" is necessary of itself, so is the divine "to will" and the divine "to know"; but the divine "to know" has a necessary habitude to the thing known; not the divine "to will," however, to the thing willed. The reason for this is that knowledge is had of things as they are in the knower; the will, however, is compared to things as they are in themselves. Since, then, all other things have a necessary "to be" inasmuch as they are in God, but have no absolute necessity in so far as they are in themselves, it follows that God knows necessarily whatever He knows, but does not will necessarily whatever He wills.[61]

We conclude: Since, then, God wills His own goodness necessarily, that is, with absolute necessity, but other things not necessarily, that is, only by necessity of supposition, He has free choice (*liberum arbitrium*) with respect to all other things besides Himself.

The Will of God Has No Final Cause: Why does God will other beings besides Himself? (1) Because He wills to communicate His goodness. (2) His goodness, however, although the end to which all things are ordered, is not the final cause of His willing the "to be" of creatures. We shall establish both propositions.

1. First, let us state a principle. Not only does a being (*res naturae*) tend toward its proper good when it is lacking it, not only does it rest in the possession of such a good when it possesses it, but it possesses a natural inclination, necessary in an inanimate being, *free in a free nature,* to communicate the good which it possesses. For a being acts in so far as it is in act in accordance, of course, with its nature.

It is in this fashion that we must consider why God wills other beings besides Himself. He wills His goodness to be participated by others. In no way does He will a creature in order to obtain His own good. To do so would be a contradiction, since He is Goodness Itself. The end of His act of willing, therefore, is not the desire to attain a desired good; nor are creatures means that God might possess His own goodness. On the contrary, God wills other beings besides Himself, because He wills to communicate His own goodness.

---

[61] *S. Th.*, I, 19, 3, ad 6[m].

2. Although the goodness of God is the end of His act of willing, nevertheless it is not its final cause. The reason is that a final cause is distinct from the agent, for it is the effect *as desired* and not yet possessed. Now the act of willing in God, the "to will," is identical with His goodness. Hence, while God is not moved to action by a final cause, He not only has an end, but that end, His own goodness, is Himself. God, then, wills creatures as well as His goodness by the same unique "to will."

In creatures the will is an inclination to an end sought but not yet possessed, and consequently, the act of the will in creatures imports a final cause. There can be, as we remarked, no final cause in God, since God is "To Be." We speak, however, of God's goodness which is not sought but is loved by the will of God because possessed. It would be, of course, ridiculous to say that the things willed by God are means to the end, since the end is already possessed, and therefore there can be no question of means. Creatures are, however, ordered to the end which is God's goodness. By willing them to be, God orders them to their end. He wills them to be, not that He may obtain the end which is Himself, but that the divine goodness may be manifested.

No Necessity of the End in God: This truth is an added argument for God's freedom regarding the created world. God's will is not necessitated but is absolutely free regarding the existential actuation of creatable essences; for the divine will is not determined to its operation by a final cause which it must seek. Indeed, in the very act of willing necessarily His goodness, which act is the "To Be," God freely wills creatures to be, not as means, but as ordered to the end which is Himself. God therefore wills to order them to their end by actually placing them in the order of existence. "He wills them *to be* because of His goodness; He does not will them in order that He might obtain His goodness."[62] There is, therefore, in God no necessity of the end in willing the creature.

---

[62] Thomas expresses all the above in a lapidary phrase: *"Vult hoc esse propter hoc, sed non propter hoc vult hoc."* It seems an unfortunate translation of the first part of the above to render *"vult hoc esse propter hoc,"* as "He wills this to be as *means* to that." That is exactly what God does not will and cannot will, since

Divine Will Not an Appetite: It appears from all this that unlike a created will, the divine will is not an appetite in the strict sense, for an appetite is an inclination to something distinct, not yet possessed but sought by the subject. Now the end of God's will is His own goodness which He is. The will of God, therefore, is not an appetite.

ARTICLE III: Does the Will of God Impose Any Necessity on the Things Willed?

Problem: The will of God, we have seen, is not necessitated regarding anything except His divine goodness. Whatever happens in the universe happens either because the will of God freely causes it, as in the case of the creation of the world, or because God at least allows it to be by freely willing the existence of any being, of any operation, that exists. Now we come to a more subtle problem. Granted that God wills these things freely, nevertheless, God wills them from all eternity; He wills them efficaciously. Consequently, whatever He wills must necessarily take place, for His will is immutable. In view of all this, should we not grant that while God's action may be perfectly free, nevertheless the act of the creature can be neither free nor contingent; it is necessitated.

This question, as proposed in the celebrated eighth article of question nineteen, has been greatly misunderstood and often misinterpreted. St. Thomas, in this article, refutes an erroneous opinion and offers the true solution to this problem.

Erroneous Solution: The erroneous solution which St. Thomas undertakes to refute is this: the operations of secondary causes are contingent *only* because the causes are contingent. This answer amounts to saying that the will of God is not efficacious. For, according to this opinion, the contingency of the operations is due to the imperfection of the secondary causes in this way, that the effect of the first cause, which should be necessary since the cause

---

creatures are definitely not means by which God attains His divine goodness. For the will of God, as well as the divine goodness, is "To Be."

is necessary, is hindered by the deficiency of the secondary causes.

Doctrine of St. Thomas: St. Thomas refutes this error and at the same time gives a solution to the problem. The reason for the contingency and freedom of some of the operations of certain creatures, while immediately attributable to the freedom and contingency of the creature, do not result from the deficiency of the creature. We must deny absolutely that the effect of the first cause is hindered by the weakness and deficiency of the secondary cause. Indeed such an explanation is an explicit denial of the efficacy of the divine will. It is an implicit denial of the omnipotence of God.

On the contrary, the freedom and contingency of the creature's operation are attributable to the efficacy of God's will first and foremost. For God willed these operations to be free and contingent, because He prepared (*adaptavit*) certain natures to be free in their operations. This preparation signifies that God willed to actuate in the order of existence, that is, to create, certain free natures which, because of their intelligibility, rooted in the divine essence, were known by the divine intellect. To quote the words of the Angelic Doctor: "God has *prepared contingent causes* for them [the effects, the operations], because He willed that they [the effects, operations] might happen contingently."[63]

No Predetermination: Nothing seems more obvious, nothing could be clearer, than this simple statement. Yet it has been suggested that in this article, St. Thomas proposes that the free acts of man, although predetermined by a divine motion, are perfectly free, because God has willed them to be free in this way, that God in the predetermining motion gives them their mode of liberty. It seems fantastic to extract such tortuous meaning from the simplicity of St. Thomas' explanation. The fact of the matter is that St. Thomas has never admitted a predetermining motion, and that he has explained time and time again that the free act of a creature is caused by a free nature and not by a predetermining motion. "Therefore," he explains, "to some effects He has made ready unfailing necessary causes; to others [He has made ready]

---

[63] *S. Th.*, I, 19, 8, c.

contingent causes from which the effects arise contingently."[64]

The truth of the matter, then, is that these operations are contingent and free, not because they are produced immediately by a secondary cause which, on account of its weakness and deficiency, fails in co-operating with the divine motion, but because God, in accordance with His knowledge of *simple intelligence* has willed to create causes which of their very essence are free and contingent. This is exactly what is meant by the following statement. "From the very fact that nothing [efficaciously] resists the divine will, it follows not only that those things happen that God wills to happen, but that they happen necessarily or contingently according to His will."[65]

The fact, then, of God willing this act of man to take place, that is, to exist, does in no way interfere with the freedom. For, as we have explained in the treatise on God's knowledge, the will of God does not determine the nature of a free act but only the fact of its existence. The nature as a possible and futurable is seen by God's intellect in the divine essence. God's will merely determines the fact of its existence in time. There is, then, no intrinsic determination from the will of God. That is why St. Thomas can declare: *"Non sunt incompatibilia: Deus vult istum salvari, et ille potest damnari."*[66]

APPENDIX: Does God Will Evil?

Problem: Let us recall an essential distinction between physical evil which is either evil of nature or evil of punishment, and moral evil which is evil of sin or of fault.[67] St. Thomas declares that God, *per accidens,* can will evil of nature and of punishment, but never evil of sin; He can only *allow* it. The reason for this statement is obvious. God cannot will that which is opposed to His divine goodness. Evil of sin is directly opposed to the divine

---

[64] *Loc. cit.*
[65] *S. Th.*, I, 19, 8, ad 2m.
[66] *De Ver.*, XXIII, 5, ad 3m.
[67] Cf. *The Philosophy of Being,* p. 184.

goodness. Hence God cannot ever will evil of sin. On the other hand, physical evil is not necessarily opposed to the divine goodness. Indeed, such evil may be connected with a greater good. God, therefore, may will such an evil *per accidens,* that is, because He wills the good of the universe which is greater than a particular evil. In willing, for example, the preservation of nature, God wills *per accidens* that some things be naturally corrupted.

Difficulty: The seemingly weak spot in this otherwise acceptable doctrine lies in this: What is meant by the statement, "God allows or permits evil of sin"? The difficulty is this: We know, of course, that nothing can exist unless God wills it to exist, since the will of God is absolutely efficacious and the cause of existence. Evil of sin exists. God, therefore, must will it to exist. We should conclude, God does not merely permit evil of sin; He wills it. When we say, then, that God merely permits such evil, we are presumably using words to cover up what is an impossible situation. God should not will evil of sin. Evil of sin does happen. Yet nothing can happen unless God wills it to happen. Can we salve our intellectual integrity by stating that God does not really will evil of sin, that He merely permits it, and then try to forget that to permit is an act of the will, and that the act of the will of God is the cause of the existence of this evil? That God permits evil, then, seems tantamount to saying, "God wills it."

Solution: While St. Thomas, to the author's knowledge, has not proposed this difficulty directly, he has laid down some elucidations regarding the knowledge and the will of God which indicate at least a definite direction toward a solution. Let us recall these.

Evil of sin supposes a free operation and, therefore, a subject endowed with liberty of choice. This subject or nature as well as the free operation are rooted as pure possibles in the divine essence. From all eternity, God, contemplating His divine essence, sees and understands this free operation as well as its opposite (contradictory) — for example, that Peter will sin and that Peter will not sin — in His knowledge of simple intelligence. Moreover, since one of these contradictories, for example, Peter will sin, has as a futurable greater intelligibility than the other, God in the knowledge called middle science knows it as futurable.

We should note that, regarding this twofold knowledge, the will of God in no way enters as a factor in determining the free act of Peter. All this is in the order of knowledge, of specification. Finally, with His will joined (*adjuncta*) to this knowledge, God wills to actuate Peter's free act. Peter, then, does sin in time. In His science of vision, God from all eternity sees Peter freely sinning at the appointed time.

What part does the will of God play regarding the determination of the evil act of Peter? No part whatever. The creation of Peter merely places a creatable free essence in the order of existence. The actuation of Peter's free action by God's will in no way determines the direction of the act, for the *free* determination of an action is in the order of the nature, of the essence, and is not found in the actuation by the "to be" which merely makes it exist. God, in the words of Thomas, can will any act *to be* or *not to be*,[68] but such actuation is not in the order of the nature of the act, whether good or evil. The determination as regards good and evil depends entirely on the will of Peter. Peter, not God, freely wills the act; Peter, not God, therefore, wills the evil of the act. God wills to give the "to be" of Peter's operation; in doing so, He only allows the evil; He does not will it.

If the difficulty were urged that not only does God actuate the nature by giving existence, but that He must also actuate the will by a divine motion in the order of exercise which pertains to the order of nature, we answer with the Angelic Doctor: Whatever motion may be given in the order of nature does not predetermine the will to this act; for God cannot force the will.[69] The will of man, even when moved by God, is free and therefore solely responsible for the evil of the act. God does not will the determination of the act. He wills to actuate a free act of man. "He wills," says

---

[68] *S. Th.*, I, 19, 10, ad 2m.
[69] Cf. *The Philosophy of Man*, p. 195 ff. Many relevant texts of St. Thomas are quoted in these pages.

St. Thomas, "to permit the evil to be done, and this is a good."[70]

On the other hand, if an operation does not depend upon a free secondary cause — as for example in the case of a flood, an earthquake, a storm — we must say that God wills the physical evil *per accidens*, for not only does He give the operation its "to be," but He gives the initial motion which, because of the nature of the secondary cause, is determined only to this one effect. God, then, wills this physical evil, but only *per accidens*, that is, for the good of the universe.[71]

S U M M A R Y — Question III

THE WILL OF GOD

1. **Problem:** The will of God as well as its operation is a necessary and an immutable being, since it is identical with "To Be." How can such a being be free?

2. **Prologue:** *In the production and governance of the world God does not act by a necessity of nature,* because such necessity is not intelligible unless there be an exemplary as well as a final cause in a superior intellectual agent. God, however, is the first uncaused cause; hence, He does not produce the world by necessity of His nature but by intellect and will.

ARTICLE I: What Is the Will in God?

The will in God is an inclination which follows knowledge. In God, it is primarily a necessary inclination to love his own goodness. Because the will as well as the operation of willing is one with "To Be" which is His goodness, we declare that God acts and, therefore, wills by His essence. This is quite different from saying that He acts by necessity of nature.

---

[70] *S. Th.,* I, 19, 9, ad 3^m.

[71] We can surmise from the above how the tract on the governance of the world will depend largely on the relative functions of the divine intellect and will.

ARTICLE II: God Wills Freely All Things Other Than Himself.

1. God's will is necessitated to love His own infinite goodness. Hence, He is not necessitated but is free to love, i.e., to will the limited "to be" of any of the possible essences.

   a) He wills His own goodness *with absolute necessity.*

   b) He wills all other things *freely.*

   c) Supposing His free act from all eternity which freely wills all existing creatures, we should add that He can no longer not will them, since His will is immutable. He does not, however, will these with absolute necessity but *with the necessity of supposition.*

2. **The act of the will of God has no final cause.** Divine goodness is its end but not its cause. The reason is that a final cause is desired and sought, not possessed. Now God's goodness is identical with His will.

3. **There is no necessity of the end in God.** Since God is His end, God does not will the creature as a means in order to attain the end. On the other hand, in the created will whenever the end is willed, the means which are necessary for the attainment of that end are willed by necessity of the end.

ARTICLE III: The Will of God Imposes No Necessity in the Things Willed.

1. If a created nature is not endowed with a free will, its operations which in the last analysis result from a motion of the divine will are not free but determined because of the nature which is not free; for example, an earthquake is necessarily caused by the forces of nature.

2. The freedom of a creature results from its nature, not from the divine motion. If a created nature is free, that is, endowed with intellect and will, the operations of the created will which result from the divine motion are not determined to one by this motion; they are free, that is to say, the will may or may not act; it may freely place this or that action. The will of

creatures, therefore, is not predetermined by the divine motion. Hence, neither does the motion of God's will impose necessity on the operations of the created will, nor does the divine will determine the act of a created nature to be free by actuating such a nature and its free operation in the order of existence, that is, by giving it a "to be."

N.B. We recall that the infallibility of God's knowledge regarding the essence of the free act is had in His knowledge of His own essence in which all intelligibility is found, as explained in the question on God's knowledge.

APPENDIX: Does God Will Evil?

1. God wills physical evil *per accidens,* for the good of the universe (that is, primarily for the good of the higher natures, the rational creatures).
2. He does not will moral evil, but He permits it. In other words, God does not predetermine the evil act of man by moving his will. He merely wills to give existence to a free act which is already seen in the divine knowledge of His essence as a possible (simple intelligence) and as a futurable (middle science).

Question IV

THE CONSEQUENTS OF THE DIVINE WILL:

LOVE, JUSTICE, MERCY

There will be three articles in this question: (1) divine love, (2) divine justice, and (3) divine mercy.

ARTICLE I: Divine Love

Love is the first, the most fundamental, and the principal act of the will. Whenever other operations of the will are elicited, whether desire or hatred, joy or despair, they presuppose the *initial inclination to the good* which is an act of love.

Love Is First: In order to establish this fact, that the act of love is the first act of the will and that upon which all other motions of the will depend, we should explain what love is. Love is the natural inclination of the will to its proper object, the good. Now the first, the principal motion of any operative potency is to its proper object. Hence, those acts of the will which look to the good, such as love and desire, must precede those, as for example, hatred and despair, which result from the consideration of evil; for we hate an evil because it is opposed to the good which we love. Moreover, the more universal, more general, more common (*communius*) object is first in the determination of an operative potency. Now we *desire* the good which we do not possess; we *enjoy* that which we possess. The act of love, on the other hand, which looks to the good without any particularization must necessarily precede all other operations of the appetite.

There Is Love in God: The act of love, then, is the first act and the root of all other operations of the will. Now we have established that there is will in God; consequently, there must be love. Indeed, since the will of God as well as the "to will" is "To Be," it follows that the "to love" in God is "To Be." God is Love. *"Deus est caritas."*

Love in God Is Not a Passion: In order to understand the reality that is divine love, we should explain that love in God is not a passion. It is a common fact that men in practical life seldom distinguish the passion of love which is an operation of the sense appetite, the concupiscible power, from the act of the intellectual appetite, the will, which tends to the good. In the philosophy of man, we showed that one of the essential factors of a passion is the material change which occurs in the body or organ or glands — what St. Thomas calls a *"transmutatio corporis."* There can be, of course, no organic change in the will and, therefore, no passion of love, since the will is purely immaterial. It often happens, however, that an intense act of the will in man will redound into the sensible appetite and thus arouse the passion of love with its accompanying bodily mutation. This, of course, is due in man to the unity of the human supposit, a unity which results from an existential composition of matter and form. In God, on the contrary, we can never speak of the passion of love, for God is pure spirituality.

Predication: We note, moreover, that not every operation of the human will is attributable to God. Although no operations of the will, because spiritual, imply an organic change, nevertheless, certain actions such as desire and hope imply some formal imperfection, that is, some potency in the subject for the good not yet obtained. Consequently, these are not attributable to God except metaphorically. On the other hand, love and joy do not indicate such imperfection. Hence they are properly attributed to God. Moreover, as in every direct predication of a divine name, they are said of God substantially and according to what they signify. The mode of representation, however, is that of creatures. In this direct predication, the perfection is identified with "To Be" by an analogy of proportionality. God is Love.

Difficulty: Love is often spoken of as a unitive, a binding force. Now God is absolutely simple. Hence, there is nothing to bind, nothing to unite.[72]

Solution: In answering this difficulty, St. Thomas first gives an analysis of the nature of love. The act of love, he explains, has a twofold direction, a twofold inclination: (1) toward the good one wills somebody (self or another); (2) toward him (self or another) to whom one wills the good.

The first inclination is called love of concupiscence or of desire;[73] the second, the love of benevolence. This latter is termed "love

---

[72] This difficulty, when viewed from the love that God has of Himself, is studied in revealed theology in the treatise on the Trinity.

[73] In spite of its name, the love of concupiscence — hereafter we shall call it the love of desire — is not necessarily an evil act, e.g., I love wine, food, etc. In practice, the love of concupiscence is had when one wills the good to himself. "*Amor dividitur per amorem amicitiae et concupiscentiae. Nam, ille proprie dicitur amicus cui aliquod bonum volumus, illud autem dicimur concupiscere, quod volumus nobis.*" (*S. Th.*, I–II, 26, 4, ad 1m.)

of friendship" when a mutual inclination exists between rational supposits.[74]

We may now establish the truth that love is a unitive, a binding force. Whenever one loves himself, he wills some good to self. He wills the good to be his, that is, to be united with him, in so far as such a union is possible, according to the nature of the subject and object. Love, then, is a unitive force. In God, however, because of His absolute simplicity, the union between God and His own goodness is a union of identity, not a union of composition.

It may be asked: If we will a good to someone else by a love of benevolence and friendship, how does such a love unite and bind? *"Amans est in amato"*: the lover is in the beloved; he *is* the beloved in a certain manner. In willing a good to another, we use (*utitur*) the other, that is, we consider the other as if he were ourselves. In other words, we project ourselves in his place so that we look upon him as ourselves. In this way, love is really a binding force (*vis concretiva*), for it aggregates the other to ourselves, so that we are to him what we are to ourselves: *"habens se ad eum sicut ad seipsum,"*[75] considering his welfare as our own. Now God binds us to Himself by His love of friendship, for all the good we possess He wills to us. God loves us by a love of friendship; He loves irrational creatures by a love of quasi-desire.[76]

Does God Love All Things?: Which is correct to say: God loves us because we are good, or we are good because God loves us? St. Thomas states that the second proposition is true: we are

---

[74] *"Nec benevolentia sufficit ad amorem amicitiae, sed requiritur quaedam mutua amatio quia amicus est amico amicus."* (S. Th., II–II, 23, 1, c.)

[75] S. Th., I, 20, 1, ad 3[m].

[76] "Friendship cannot exist except towards rational creatures who are capable of returning love and of communicating with one another in the various works of life, and who may fare well or ill according to the changes of fortune and happiness; even as towards them is benevolence, properly speaking, exercised. But irrational creatures cannot attain to loving God, nor to any share in the intellectual and beatific life that He lives. Strictly speaking, therefore, God does not love irrational creatures with the love of friendship, but as it were, with the love of desire in so far as He orders them to rational creatures, and even to Himself. Yet this is not because He stands in need of them, but only because of His goodness, and of the services they render to us. For we can desire a thing for others as well as for ourselves." (S. Th., I, 20, 2, ad 3[m].)

good because God loves us. The reason is not far to seek. A being is good in so far as it exists; indeed existence is the supreme good in the order of being, for the act, the perfection of being is "to be." Now the will of God is the cause of the existence of all things. God, then, in giving existence, wills a good to a creature. But to will a good is to love. God, therefore, loves all existing realities. They *are,* or in other words, they are good, because of God's love. For God by creating, by giving existence, pours goodness into all things. In the last analysis, if we exist at all, if we are able to perform good actions, if we acquire various perfections, it is because of His love which communicates these participations in His "To Be."

Difficulty: Many will object to the sweeping statement that we are good because God loves us. One reason for their refusal to accept this doctrine is founded on a common experience. We love this or that object because it is good; the object is not made good because we love it. This fact of experience they apply to the divine love. They forget that such a comparison, such an application, is without foundation. Our will is not the cause of the goodness of the object; whereas, as we have seen, God's will is the cause of all that is.

Another reason for denying the truth of the proposition: we are good because God loves us, is that one might fear that such an affirmation will endanger, impair, and destroy the freedom of man; for if the goodness of a free act is caused by God and not by man, then man is not free to place a good act. This, however, is not too difficult a point if we recall the treatise on the intellect and will of God.

Solution: In the strictest philosophical sense, when we speak of goodness we mean existing goodness, for "To Be" is the supreme perfection. The fact of the matter is that the determination of the free act of man is not from God but from man. This act is known by God because of its intelligibility. It is seen in the knowledge of simple intelligence and of the middle science. But the operation itself, like every other created thing, cannot exist unless God gives the "to be." Now, the "to be" establishes the transcendental goodness of the act in the existential order. God's love is the cause of the "to be"; God's love is the reason why the operation is, why it is good. We are good because God loves us.

Let us restate the difficulty and its solution: If the fact that we are good depends upon God's love which is the cause of our goodness whether we want it or not, then we are not free. To state the difficulty thus is a gross misconception of divine causality regarding a free act of man. God, we answer, does not determine the human act; He merely actuates it in the order of existence.

But, we may ask, does not such an actuation manifest the dependence of God's will upon that of the creature who wills or does not will this operation? Not in the least. God is not moved or determined by the will of man. He wills to actuate or not to actuate a creatable nature seen in the divine essence, according as He loves or does not love.[77] God wills to actuate this act. The man *is* good because God loves him. We may add that *God loves him in so far as he is good,* but not in the sense that God's love depends upon man's action. In other words, man is good, and God loves him; but God's love is not caused by man's goodness.

Love is a marvelous power. It places the lover outside himself and, in a fashion, identifies him with the beloved. Not that the lover really loses his identity; but by his love he, as it were, transfers himself into the beloved, for he considers the beloved as himself, in so far as he wills good to the beloved as to himself and works for the beloved as for himself. Thus God loves man.

God Does Not Love All Equally: It appears from the above that God loves some beings more than others, since he wills greater good to one than to another. This by no means indicates that the divine act of love is more or less intense. God loves all in the same identical act of the will which is "To Be." It only means that He wills greater gifts to some. In the words of St. Thomas, "Some are better because God loves them more."[78] We should not forget, however, that such a statement in no way impairs the freedom of man's will.

---

[77] "Although creatures are not [*non fuerint*] from eternity, except in God, yet because they have been in Him from eternity, God has known them eternally in their proper natures, and for that reason has loved them." (*S. Th.,* I, 20, 2, ad 2[m].)

[78] *S. Th.,* I, 20, 4, c.

ARTICLE II: The Justice of God

In man, justice is a moral habit; it is a virtue.[79] Unlike the other moral habits of fortitude and temperance, justice is not found in the sense appetite, but it is rooted in the will. For this reason, it does not import the essential material limitation of the sense faculty and can therefore be attributed to God. Of course, what we predicate of God when we say that God is just, that He is justice, is not the habit which is an imperfect act, but the act (operation) of justice.[80] On the other hand, the moral virtues of temperance and fortitude are rooted in the sense appetites, for they are concerned with the control of such passions as concupiscence and fear. They imply, therefore, an essential imperfection. That is why they cannot properly be attributed to God.

Division: We shall consider two points: (1) Should we attribute justice to the will of God; can we properly, not merely metaphorically, say that God is just, that He is Justice? (2) Should we predicate truth of God's justice; that is, should we say that God's justice is truth, notwithstanding the fact that justice belongs to the will while truth refers to the intellect?

There Is Justice in God: Justice, as everyone knows, is a virtue of the will which enables man to render to others what is their due. Philosophers generally distinguish two types, two species of justice: *commutative* and *distributive* justice. The first, commutative justice, is concerned with mutual exchange, in mutual giving and receiving, as in buying and selling. The second, distributive justice, pertains to the distribution of goods, according to rank and needs, as a ruler to his subjects, a father to his family. This latter is, of course, the only type of justice which belongs to God.

Justice of God Is Founded on His Wisdom: Since God is not a debtor, but rather all things are indebted to Him in their absolute dependence, how can He render to anyone what is his due? In

---

[79] Cf. *The Philosophy of Man*, p. 225.

[80] Justice in God is not a habit but the act of the will, the "to will," which is identified with "To Be"; it is the divine essence. "Although justice refers to an act, this does not keep it from being the essence of God." (*S. Th.*, I, 21, 2, ad 4m.)

strict justice, God owes nothing to anyone; indeed even the existing nature of a creature is the pure gift of the Almighty. In God, therefore, there can be no question of strict justice, no question of an obligation toward the creature. We may consider, however, that having given existence to a rational nature, God is bound, not by the creature but by His own wisdom, to provide for such a nature the necessary means to its end. The reason is that justice must be in accordance with law. In man, law (Eternal Law) is distinct from his nature and is communicated to him; God, however, is a law unto Himself, and His law is His wisdom. It follows that justice in God must be in accordance with the divine wisdom. Consequently, it is impossible for God to will that which is at variance with His divine wisdom. That is why, having created a rational nature already understood in His knowledge of simple intelligence, God is bound according to His wisdom to give it the proper means to its end.[81] Thus God carries out justice when He gives to each thing what is due it according to its nature and condition.

This debt, if we may use such a term regarding God, is derived from a most radical, a most profound necessity. It is this: We must consider that all rational creatures, because of their spiritual nature, are ordered to God directly. In this way, God has a debt to Himself, for it is necessary that there should be fulfilled in creatures what is contained in His divine wisdom in order that His goodness may be manifested as He freely wills it to be. God, therefore, is just; He is Justice Itself.

Justice and Truth: The virtue of justice in man depends upon prudence, the directrix of all moral virtues. Strictly speaking, there is no prudence in God, as prudence, the moral virtue in man, implies some potency in the subject, that is, a need for deliberation and counsel owing to a possibility of error. In God, absolute knowledge, which is Wisdom and, therefore, absolute truth, rules supreme.

---

[81] Justice, which in man depends on a distinct law, is regulated by the virtue of prudence which is in the intellect. In God, justice is in accord with His wisdom. Prudence, of course, properly speaking, belongs only to a creature.

[82] Cf. *The Philosophy of Being*, p. 177.

There are two types of truth:[82] formal which resides in the intellect, and transcendental which is in the object. Truth is the conformity of an intellect with its object of knowledge. Now, God's knowledge of creatures is their exemplary cause. Hence, as a result of the formal truth in the divine intellect, we speak of transcendental truth in created things because of their conformity to their divine exemplar upon which they depend.

Now the truth of existing things results from the divine will acting with justice in accordance with the divine intellect which is Wisdom. "Therefore," explains the Angelic Doctor, "God's justice, which has established in the world of creation an order conformed to the knowledge [rationi] of His wisdom which is the law of His justice, is fittingly [convenienter] called truth."[83]

ARTICLE III: The Mercy of God

There Is Mercy in God: When we speak of mercy in God, we should be careful to distinguish the nature of mercy, which is an act of the will, from its accompanying sensible affection which is the passion of pity or sorrow for the ills of another. The effect of the act of the will which we call mercy consists in alleviating the misery of another. In this sense we attribute mercy to God in a most perfect manner. On the other hand, we can never, except metaphorically, predicate of God anything which pertains to a passion, that is, to the sense appetite. For, to use the words of the Angelic Doctor, "To sorrow over the misery of others does not belong to God; but it does most properly belong to Him to dispel that misery, whatever be the defect we call misery." What we mean, therefore, when we attribute mercy to the divine will is that God, by an act of the will which is Existence Itself, dispels the misery of rational creatures. God is merciful; there is mercy in God. God is Mercy Itself.

Mercy and Justice in God Are Not Opposed: It is commonly thought that justice and mercy are opposed to each other, so that whenever one is merciful, he is not just. How, then, can God mani-

[83] S. Th., I, 21, 2, c.

fest His justice and mercy in the same works of creation and sanctification?

We should explain that in bestowing perfections on creatures, God manifests both His justice and His mercy. We have noted in the preceding article that whatever perfection God communicates by the act of His will is in accordance with His divine wisdom and must be, therefore, befitting the nature to which the perfection is communicated. In this sense, the communication of gifts is always good and just. It is the work of God's justice. Because, however, such perfections remove the defect and misery of the creature, the giving of these belongs to the mercy of God. God acts mercifully, not by going against His justice, but by doing something more than what mere justice requires. Mercy, therefore, does not destroy justice. It is its fullness; it is a superabundance of justice. An example will clarify this statement. If I were to give a creditor much more than I owe him, I should not thwart justice, but I would be liberal, generous, merciful to him. In the same manner, in forgiving one who has done me wrong, I not only satisfy justice; I do much more than that. Instead of balancing the wrong he has done by punishment, I give him forgiveness of the wrong, and this is the superabundance of justice. "Mercy exalteth itself above judgment."[84]

Goodness and Justice, Liberality and Mercy: St. Thomas explains that in giving perfections to creatures, God manifests four of His divine attributes: His goodness and justice, His liberality and mercy. We quote the entire text.

> It must, however, be considered that to bestow perfections on things pertains not only to the divine goodness, but also to the divine justice, liberality, and mercy; yet under different aspects. The communicating of perfections, absolutely considered, pertains to goodness, as was shown above; in so far as perfections are given to things according to what is due them, it is a work of justice, as has been already said; in so far as God does not bestow them for His own use, but only because of His goodness, it belongs to liberality; in so far as perfections given to things by God expel defects, it belongs to mercy.[85]

---

[84] James 2:13.   [85] *S. Th.*, I, 21, 3, c.

CONSEQUENTS OF THE WILL

ARTICLE I: Divine Love.

1. Love in God.

a) Love is an inclination to the good; it is the first, the principal act of the will. Because there is will in God, there is love. *God is Love.*

b) In man, we distinguish between the love which is a passion, an act of the sense appetite, and the act of the will. In God, love is not a passion; it is the act of the divine will.

c) **Predication:** After removing all the imperfection of created love, we identify the act of divine love with Existence.

2. Love unites: it is a binding power.

a) We distinguish between:

1) love of desire — toward the good desired, e.g., food;

2) love of benevolence (or friendship, only toward a rational individual) — toward the object *to whom* we will a good: I will to give food to Peter.

b) Application:

1) Regarding the *primary object* of God's love, i.e., Himself, there is perfect union of love, i.e., a union of identity (there is no question here of love of desire).

2) Regarding the *secondary object* of God's love, i.e., creatures:

(*a*) God loves *rational* creatures with a love of benevolence and friendship. This love unites rational creatures to God in this fashion: the lover (here, God) projects Himself into the beloved (rational creatures). He wills good to the beloved as if he (the beloved) were Himself. Hence, by communicating to us all that we are and possess, God unites us to Himself.

(*b*) God loves irrational creatures by a love of *quasi-desire*, because He loves them for the good of rational creatures. In this manner, divine love unites irrational creatures to God through rational creatures.

3. We are good (transcendental goodness) **because God loves us.** God loves all creatures primarily in this manner, that He wills to give them existence which is the supreme good in the order of being. In that way we are good because He loves us. We cannot say that He loves us because we are good, since the actuation of existence given by His will does not depend on the creature. God loves us in so far as we are good, but we are not the cause of God's love, since He is the First Uncaused Cause.

ARTICLE II: Divine Justice.

1. Justice in God is not a habit; it is an act.

2. There is justice in God: Justice, by which one renders to another what is his due, in God signifies not commutative but *distributive* justice. In God, justice is founded not on the rational creature's rights, but upon divine wisdom in this way: Having willed a rational creature to exist, God owes it to Himself, to His wisdom, to provide the necessary means to the end.[86]

3. God Is Justice Itself: The act of the divine will by which, in accordance with divine wisdom, God provides the rational creature with the necessary means to its end, is identified with subsisting "To Be." Hence not only is God just, but He is Justice.

4. Justice in God may be called Truth: God's justice establishes an order conformed to His wisdom which is the law of His justice. Hence, the Justice which establishes such conformity may be fittingly called Truth.

ARTICLE III: Divine Mercy.

1. Mercy is the act of the will by which God alleviates the misery,

---

[86] Note well that the act of justice is a free act. God is not necessitated with *absolute necessity* but only with *necessity of supposition*.

the defects, of rational creatures. God is merciful. He is Mercy Itself.

2. **Mercy and justice are not opposed.** Mercy is the fullness, the superabundance of justice.

3. **Goodness, Justice, Liberality, and Mercy** are manifested in the works of God, in giving perfections to His creatures.

Question V

THE PROVIDENCE OF GOD

This question will contain two articles: (1) Providence belongs to God. (2) All creation is subject to divine providence.

ARTICLE I: Providence Belongs to God

Providence and Governance: In common parlance we do not generally distinguish between the providence of God and the divine governance of the world. We include both under the word "providence." Speaking more accurately as philosophers, we must say that, although dealing with the same object, to wit, the ordering of the world to its end, providence and government are not identical. The difference lies in this, that providence is the order of the world to its end as conceived in the intellect of God, whereas government means the execution of the divine plan, that is to say, the actual establishing of this divine design, of this divine idea, in the order of existence.[87]

Problem: Providence is the knowledge (*ratio*) of the things to

---

[87] "Two things pertain to the care of providence — namely, the *ratio of order*, which is called providence and disposition; and the *execution of order*, which is termed government. Of these, the first is eternal, and the second is temporal." (*S. Th.*, I, 22, 2, ad 2[m].)

be ordered toward their end, which knowledge pre-exists in the intellect of God. Regarding this definition we shall consider two points: (1) What is the profound meaning of this knowledge of order, that is, what does the definition signify? (2) What do we understand when we attribute providence to God?

FIRST PROBLEM: Meaning of Definition

Analysis of Definition: Providence is a knowledge (*ratio*). The word *ratio* has sometimes been erroneously translated by "exemplar." This is certainly not the meaning of *ratio*. In a previous article on the divine ideas,[88] St. Thomas explains that the idea is sometimes called *exemplar* and sometimes *ratio*. Whenever it signifies a principle of knowledge, it is called *ratio*. On the other hand, should it be connected with the divine will which, as the efficient cause, wills to produce a creature, then and only then is it to be designated as *exemplar*. The reason is that the exemplar is a real, an existential cause which, as cause, must have here and now an influx in the determination of the effect. In what manner does the exemplar have an influx upon the effect? The answer is that the exemplar has an influx by specifying the nature of the effect caused by the action of the agent. Here, this action is the act of God's will. Consequently, in order that the idea be an exemplar, there is need of the act of the will. Now providence, as we shall show, is not in the will but in the intellect; moreover, it does not include an actual determination of the act of the will which follows it and which establishes the order, but it prescinds from it. Hence, providence cannot be defined as an exemplar. It is a *ratio,* that is, the knowledge of the practical intellect which looks to but does not include a determination of the will.

Providence and Prudence: To make this even more evident, after stating that providence is a *ratio,* not an exemplar, St. Thomas continues, "Providence is a part of prudence." Now prudence, which is the true knowledge of the things to be done (*recta ratio agibilium*)

---

[88] *S. Th.,* I, 15, 3.

is in the practical intellect. It looks to the will but does not include any operation of the will as a constitutive element.

It is true, knowledge which is in the practical intellect pre-supposes knowledge of the speculative intellect; it presupposes a previous operation of the intellectual appetite willing the end. In its formal aspect, however, although depending upon the virtue of this previous act of the will willing the end,[89] and although looking to the succeeding act of the will which is the act of choice, prudence does not include any operation of the will as a constitutive factor.

Providence Is Not Governance: To make this clear, St. Thomas distinguishes sharply between the following: first, speculative knowledge of the end; then, the love of the end which follows upon knowledge; providence which is the third step and the *ratio* of the order to the end, of the things related to the end; then power or omnipotence (*potentia*) which embraces this knowledge of the intellect together with the efficacious act of the will so that the *ratio* now becomes an exemplar; finally, the execution of the act of the divine will which is called governance.[90] This governance — which takes place in time — is the establishing, the placing, the working-out of the plan which pre-existed as providence in the divine intellect and is willed by the power of God.[91] This, then,

---

[89] "Providence is in the intellect; but it presupposes the act of willing the end. For no one commands concerning things done for an end unless he wills that end." (*S. Th.*, I, 22, 1, ad 3^m.) It is because of this previous act of the will that we place providence which pertains to the intellect after the tract on the will.

[90] "*Ex dictis igitur patet quomodo providentia se habet ad alia quae de Deo dicuntur. Scientia enim communiter se habet ad cognitionem finis, et eorum quae sunt ad finem: per scientiam enim Deus scit se et creaturas; sed providentia pertinet tantum ad cognitionem eorum quae sunt ad finem, secundum quod ordinantur in finem; et ideo providentia includit et scientiam et voluntatem; sed tamen essentialiter in cognitione manet, non quidem speculativa, sed practica. Potentia autem executiva est providentiae; unde actus potentiae praesupponit actum providentiae sicut dirigentis; unde in providentia non includitur potentia sicut voluntas.*" (*De Ver.*, V, 1.)

[91] It should be noted that the power or omnipotence of God is not a third principle of operation besides intellect and will. Rather, it includes both. "Power is predicated of God not as something really distinct from His knowledge and will, but as differing from them logically; inasmuch as power implies the notion of a principle putting into execution what the will commands and what knowledge directs; which three things in God are identified." (*S. Th.*, I, 25, 1, ad 4^m.)

is the sequence which St. Thomas proposes: (1) speculative knowledge of self and of possible creatures; (2) love of the end; (3) knowledge of the things to be ordered to the end (providence); (4) will to establish such an order (power); (5) actual placing of order (governance).

We conclude: Providence is in the intellect; it does not include the actual determination of the will; it is knowledge (*ratio*) of the order, not the exemplary cause.

SECOND PROBLEM: Meaning of Predication

Problem: The statement that providence is a part of prudence may be questioned, since prudence in man is a virtue which implies some imperfection in the subject. Hence, the problem arises, how can providence which is a part of prudence be properly predicated of God? How can we say that providence belongs to God, that God is Providence?

Analysis of Prudence: 1. Three Distinct Operations: The solution of this problem can be discovered only by a serious analysis of prudence as it functions in man. To begin with, we should observe that there are *three distinct operations* necessary for a complete, a perfect act of the virtue of prudence. (*a*) There is the act called *counsel* which considers the things that are related to the end. (*b*) Then man judges what is better for the attainment of the end. (*c*) A *command* follows (*praeceptum*) which consists in the application of the things counseled and judged as ordered to the end. This command is an act of the practical intellect, for it looks to the work to be willed, to be done. It is the principal, the perfect act of the virtue of prudence. In its make-up, this act does not imply imperfection in the subject.

Now as we analyze the various parts of prudence which are necessary for placing the three acts, we shall discover that providence is the integral part which results in the third act, the act of command.

2. The Parts of Prudence: In all virtues there are various kinds of parts to be considered: subjective parts, potential parts, and integral parts.

a) **The subjective parts** are those virtues which are related to prudence as various species are related to a common genus. We may mention as one subjective part of prudence the personal virtue which is concerned only with the human acts of the individual subject. The other specific virtue under prudence looks to the direction and government of others. It belongs to one in authority, whether of a community or state or family.[92]

b) **The potential parts** embrace those subsidiary virtues which are connected with the primary virtue and dispose the subject to the perfect act of prudence. They are quasi-faculties of the principal virtue and are ordered to the less perfect, to the less important operations of prudence. St. Thomas mentions them in this present article. They are the virtue of *eubulia* which looks to the first operations called counsel, and the virtue of *synesis* which is concerned with judging.[93]

c) **The integral parts** are those various dispositions which concur to the perfect act of the virtue. There are some eight distinct integral parts of the virtue of prudence. In the question on divine providence, St. Thomas mentions the three more important parts: the memory of the past, the understanding of the present, and the conjecture of the things to be provided for. This last disposition is providence (in man) from which the knowledge and command (*ratio praeceptiva*) of the order to the end issues forth. This command of reason is the perfect act of prudence; it is the act of the part of prudence which we call providence. Hence, providence in man is that disposition of the intellect whose act inclines the will by a command to establish, in accordance with the proper order to the end, those things that are related to the end.

Providence in Man: It is evident that providence is the principal integral part of prudence and that it is a disposition of the intellect,

---

[92] "A prudent man orders his actions in regard to himself or in regard to others subject to him in a family or state." (*S. Th.*, I, 22, 1, c.)

[93] "*Eubulia* rightly counsels and *synesis* rightly judges." (*S. Th.*, I, 22, 1, ad 1m.)

for all the other parts of prudence concur to this, that by a command of reason something be rightly ordered to its end. For the principal act of prudence is to command the true order of the work to be done.[94]

We have stated that the knowledge of command belongs to providence[95] and that it is in the intellect. It may be asked, is command an act of reason or an act of the will? St. Thomas explains[96] that to order by command (*praeceptive ordinare*) belongs to the intellect; nevertheless it supposes a previous act of the will. The virtue of this act of the will remains in the intellect and enables it to command.[97]

In God, Providence Is "To Be": Providence, which is the prin-

---

[94] Cf. *S. Th.*, II–II, 47 to 52. It should be noted that in man this command which is the supreme act of the virtue of prudence and which is an act of the intellect must precede the act of choice which is in the will. The reason is that prudence, which is concerned with the moral act, must precede the internal act of the will which is the moral act *par excellence*. There is, of course, another command (*imperium*) which occurs after choice and which is necessary for the proper *use* of the other faculties and members in the external operation.

[95] "*Providentia est ratio in intellectu existens praeceptiva ordinationis aliquorum in finem.*" (*S. Th.*, I, 23, 4, c.)

[96] Cf. *S. Th.*, I–II, 17, 1, c. "Command is an act of the reason, presupposing, however, an act of the will. In proof of this, we note that, since acts of the reason and of the will can be brought to bear on one another, in so far as the reason reasons about willing, and the will wills to reason, it follows that the act of reason precedes the act of the will, and conversely. And since the power of the preceding act remains in the act that follows, it happens sometimes that there is an act of the will in which there remains virtually something of the act of the reason, as we have stated in reference to use and choice; and conversely, that there is an act of reason in which there remains something of the act of the will."

[97] This is the first act of the will willing the end as explained above. (Cf. *S. Th.*, I, 22, 1, ad 1m.) We should like to state further that the three acts of prudence in man occur before the act of choice. Counsel occurs after the "intention" to the end and before the "consent" to the means *in globo*. Counsel is a discussion of the aptness of the respective means; then judgment as regards the best suited means takes place: "This is best"; finally there follows command of reason to the will, "This must be done." The act of the will called "choice" follows immediately. Prudence, therefore, is necessary for every good choice by the human act. That the act of counsel, which belongs to prudence and is an operation of the intellect, takes place between two distinct acts of the will should not be surprising. In the process of a deliberation, there may occur a large number of correlated acts of intellect and will. The acts of prudence would be found among the various intellectual operations. They are directive norms of the process of deliberation in the order of specification.

cipal part of prudence, does not in its formal definition include limitation, potency, imperfection. It is the *"ratio praeceptiva,"* the knowledge of the things to be ordered to their end. Hence, it can be attributed to God, not, of course, as a habit but as an act which is "To Be."

Proof: There Is Providence in God: God, the supreme intellect, is, because of His knowledge, the specificative cause of all creatures. Hence, the knowledge (*ratio*) of any possible effect must pre-exist in His intellect. Now the order of things to their end is a possible effect. Therefore, the knowledge of this order must pre-exist in the intellect of God. This knowledge (*ratio*) is providence.

It is necessary to attribute providence to God. For all the good that is in things has been created by God, as was shown above. Now in things, good is found not only as regards their substance, but also as regards their order towards an end and especially their last end, which, as was said above, is the divine goodness. This good of order existing in created things is created by God. Now God is the cause of things by His intellect, and therefore it is necessary that the knowledge [*ratio*] of every effect should pre-exist in Him, as is clear from what has gone before. Hence, the *ratio* of the order of things towards their end must necessarily pre-exist in the divine mind; and the *ratio* of things to be ordered towards an end is, properly speaking, providence.[98]

Conclusion: Because God is pure act, absolute perfection, simplicity itself, it is not sufficient to say that there is providence in God. We must add, *God is Providence.*

ARTICLE II: Are All Creatures Subject to the Providence of God?

All Creation Is Subject Absolutely to Divine Providence: This truth is a necessary inference from the established fact that God and only God by His will gives "to be" to all existing beings. Hence, nothing can, nothing does happen except in so far as God from all eternity wills to actuate the knowledge of the order of

---

[98] *S. Th.,* I, 22, 1, c.

things to their end. This is admirably expressed in these words: "Since the providence of God is nothing other than the knowledge [*ratio*] of the order of things towards their end, it is necessary that all things be subject to the divine providence in so far as they participate existence [*in quantum participant esse*]."[99]

Consequently, it should not prove difficult to refute the error of those who attribute to God a providence which looks only to the general direction of the world as a whole, but is not concerned with the government of each individual nature, of each particular event. This opinion has been proposed repeatedly by pseudo-philosophers. For, they explain, it would be beneath the perfection of God to be bothered with such inconsequential happenings as the change of weather, the gyrations of a housefly, or the loosening of a shoestring. These statements manifest how little their authors understand what is meant by a God who is "To Be."[1] Far from being an imperfection, the communication of existence to a creature as well as to the operations of creatures can be attributed only to the One who is Existence.[2]

No Chance Happenings: It follows also that, absolutely speaking, there is not such a thing as chance; for while to man, who is not acquainted with the designs of divine providence, many events and circumstances happen as if by chance, nevertheless we know that these have been fully foreseen in the divine plan and willed by God. The reason is, of course, that they exist, that they have a "to be" which can come only from God.

Providence and Evil: Again, when we reflect upon the many evils which take place constantly throughout the world, we may infer with absolute certitude that God wills to allow these because of the greater good of the universe in accordance with the goodness of the divine plan.[3] Since God is Wisdom Itself,

---

99 *S. Th.*, I, 22, 2, c.

1 The famous saying of Christ, "Not a sparrow shall fall on the ground without your Father" (Matthew 10:29), is literally true. Every change means, at least, a new accidental "to be."

2 This point was brought out in *The Philosophy of Being*, p. 133 ff.

3 The phrase, "for the good of the universe," means primarily "for the good of souls, of spiritual beings" which are the most perfect part of this created universe.

neither chance — as we call it — nor evil is removed from the care of divine providence.

Providence and Man's Free Act: Hence, although man's free will is in no way predetermined by the will of God,[4] nevertheless, man is subject to divine providence. The reason is that the cause of the free act, *in so far as it exists,* is God Himself[5] who freely wills to actuate, that is, to give existence to, the futurable act as seen in His essence. Moreover, God extends His providence to men inasmuch as He does not allow too many evils and temptations to overburden the life of rational creatures.

We must state, therefore, that regarding man, God has a special providence. Indeed, because of his free acts, man becomes worthy of praise or blame, of rewards or punishments. These are bestowed on man in the execution of the divine plan.

No Predetermination of the Human Will: What of the conflict between the free will of man and the determination of the divine plan? How can God in His divine providence foresee and order man to his end, when the latter is free in his human actions? St. Thomas makes some precious remarks on this difficult point.

He begins by declaring man's freedom and rejecting absolutely any predetermination of the will of man by God. The words of the Angelic Doctor are significant: *"Non praefigitur homini virtus operativa determinata ad unum."*[6] There is no predetermining virtue prefixed by divine providence. How, then, can we say that even man is subject to divine providence? Let us once more quote Aquinas. We can say, we must say, that those things which happen from free choice are subject to the divine providence, because "the very act of free judgment and choice is traceable [*reducitur*] to God as [*sicut*] to its cause."[7] These words are extremely

---

[4] *"Non praefigitur homini virtus operativa determinata ad unum."* (S. Th., I, 22, 2, ad 4m.) This significant phrase seems an absolute rejection of a predetermining motion (*virtus*).

[5] *"Ipse actus liberi arbitrii reducitur in Deum sicut in causam."* (Loc. cit.) The essence of God as understood is the specificative cause of the intelligibility of the essence of the action of a creature; the will is the efficient cause of the existence of a free act.

[6] *Loc. cit.*   [7] *Loc. cit.*

important. St. Thomas here is speaking of an existential cause, of the cause of the "to be." The "to be" of the free act is caused by God. Without this causality on the part of God, this free act would never exist. Hence the free act is traceable to, derived from, God as (*sicut*) its cause. Note the word "*sicut.*" We do not say that God is simply the cause, but that the act is traceable to God as to its cause; for although God in no way predetermines the act, as was stated just a few lines before, nevertheless it could never take place without God causing its "to be." Divine providence is not only compatible with the free acts of man; it is necessary for the actuation of such freedom.

S U M M A R Y — Question V

DIVINE PROVIDENCE

ARTICLE I: Providence Belongs to God.

1. **Definition:** Providence is not governance of the world. Governance is the execution of providence. Providence is the knowledge (*ratio*) of the things to be ordered to their end. Hence, providence is not the exemplar which implies the act of the divine will; it is a knowledge, *ratio,* of the order and belongs to the intellect alone. This is confirmed by the fact that providence in man is a part of prudence which is in the intellect.

2. **Predication.**

   a) **Problem:** We look for a true concept of providence in creatures, which concept we shall predicate of God after removing all the imperfection of the creature. Now, since providence is a part of prudence, we try to discover the true meaning of the perfection of providence by an analysis of prudence in man. It is obvious, of course, that prudence as such cannot be predicated of God. Hence the problem: How can providence, which is a part of prudence, be predicated of God?

b) **Analysis of prudence in man.**
1) There are three distinct operations: counsel, judgment, command (perfect act).
2) There are three kinds of parts of the habit:
   (*a*) Subjective parts, which are specific virtues *related* to prudence as to their *genus*.
   (*b*) Potential parts, which are subsidiary virtues that, by their actions, *dispose* man to the perfect act of command.
   (*c*) Integral parts, which are various dispositions that *concur* to the perfect act; the most perfect is providence.
c) **Providence in man** is that disposition which enables him to enact the knowledge and command which is the perfect act of prudence. This is a concept of a perfection which does not necessarily include imperfection.
d) **In predicating this perfection of God,** who is the cause of all human providence, we remove the imperfection of the creature. Providence in God is not a disposition; it is an act. Then we identify it with Existence: God is Providence.

3. **Proof: There is providence in God.** God's knowledge is the specificative cause of all creatures. Hence, providence, which is the *knowledge* of the order of creatures to their end, must pre-exist in the divine intellect.

ARTICLE II: All Creatures Are Subject to Divine Providence.

Since God's will is the free efficient cause of the existence of all creatures, such existence must be according to the knowledge of the divine plan, that is, in accordance with divine providence. Hence:
1. Absolutely speaking, there is no such thing as pure chance; whatever happens happens because God, in accordance with divine providence, wills it to happen.
2. Evil is not removed from the care of divine providence.

3. Although the will of man is not predetermined, the actuation of existence of the free act of man by the divine will is in accord with and subject to the divine plan of God's providence.

Question VI

THE OMNIPOTENCE OF GOD

There will be two articles to this question: (1) Is God omnipotent, that is, is there infinite power in God? (2) In what does God's omnipotence consist, that is, are there limitations to His power?

ARTICLE I: God Is Omnipotent

Potency and Power: The Latin word, *potentia* (potency), is a difficult term to render properly into the English language. Its root, which is the verb *posse,* signifies "to be able," "to be capable of." Hence, potency means primarily ability for doing something; it means a power for action; it is an *active* potency. The secondary or derived meaning of potency is a capacity, not for doing, not for giving, but for receiving and limiting a perfection, for undergoing a change. Such a capacity we call *passive* potency. In this latter sense, we have used the word potency throughout metaphysics. Potency has come to signify ordinarily a limiting principle, a capacity which looks to the reception of an act.

Later, in *The Philosophy of Man* in which we discussed the problem of the operative potencies, we noted a difference in our understanding of potency. The faculties of man which we termed operative potencies were discovered to be primarily passive. The intellect, for example, has to be actuated by a representative species distinct from it. As soon as it was put in act, the intellect could no longer be considered a mere passive potency. It became a power for action, an active potency.

Finally, in this treatise of THE PHILOSOPHY OF GOD, we have established at length that God is pure act and that there is no potency in Him, meaning, of course, no passive potency. Consequently, when we come to inquire about the omnipotence of God, we are not concerned with passive but with active potency or power. We do not ask whether there is in God a capacity for change, but whether there is power to produce effects, and in what does this power consist.[8]

Definition: We may infer that power (active potency) is not opposed nor contrary to act but founded upon it, since everything acts according as it is in act. Power, then, is an active principle; it is defined as *the principle of action in another*.[9]

When applied to God, this definition will need to be modified. God's action is not distinct from His power, since both power and action are His essence: they are the supreme act which is "To Be." In creatures, on the contrary, the action is in another.[10] In God, then, we may say that power (active potency) is the effective, the active principle. It is the principle of an effect.[11]

There Is Power in God: Power most assuredly belongs to God in the highest degree.

> For it is manifest that everything, according as it is in act and is perfect, is the active principle of something; whereas everything is passive according as it is deficient and imperfect. Now it was shown above that God is pure act, absolutely and universally perfect; there is no imperfection in Him. Whence it most fittingly

---

[8] In order to avoid confusing the reader, we shall use the term power or omnipotence of God rather than active potency.

[9] Aristotle, *Metaphysics*, IV, 12, 1019a, 19.

[10] "*Actio est in passo.*" This, of course, refers to a transient (predicamental) action. Now a transient action is a motion from the agent which is in the patient. It is therefore distinct from the agent.

[11] "In creatures, power [*potentia*] is not only the principle of action but also the principle of effect. In this way, the notion of power [*potentia*] is preserved in God as principle of effect, not as principle of action, since the action is the essence." (*S. Th.*, I, 25, 1, ad 3m.)

belongs to Him to be an active principle, and in no way whatsoever to be passive. On the other hand, the nature of active principle belongs to active power. For active power is the principle of acting upon something else, whereas passive power is the principle of being acted upon by something else. . . . . It remains, therefore, that in God there is active power supremely.[12]

God Is Omnipotent: "Active power exists in God according to the measure in which He is in act. Now His 'To Be' is infinite, inasmuch as it is not limited by anything that receives it, as is clear from what was said when we discussed the infinity of the divine essence. Therefore, it is necessary that the active power of God should be infinite. For in every agent we find that the more perfectly an agent has the form by which it acts, the greater its power to act. For instance, the hotter a thing is, the greater power it has to give heat; and it would have infinite power to give heat were its own heat infinite. Whence, since the divine essence, through which God acts, is infinite, as was shown above, it follows that His power likewise is infinite."[13] In short, God is omnipotent.

In God Power Is Not a Third Principle of Operation Besides Intellect and Will: We may infer also that although in man the operative potencies of intellect and will are not identical with power (active potency), since the soul of man is also the principle of vegetative and sentient operations, in God nevertheless we must affirm that power does not differ really (*secundum rem*) from intellect and will but only rationally (*secundum rationem*). For although power implies the notion of a principle which accomplishes what the will demands and what knowledge and intellect direct, nevertheless in God power is in no way distinct from these, so that we may say that intellect or will include the effective principle which we call power.[14]

The truth that power in God is not a distinct principle of action can be established in this manner. God is a purely spiritual being. Now in such a being, there can be no effective principle which is

---

[12] *S. Th.*, I, 25, 1, c.
[13] *S. Th.*, I, 25, 2, c.
[14] Cf. *S. Th.*, I, 25, 1, ad 3ᵐ; I, 25, 5, ad 1ᵐ.

not intellectual and does not operate the action of knowledge or love; any other operation has no meaning in such a being. "If we speak of immaterial beings," affirms St. Thomas, "there can be no other faculty, no other operation, except that of the intellect and will."[15] The reason is that virtue (power) and operation must follow nature. Now a purely spiritual being is not intellectual in part as is the soul of man, which is also the principle of vegetative and sentient operations, because it is the form of the body. It is intellectual as to its whole nature. Consequently, there can be no virtue, no power, in a purely spiritual being except intellectual knowledge and intellectual appetite.

ARTICLE II: What Is the Object and Extension of God's Omnipotence?

The Problem: This statement is often heard: If God is omnipotent, there is nothing that is not in His infinite power; He can do all things. We ask: Is the omnipotence of God limited, that is, restricted to certain objects? What is the meaning of that phrase, "God can do all things"? Could God create a square circle; could He make yesterday be tomorrow; can He make the impossible become possible?

Erroneous Solution: We know that voluntarist philosophers such as Ockham and Descartes thought that the power and the will of God were supreme. Consequently, according to these authors, the most profound reason why something is impossible is that God does not will it. Such a fundamental principle — as we have sufficiently noted in the philosophy of being — can only lead to skepticism, for it implies the relativity of truth.[16]

Doctrine of St. Thomas: Our solution is founded on the principle of intelligibility: being only is intelligible. Hence, whatever is not intelligible is not being; it is nothing; and therefore it cannot exist. That is why being is denominated from "to be" (*ens denominatur*

---

[15] *De Malo*, XVI, a. 1, ad 14m.

[16] The nature of the possible beings was discussed in metaphysics. Cf. *The Philosophy of Being*, p. 108 ff.

ab esse); that is why we declare that being is that whose act is "to be." The inference from this truth is that whenever the intelligible content of what is thought to be an essence implies a contradiction, as for example a square circle, then there really can be no capacity for existence. For a contradiction which signifies nothing cannot be ordered to the supreme act of existing, the "to be." It cannot exist because it is not possible, and it is not possible because not intelligible. It is not being; it is nothing.

> Nothing is opposed to the notion of being except non-being. . . . Whatever, therefore, implies a contradiction does not come under the divine omnipotence, because it cannot have the nature of possibility.[17]

Hence, when we say that God is omnipotent, we mean that He has the power to cause whatever is capable of existence, whatever is intelligible. He has power over all beings. The reason is that God is subsisting, infinite "To Be" and, consequently, that He alone can communicate existence to any effect. "The divine 'To Be' upon which the nature of the power of God is founded, is infinite; it is not limited to any class of beings, but possesses within itself the perfection of all existence. Whence, whatsoever has or can have the nature of being is numbered among the absolute possibles, in respect of which God is called omnipotent."[18]

It is not because of a defect in the power of God that that which implies a contradiction is not within the divine omnipotence, but because such a contradiction has no habitude (relation or order) to existence. Such a contradiction is not possible and, therefore, it cannot receive "to be," because it is not intelligible; it is non-being, absolutely nothing.

We conclude: God's omnipotence consists in this, that because God is "To Be," He has absolute power over all existence, and therefore His omnipotence embraces all beings.

In order to clarify this abstract doctrine, St. Thomas proposes two concrete problems whose solutions depend upon our under-

---

[17] *S. Th.*, I, 25, 3, c.
[18] *Loc. cit.*

standing of divine omnipotence. The first is, whether God could do what He does not do; the second, which complements the first, is, whether God could create a better world than the present.

1. Could God Do What He Does Not Do? This may seem at first glance to be an idle question. For we have established not only that God has power over all possibles, but that He does not produce an effect by a necessity of His nature. Moreover, we have seen that God's will, which is the cause of all existence, cannot be necessitated by a created and limited good, because God's will is identified with the divine goodness which is "To Be." Consequently, the course of events in the present order of things does not in any manner result from a divine necessity. All this is fairly obvious.

The real difficulty may be proposed thus: The power of omnipotence of God is determined to this present order of the universe because it is in accord with the divine wisdom and justice. Wisdom directs, will commands, power must fulfill. Now a wise ruler chooses the order which will bring about most perfectly the end desired; he chooses means that are truly proportioned to their end. God, therefore, who is infinitely wise, cannot but choose this particular order of the universe which must be best suited for the attainment of the end. It follows that power must follow wisdom and must be determined necessarily to this order. God could not do anything else except what He does.

In answering this difficulty, St. Thomas points out that such a manner of reasoning cannot be applied to God. The reason is that divine goodness is an end which exceeds all creatures and, moreover, that such an end is not desired but already possessed. Hence the divine wisdom is not determined to any particular order,[19] to any particular world, as means to an end; consequently, neither is His omnipotence. We must state unqualifiedly (*simpliciter*) that God could do what He does not do.[20]

---

[19] St. Thomas has expressed this thought by a strong phrase: "*Divina sapientia totum posse potentiae comprehendit.*" (*S. Th.*, I, 25, 5, c.)

[20] We should recall a distinction which was explained in the treatise on the will. Once God has willed from eternity a certain order, He cannot *ex suppositione* will

Potentia Absoluta et Potentia Ordinata: In order to clarify matters further, we should distinguish between God's absolute power and His preordained power. The first is absolutely infinite and looks to being. Absolutely speaking, God can do all things, for being is that whose act is "to be," and God's power is Subsisting Existence. On the other hand, we speak of God's preordained power as related to the order of the universe which divine wisdom and providence have proposed to be established. Regarding such a universe, God will not do otherwise than what has been preordained, although, absolutely speaking, He has power to do otherwise. To express this succinctly, we may say that God does this by preordained power because He wills it. But we must add, absolutely speaking, by absolute power, God could do other things because His omnipotence embraces all beings.

2. Could God Create a Better World? From the concluding remarks of the preceding paragraph, we immediately infer that, absolutely speaking (*potentia absoluta*), God could create more and better beings, better either in their nature or in their accidental perfections. This, however, is not precisely the question.

St. Thomas admits that this present universe is by no means the best, since God could create a world of more perfect beings. But, and this is the point, he adds almost in the same breath that in a certain sense this world could not be bettered. "Given the things which actually exist, the universe," he declares, "could not be better."[21] These are strong words, but their meaning is extremely delicate and finely balanced. Hence, unless properly understood, they could lead to grave error. St. Thomas himself explains that the reason why such a world could not be improved is that God in His wisdom has established the most fitting order for the things He has created. In this order does the good of the universe consist. Hence, if the perfection of one being were increased without the proper readjustment for the rest of the universe, the perfect

---

another. This statement is not opposed to our solution that unqualifiedly God could do what He does not do.

21 *"Universum, suppositis istis rebus, non potest esse melius."* (*S. Th.,* I, 25, 6, ad 3ᵐ.)

balance of this order would be destroyed, and the universe would become less perfect. It is true, God could create other beings and add new perfections to the present creation. In such a case, the world might be more perfect but not the same; it would be a different world. Taking things as they are, this universe could not be better.[22]

S U M M A R Y — Question VI

THE OMNIPOTENCE OF GOD

Article I: God Is Omnipotent.

1. **Active and passive potency.** Active potency is capacity or power for action; passive potency is capacity for reception, for limiting.
2. **Active potency or power** is the principle of action in another. Such a definition imports a predicamental action which is distinct from the agent. Hence the definition has to be modified, since God is His own action. In God we say that power is the principle of an effect.
3. **There is power in God.** A being is able to act, to produce an effect, inasmuch as it is in act. God is pure act. Hence, not only must we say that there is power in God, but we must add that His power is infinite. He is omnipotent.
4. **Power in God is not a third principle of operation besides intellect and will.** This is true of any pure spiritual form. There can be no other operation and, therefore, no distinct principle

---

[22] This doctrine is poles apart from the Leibnitzian error that this is the most perfect world possible. We quote the words of the Angelic Doctor: "Although the present order of things is restricted to what now exists, the divine power and wisdom are not thus restricted. Whence, although no other order would be suitable and good for the things which now exist, yet God can make other things and impose upon them another order." (*S. Th.,* I, 25, 5, ad 3ᵐ.)

of action in a spiritual form except intellect and will. For the
nature of such a being is purely intellectual. In man, on the
contrary, power is exercised through the members of the body.

ARTICLE II:　Object and Extension of God's Omnipotence.

1. Being is the object of God's omnipotence.

a) God has power over all beings. For being is that whose act
is "to be," that is to say, it has a relation to existence. Now
God has power over "to be," since He is subsisting "To Be."
Hence His omnipotence is extended to all beings without
exception.

b) A contradiction, because it is not intelligible, because it is not
being, is not the object of God's omnipotence.

2. Inferences.

a) **Can God do what He does not do?** Absolutely speaking,
He can, because His absolute power extends to all beings.
The reason is (1) God does not seek an end, and (2) the
divine goodness infinitely exceeds all creatures. If, however,
we speak of God's *preordained power,* that is, the execution
of the divine plan which is in accordance with divine wisdom
as regards this present world, we must deny that God can
do what He does not do.

b) **Could God create a better world?** Certainly God has power
to create a world of superior beings. Such a world would be
more perfect. If, however, we speak of the present world
whose order is in accordance with divine wisdom, St. Thomas
is of the opinion that this world could not be bettered. For
an improvement in any being would necessitate a proper readjustment of the whole; and such a readjustment would
result in a world that is not only a better but a different world.

Question VII

CREATION

Prologue

Problem: God is the existential cause of all that is; He communicates the "to be." This truth, so often presented, so well established, is the reason why we declare that God is the Creator of the world, that He alone produces the world by creation. For, unlike the eduction of a form which presupposes an existing subject, existence is not a further actuation of an already existing reality. It is that because of which the subject is an existing reality, for without the "to be," the subject is nothing in the world of existing beings.[23] By communicating existence, by giving "to be," God produces the world. He creates. The problem of creation, then, in the existential philosophy of St. Thomas is not so much to discover that God is the existential cause of all that exists, as to show that the production of the entire existence of a being is what is meant by creation.

Creation in Existential Thought: We might wonder, then, why St. Thomas presents the problem of creation as a distinct problem and devotes considerable space to its solution. It seems to me that, besides the need for clarification and precision in a problem which has so seldom been solved satisfactorily by great thinkers — not even by Plato and Aristotle — St. Thomas wants to show that in an existential philosophy most of the difficulties that can be brought against creation vanish as soon as proposed. For, as we shall note, the fundamental difficulty against creation, the assertion that matter is uncreated, is meaningless in a philosophy whose fundamental notion of reality is based on the "to be." Being, and therefore even matter, is denominated from "to be" (*ens denominatur ab esse*), and the act of being is existence. If, then, in a material being the

---

[23] Cf. *C.G.*, II, 16.

"to be" is distinct from the entire essence which it actuates, the causing of the "to be" will imply creation of matter as well as of form.

In an essentialist philosophy in which the problem of existence is not confronted, the many changes which occur in the world of material creatures are traceable not to the existential act but only to the corruption and eduction of form. Hence, while the change of form postulates an extrinsic agent, an efficient cause, there is no necessary inference from this to warrant a dependence of the subject of that change, namely matter, upon a creator. For in an essentialist philosophy, matter is not distinct from its act of existing. Matter *is*. No reason, then, is seen for the affirmation of the dependence of matter upon an efficient cause for its "to be." On the contrary, in the doctrine of St. Thomas, the entire essence, that is, matter and form, are the potency, the capacity for the existential act. They simply cannot be thought of as existing realities without a "to be" which, being distinct from them, is unintelligible without an efficient cause.

Definition: This clear-cut opposition between an essentialist and an existentialist position regarding the truth of creation will appear even more completely when we compare the definition of creation proposed by some essentialists who admit creation with that of St. Thomas.

Some of these essentialist philosophers thus defined creation: "Creation is the production of a thing out of nothing, either of the form or of the matter."[24] St. Thomas, on the other hand, states repeatedly that "creation is the emanation of the entire 'to be.' "[25]

The cause of the profound difference between these two definitions has already been suggested. To a philosophy which does not

---

[24] *"Creatio est productio rei ex nihilo sui et subjecti."* We do not deny the truth of this definition. Indeed, in a philosophical system which does not accept the actuation of potency by a distinct existential act, this definition is the only one possible. Our point is that St. Thomas never proposed such a definition, because in the philosophy of the "to be," creation is more intelligible when expressed with regard to existence than with regard to essence.

[25] *"Creatio est emanatio totius esse."* (*S. Th,.* I, 45, 1, c.; I, 45, 2, c.; I, 45, 2, ad 1m; I, 45, 3, c.)

accept the distinction between act and potency in the existential order, it seems necessary, in defining creation, to state that creation must exclude not only a pre-existing form but a pre-existing matter as well. On the other hand, in the definition given by the Angelic Doctor, *"emanatio totius esse,"* it is obvious that such a production excludes absolutely an existing element whether formal or material, whether accidental or essential. For without existence, nothing, absolutely nothing, is. Creation signifies, therefore, the production of the *whole* being.

Emanation: The word "emanation" (*emanatio*) which is used by Aquinas has acquired an unsavory connotation in the history of thought. It has come to signify the breaking off of a piece, a part of reality, from the parent stem. It is as if an efficient cause, in producing an effect, would lose and project part of its substance. This part of the efficient cause, now being cut off and completely distinct, becomes the effect. We have already refuted vigorously this materialistic theory of efficient causality,[26] a theory which explains nothing and destroys the true notion of cause. Emanation in the Philosophy of St. Thomas means nothing of the sort. Let us analyze the true metaphysical meaning of this term.

We should note in the first place that in creatures, efficient causality, which is defined as the exercise of action, is not an emanation in the strict sense. The reason is that predicamental action, which is *motion as from this,* is in the patient. It supposes, therefore, an existing patient out of whose potency the effect which terminates the motion of the action is educed by this action. It follows that the producing of an effect by the efficient causality of a creature is not an emanation but an eduction.

We became acquainted with the term "emanation" in the philosophy of man when we analyzed the act of knowledge which is the act of a perfect being. There it was pointed out that although the actuated operative potency is the efficient cause of this immanent action, nevertheless there is no question of a predicamental action; there is no question of a motion, of a passage from potency

---

[26] Cf. *The Philosophy of Being,* p. 139.

to act, terminating into a form which is educed.[27] The act of understanding which results from the actuated intellect and terminates in the production of the "word" (*verbum*) cannot be an eduction, since the intellect which produces it is in act and not in potency. Consequently, the act of understanding in man, together with the "word," *flow* from the actuated intellect by a sort of resultance (*per quamdam resultantiam*) which St. Thomas calls "emanation."[28]

It might well be asked why, then, the act of understanding, the emanation of the word, is not called creation. The answer is simple, clear, and complete. A creature can never cause existence. Hence the production of the "to understand" as well as of the "word" by the actuated intellect is not the emanation of the whole "to be." At best we may call it the emanation of the form, of the essence. For, like all created beings, the act of understanding and the "word" exist not because of the efficient causality of the intellect of man, but because God, subsisting existence, gives them "to be."[29]

The signification of the definition proposed by St. Thomas, *emanatio totius esse,* can only be attributed to God, for such causality means really an emanation of the whole being (*emanatio totius entis*). It means that "God from nothing produces a being, the whole being, into existence."[30]

There will be three articles in this question: (1) God is the Creator of the world. (2) How does the world emanate from God? (3) Was the world created from eternity or in time?

ARTICLE I: God Is the Creator of the World

We shall establish first that God is the Creator of the world,

---

[27] Cf. *The Philosophy of Man*, pp. 14, 82, 132.

[28] Let us note that this emanation does not mean a loss on the part of the intellect. There is no loss in an agent as agent. (Cf. *The Philosophy of Being*, p. 139.) On the contrary, as a result of this production of the word, the intellect acquires an intellectual habit.

[29] There are other reasons why this emanation is not a creation: (1) it supposes a remote potency in the subject; (2) it is an accident.

[30] "*Deus est causa universalis totius esse. Unde necesse est dicere quod 'Deus ex nihilo res in esse producit.'*" (*S. Th.*, I, 45, 2, c.) "Creation is that by which the whole substance is produced." (*S. Th.*, I, 45, 2, ad 2m.)

since He gives the entire "to be" of every limited being. Second, we shall show that He is the creator of matter. Finally, we shall explain that the supreme cause which acts by intellect and will is the exemplary as well as the final cause of the world.

God Is the Cause of the Entire "To Be" of Participated Beings: The first article of question forty-four of the first part of the *Summa Theologica* is undoubtedly one of the great pages of the writings of the Angelic Doctor. In the body of the article, St. Thomas explains that the participated existence which is observed in the multitude of beings which surround us[31] supposes and depends upon the absolute "To Be" which causes it and, consequently, causes the whole participated being. God, then, because He is the efficient cause of the whole "to be" of participated beings, is their Creator.

> It must be said that everything that in any way *is* is from God. For whatever is found in anything by participation must be caused in it by that to which it belongs essentially, as iron becomes heated by fire. Now it has been shown above, when treating of the divine simplicity, that God is self-subsisting "To Be" itself, and also that subsisting "To Be" can be only one; just as, if whiteness were self-subsisting, it would be one, since whiteness is multiplied by its recipients. Therefore all beings other than God are not their own "to be," but are beings by participation. Therefore, it must be that all things which are diversified by the diverse participation of "to be," so as to be more or less perfect, are caused by one First Being, who possesses "To Be" most perfectly.[32]

We should note that the concept of creation in St. Thomas results from the fact that creatures have a participated "to be" while God is unparticipated Existence. In other words, the Thomistic notion of creation includes the analogy of proportionality.

We should note also that the notion of efficient causality results from the fact that the participated "to be," because limited, is

---

[31] Being many, they are limited and, therefore, composed of a limited "to be" and a limiting essence.
[32] *S. Th.*, I, 44, 1, c.

distinct from its potency which is the essence. For from the fact
that a being has a participated, a limited existence, it follows that
it must be caused.

> Although relation to its cause is not part of the definition of a
> thing caused, still it follows as a result of what belongs to its
> make-up [*ratio*]. For, from the fact that a thing is being by partici-
> pation, it follows that it is caused. Hence, such a being cannot be
> without being caused, just as man cannot be without having the
> faculty of laughing. But, since to be caused does not enter into the
> make-up [*ratio*] of being taken absolutely, that is why there exists
> a being that is uncaused.[33]

Even Prime Matter Is Created by God: Although this truth is
sufficiently evident from the fact that God is the cause of the
entire "to be," nevertheless St. Thomas takes time to establish it
by a distinct argument. He begins by an historical survey of some
of the views regarding matter held by philosophers who preceded
him. He shows how the Greeks in particular thought that they had
explained the cause of change — both accidental and substantial —
by postulating an efficient cause which by its action educes these
forms from the potency of an eternal matter. They gave a solution
regarding the problem of the efficient cause of the mutations of a
corporeal being, in so far as an extrinsic agent causes the specific
and the individual nature by the eduction of new forms, whether
substantial or accidental. They did not touch the problem of why
such a being exists. Not observing any change in matter as such,
they did not see why matter had to be caused. Their problem was
not one of existence but one of becoming, for they were essentialists.
Now, the complete problem is not that it is sufficient to consider
"the cause of things according as they are *such* by accidental forms
or *these* by substantial forms, but according to all that belongs to
their '*to be*' in any way whatever."[34]

To solve the problem of corporeal being, one must rise to the
cause of its entire "to be." Such a cause will need to be the cause

---

[33] *S. Th.*, I, 44, 1, ad 1[m].
[34] *S. Th.*, I, 44, 2, c.

of prime matter. Matter, therefore, is created by the universal cause of the entire "to be."

It appears, then, that in the metaphysics of the Greek essentialists, there is no place for the problem of creation, for it is strictly an existential problem. On the other hand, some of these philosophers faced and solved the problem of becoming by means of Aristotelian hylemorphism. Accordingly, change is truly explained by an extrinsic agent which by its action educes the form, whether substantial or accidental, from the potency of matter. Matter, however, does not change. Hence, there is no problem regarding matter; it is uncaused, eternal, and necessary.

Without either an existential position or the revealed truth of the fact of creation, it is not easy to see how the problem of creation could be proposed; and it is even more difficult to understand how it could ever be solved. That is perhaps why so many great philosophical minds, buried in material essentialism, never rose to the question of the absolute necessity of creation.

God Is the Exemplary Cause of the World: The problem of the exemplary cause of the world presents little difficulty at this point. We have shown in the Fourth Way that no limited perfection is completely intelligible without a First Exemplary Cause which, because it is "To Be," is the First Efficient Cause of all existing reality. Now the First Efficient Cause, which acts by intellect and will, by contemplating His essence knows all the essences which He freely wills to create. These ideas are the exemplary causes of the world and are identified with the divine existence, since God is absolutely simple. God, therefore, is the exemplary cause of the world.

> God is the first exemplary cause of all things. In proof whereof we must consider that for the production of anything an exemplar is necessary, in order that the effect may receive a determinate form. For an artificer produces a determinate form in matter by reason of the exemplar before him, whether it be the exemplar beheld externally, or the exemplar interiorly conceived in the mind. Now it is manifest that things made by nature receive determinate forms. This determination of forms must be reduced to the divine wisdom as its first principle, for divine wisdom devised the order

of the universe residing in the distinction of things. And therefore we must say that in the divine wisdom are the models of all things, which we have called *ideas,* that is, exemplary forms existing in the divine mind. And although these ideas are multiplied by their relations to things, nevertheless, they are not really distinct from the divine essence, inasmuch as the likeness of that essence can be shared diversely by different things. In this manner, therefore, God Himself is the first exemplar of all things.[35]

God Is the Final Cause of the World: We do not mean by this that God, in creating the world, has a final cause which is Himself. God has no cause. "For it does not belong to the first agent who is agent only [and not patient] to act for the acquisition of some end. He intends only to communicate His perfection which is His Goodness."[36] We say that the divine goodness is the end and not the final cause of His creating the world. This has been explained in the treatise on the will.

In the present article, St. Thomas states that the world of creatures seeks the good, for each creature seeks to acquire its own perfection. Now the perfection of a creature is a good, and therefore it is either the supreme good or the likeness of the divine perfection and goodness. Consequently, we must state that God is the final cause of the world.

Because God is the Creator of the world, that is, because God gives the entire "to be" of every being, it follows that He created matter and that He is the exemplary cause as well as the end of all creatures.

ARTICLE II: How Does the World Emanate From God? or The Nature of Creation

In the prologue of this question, we proposed the existentialist definition of creation: *the emanation of the entire "to be."* In the analysis of this definition, we noted that no existing reality is presupposed as the recipient of this emanation. Indeed, were it so, creation would be reduced to a mere generation, to a change in

---

[35] *S. Th.,* I, 44, 3, c.   [36] *S. Th.,* I, 44, 4, c.

an already existing subject. The resulting being would not be made from nothing, and our definition that creation is the emanation of the *entire* "to be" would not be applicable. In the true notion of creation, then, as expressed by this definition, nothing, absolutely nothing, is presupposed to the emanation of the entire "to be." Creation, therefore, is not a change, for strictly speaking, a change indicates that something becomes something else. In creation, on the contrary, the whole substance of a thing is produced from nothing.

Active and Passive Creation: We understand what creation does. We should like to know what it is in itself. Creation viewed actively is the divine action which comprises knowledge and will. It is, therefore, the essence of God, the divine "To Be" with a relation of reason to the thing created.

> Creation signified actively means the divine action, which is God's essence with a relation to the creature. But in God, relation to the creature is not a real relation, but only a relation of reason; whereas the relation of the creature to God is a real relation, as was said above in treating of the divine names.[37]

Viewed passively, however, creation posits a real predicamental relation in the creature. This relation establishes the dependence of the entire "to be" of the creature upon the Creator. It is the relation of an effect to its existential cause.

> Creation posits something in the created thing only according to relation; for what is created is not made by motion or by change. For what is made by motion or by change is made from something pre-existing. This happens, it is true, in the particular productions of some beings, but it cannot happen in the production of the entire "to be" by the universal cause of all beings, which is God. Hence God, in creating, produces things without motion. Now when motion is removed from action and passion, only relation remains, as was said above. Hence creation in the creature is only a certain relation to the Creator as to the principle of its "to be"; even as in passion, which supposes motion, is implied a relation to the principle of motion.[38]

---

[37] *S. Th.*, I, 45, 3, ad 1[m].
[38] *S. Th.*, I, 45, 3, c.; cf. *De Potentia*, III, 3, c.

Relation of Dependence Establishes Existential Cause: This relation of dependence of the entire "to be" indicates two things. First, that every created being must be a composite, at least in the order of existence, for unless the existential act is distinct from and limited by the essence, there can be no relation of dependence and therefore no creation. This predicamental relation, which establishes creation in the creature, manifests the dependence of an effect upon its existential cause. Hence if this effect were not a composite, there would be no real predicamental relation to the cause: there would be no creation.

Subject of Relation Is Substance: Second, this relation of dependence of the entire "to be" indicates that the mode of existence of the subject of this relation must be a substance and, therefore, that the term of creation cannot be a mere accident: it must be a substance. The reason is that " 'to be' belongs properly to that which has existence and which is subsisting in its 'to be.' "[39] On the other hand, we do not speak of the entire "to be" of an accident, since the mode of existing of an accident is to be in another. Indeed, remarks the Angelic Doctor, an accident is not really being in a strict sense, but rather it is *of a being*. Now being, not *of a being,* is the term of creation, since creation is the emanation of the entire "to be." Accidents, then, are said to be concreated rather than created.

God Alone Can Create: Because nothing exists unless caused by God who alone causes existence, we must declare that God alone can create. This truth appears most forcefully from the fact that God as the universal cause of all reality is the cause of the act of being, the "to be," since the "to be" is the most universal reality.

> It is sufficiently apparent at first glance that to create can be the proper action of God alone. For the more universal effects must be reduced to the more universal and prior causes. Now among all effects the most universal is "to be" itself; and hence it must be the proper effect of the first and most universal cause, which is God. . . . Now to produce "to be" absolutely, not merely as this or

---
[39] *S. Th.,* I, 45, 4, c.

such, pertains to the nature of creation. Hence it is manifest that creation is an action proper to God Himself.[40]

A Creature Cannot Create: We may infer the same conclusion negatively by considering that no limited being could cause existence, for if it could cause the "to be" of any other creature, it would be capable of causing its own "to be"; and this is an obvious absurdity. Why do we infer that if a creature could cause existence in another, it could cause its own existence? The reason is that the limitation of an act results not from the agent but from the potency which receives it. Hence, if an agent could cause "to be" in one creature, it could cause it for all other creatures; for the limitation of the "to be" which was caused resulted not from the lack of power and virtue of the agent but from the capacity of the essence.

> But just as an individual man participates in human nature, so every created being participates, so to speak, in the nature of "to be"; for God alone is His own "To Be," as we have said above. Therefore no created being is able to produce any being absolutely, but only in so far as it causes it to be in this; and so it is necessary that that by which something is "this" is presupposed to the action whereby the creature makes it like to itself.[41]

A Creature Cannot Be an Instrumental Cause in Creation: A far more difficult question is this. Granted that God alone creates, since God alone is "To Be," why could not God communicate existence through the instrumentality of a creature? For, as we studied in metaphysics, it is possible for an instrument to cause an effect that is more perfect than itself. And, consequently, a highly endowed creature such as an angel might be used by God as an instrument to create a less perfect being such as a stone.

This opinion has met favor with some important Christian philosophers. St. Thomas, however, states that it implies a contradiction. He argues in this fashion. In order that a creature be a true instrumental cause, it must share somehow in the operation

---

[40] *S. Th.*, I, 45, 5, c.
[41] *S. Th.*, I, 45, 5, ad 1m.

of the principal cause producing its effect. In other words, it must exercise a causality of its own; it must, by its own proper action, dispose the patient to the effect of the principal agent. Now the proper action of a creature is to cause not the "to be" but the becoming. It is obvious that there can be no becoming in the case of creation. The reason is that becoming supposes an existing patient, for it is a motion, a passage from potency to act *in a subject*. Creation, on the other hand, which is the emanation of the whole "to be," is the production of the whole substance so that nothing is presupposed. Consequently, there can be no becoming when there is no presupposed subject which can become. It is impossible, then, that a creature be a true instrumental cause in the divine work of creation.

ARTICLE III: The Beginning of Creatures

Two Opposite Views: St. Thomas takes a position between two extremes. To understand his position, we should present first these two opposite views. Aristotle and the ancient essentialist philosophers, ignorant as they were of the truth of creation, affirmed the eternity of matter. Against these, Aquinas establishes that only God can be proved definitely to be eternal. A world, he explains, whose "to be" depends absolutely upon the divine will does not necessitate an eternal duration. The reason is that the will of God is free as to the production of the world and in no manner determined as to the "when" of such production.

In complete opposition to a world which is necessarily eternal, many Christian philosophers think it evident to human reason that the world could not have been created from eternity, but that of its very nature it must have been created in time. St. Thomas has little patience with this opinion. He wrote an entire *opusculum, De Aeternitate Mundi,* to show the absurdity of this doctrine, and in many other works he has relentlessly denounced it. He states in the *Summa* that "we hold by faith alone that the world did not exist [from eternity]; it cannot be proved by a demonstration of science; it is an object of faith." "And," he adds, "it is useful to

consider this, lest anyone should bring forward arguments that are
not cogent. For this would give unbelievers something to ridicule."[42]

Position of St. Thomas: St. Thomas' position, then, is this:
although we cannot demonstrate that the world needs to be
eternal, nevertheless, neither can we demonstrate that the world
was necessarily created in time. The determination of the beginning
of the created world is a matter which transcends the human
understanding and which can be known only by faith. Reason
shows us the impossibility of discovering such a determination. It
can be obtained only from revelation.

There are, therefore, two points to be established: (1) The world
need not be eternal. (2) We cannot demonstrate that it was created
in time.

The World Need Not Be Eternal: The erroneous opinion which
declares that the world is necessarily eternal has been already
refuted, for we have shown that matter as well as form, because
distinct from their act of existing, must depend upon God for
existential actuation. In an existential philosophy, then, the question
is not, "Is the world necessarily eternal?" but, rather, "Was it
necessary for God to create the world from eternity?" The answer
is: certainly not, for creation, which is the emanation of the entire
"to be," is the effect of the free act of God. Consequently, it
belongs to His absolute will to determine the moment of creation.
Now the absolute will of God is inscrutable to us. Hence, human
reason cannot show that the world was created from eternity. It
can, however, infer from this that the world *need not be eternal.*

> . . . The will of God is the cause of things. It is necessary for
> some things to be, according as it is necessary for God to will
> them. . . . Now it was established that, absolutely speaking, it is
> not necessary for God to will anything except Himself. It is not
> necessary, therefore, for God to will that the world should always
> exist. The world is eternal only in so far as God wills it to be,
> since the "to be" of the world depends on the will of God as upon
> its cause.[43]

---

[42] *S. Th.,* I, 46, 2, c.
[43] *S. Th.,* I, 46, 1, c.

Reason Cannot Demonstrate That the World Was Created in Time: The argumentation of St. Thomas rests on a metaphysical principle. It is this, that while existentially subordinated (*per se*) efficient causes are necessarily limited in number so that we must come to an existing first cause, accidentally subordinated (*per accidens*) causes are not so limited. This he states definitely: "There cannot be an infinite number of causes that are *per se* required for a certain effect; for instance, that a stone be moved by a stick, the stick by the hand, and so on to infinity. But it is not impossible to proceed to infinity *accidentally* as regards efficient causes, for instance, if all the causes thus multiplied should have the order of only one cause, while their multiplication is accidental, e.g., as an artificer acts by means of many hammers accidentally, because one after the other is broken."[44]

Accordingly, since it is impossible to know from observation or analysis whether such an infinite series of accidentally subordinated causes did not take place, it is also impossible for unaided reason to infer conclusively that the world was created in time. For although in the order of existentially subordinated causes — an order which transcends time and place — we must come to a first cause which here and now causes the "to be" of the world, nevertheless this is not the case with regard to accidentally subordinated causes.

Proof: A demonstration that the world need be created in time should be based either on the nature of the world itself or on certain knowledge of the efficient cause of the world. Now, we cannot arrive at a definite conclusion regarding the moment of creation either from the nature of or from the cause of the world.

In the first place, the moment of creation cannot be established from the nature of the world. The reason is that the principle of demonstration is the essence, the quiddity, of things. Now an argument based on a quiddity can have no reference to time and place, for the essences of things as conceived by the intellect of man

---

[44] *S. Th.*, I, 46, 2, ad 7m.

abstract from the here and now. Time and place result not from
the essence but from the individuation.

Likewise the fact that the world was created in time cannot be
demonstrated from the efficient cause, for the will of God cannot
be investigated by human reason except as regards those things
which God wills necessarily. Now the will of God is free in regard
to creatures. There is, consequently, no certain means to arrive at
a certain knowledge of the fact that the world was created in
time, except through revelation.[45]

S U M M A R Y — Question VII
CREATION
Prologue

1. Problem.

   a) The problem of creation in an existential philosophy is not
   so much to discover that God is the existential cause of all
   that exists, as to show that the production of existence is
   fundamentally what is meant by creation.

   b) In an existential philosophy, the truth that God is the existential principle of all that exists is easily established. It results
   from an analysis of a world of limited beings, of beings
   which are not intelligible unless their distinct existence is
   shown to depend causally upon the Subsisting "To Be." Is
   this causing of the "to be" what we mean by creation?

2. Definition: *Creation is the emanation of the whole "to be."*

3. Analysis: The emanation of the whole "to be" is not an eduction; it does not suppose an existing subject of reception. It is
   the production of the whole being into existence. This is what
   we mean by *creation.*

ARTICLE I: God Is the Creator of the World.

**1. God is the efficient cause of the entire "to be" of every limited
   being.** For a participated "to be" is not intelligible without an
   efficient cause which is "To Be."

---
[45] *S. Th.,* I, 46, 2, c.

man is one who knows how to adapt the means to the proper end. Hence, to order properly to the end belongs to the wise, and that is what we mean by good government. Now the end is the good, and the end of the universe is the Supreme Good and that is God. The divine governance, therefore, is the proper ordering of the universe to God, and this government is to us the most perfect manifestation of divine wisdom. Clearly, then, the study of the governance of the world will help us to attain more completely the wisdom we have been seeking.

Throughout The Philosophy of God, we have tried to understand — as well as our limited intellects could understand — the nature of this Supreme Good who is Wisdom and Love. Now we shall complete the term of our study by reflecting upon the manifestation of this wisdom, by considering the government of the world. For this governance, which is the execution of divine providence, is the effect of God's operation as He orders all created things to their end. This order is a true manifestation of divine wisdom, for *"sapientis est ordinare."*

Governance Is the Term of Divine Love: God, who is absolute Goodness, wills the perfection of the universe, for that is to order the universe to its end. Because the divine will is efficacious and identified with the divine wisdom, the execution of the order established by providence, that is, the governance of the universe, is the term of the cycle of divine love. This truth is made evident in the following manner.

God is; He is absolute Goodness, absolute Truth, absolute Beauty, because He is Pure Existence. Knowing Himself, He knows all the possible imitations of His divine goodness. Loving Himself, He wills to communicate His goodness by creating a world which is a manifestation of that goodness and a participation of His beauty. Because the world is a limited participation of an Unparticipated Act, it must, by its natural appetite, tend toward the end to which the Creator has ordered it. But God Himself is the end of the world.[46] Hence the universe must necessarily seek God, its

---

[46] This we proposed earlier, *Supra,* p. 202.

end, according to the measure of its capacity. This seeking and attaining the end which is the term of the cycle of divine love is brought about by the divine government. God, therefore, governs the world by ordering it to its end, the good of the universe, and that is God Himself.

> Since it is proper to the best to produce the best, it is not suitable to the supreme goodness of God that He should not lead the things produced to their perfection. The ultimate perfection of each thing consists in the attainment of the end. Consequently, it pertains to the divine goodness that as it has caused things to be, so it must also lead them to their end. This is to govern.[47]

Division: This question is divided into three articles: (1) the government of the universe in general; (2) the conservation of creatures in existence; (3) divine motion in creatures.

ARTICLE I: Government of the World in General

Difficulty: Why speak of the governance of the world by God? The universe is made up largely of beings devoid of reason and will. It is obvious from casual observation that these things (and for that matter, even those beings which have knowledge and will) necessarily tend by their nature to actions which are the perfection of their nature. They follow the laws of natural evolution. Hence there seems no need for governance by an extrinsic deity, for these natures must act in accordance with their natural inclination. Governance of the universe by God, which was universally admitted by the Schoolmen, is meaningless today in view of the development of scientific knowledge.

As to those so-called rational beings which are said to be endowed with freedom of judgment and of choice, on the supposition that they are truly rational and free, such a government by an all-powerful deity would appear not only useless but actually harmful. For if we declare that the divine rule is efficacious, the free will of man could not but conflict at times with the divine plan. Such conflict could only result in the destruction of all free natures.

---

[47] *S. Th.*, I, 103, 1, c.

Answer: Both difficulties are due to a grave misconception of divine government. The second difficulty has been solved repeatedly in the tracts on the knowledge and will of God. Some complementary explanation will be proposed in the following article on divine motion. In answer to the first objection, we can only say that in affirming the necessary determination of a nature to action and perfection, this difficulty states precisely the fundamental position of the Angelic Doctor regarding the government of the universe. For the most important factor in such rule is the natural appetite of the various creatures. Indeed the acceptance of such a natural tendency which is inferred from the observation of the operation of the various substances is the beginning of the metaphysical reflection which establishes the fact of the governance of the universe by God.

Argument of St. Thomas: Let us mark the full development of the argument of St. Thomas. He begins with a simple remark which is within the observation of all men. Just look, he says, at the world in which we find ourselves; look at nature; consider the order of the heavens. Obviously, there is order, direction, finality. Up to this point, St. Thomas and the materialistic evolutionists are saying the same thing. Here, however, they part company completely; St. Thomas affirms the necessity of divine governance; the evolutionists deny it absolutely. The evolutionists conclude that there is no need for an extrinsic agent to direct nature, for all is sufficiently explained by the intrinsic finality which we observe in the various natures. St. Thomas, on the other hand, not only accepts the fact of intrinsic finality of nature, but upon this very fact he erects the metaphysical structure of his argumentation to prove the divine government of the universe.

The metaphysical argument of St. Thomas really begins when the evolutionists have reached their declaration that nature is intrinsically and necessarily determined to operation, that finality is intrinsic. We are more than willing to admit the necessary determination of a nature to its end. Indeed this determination is, we shall recall, the foundation for the Fifth Way of the demonstration of the existence of God. This necessity of nature we call the natural appetite to distinguish it from the sense and intellectual appetite. The natural appetite is the necessary inclination of a nature to its end; it is nature itself, since nature is the principle of action to an end. We will go farther and state that every nature, even a free nature such as that of man, has a natural, a necessary appetite to its end.

Proof: The argument may be stated thus:[48] Every agent acts for an end. The reason is that the operation, the action of an agent would not be intelligible without the determination of the final cause. Without this determination, there would be no reason why this particular agent acts this action, produces this effect. Without the determination of the final cause, there could be no answer to the question, why this effect rather than another? The effect as well as the action would not be intelligible.

Now a final cause cannot be an existing reality, for it is nothing but the effect as desired. It must be, therefore, in the order of intention, the order of intellect and will. From this fact, we must infer that since a natural agent is incapable of self-determination by knowledge, by a desire of the end, that is, by the knowledge of the effect *as desired,* there must be another, a higher cause, an intellectual agent responsible in some manner for the necessary inclination of a nature to its end. This intellectual agent we have already demonstrated to be God;[49] a God who has created the various natures and has endowed them with a necessary inclination, the natural appetite, to their end. This is the most fundamental aspect of the governance of the universe by God.

The natural necessity inhering in things which are determined to one is a certain impression from God directing them to their end, just as the necessity by which the arrow is moved so as to fly towards a certain point is an impression from the archer and not from the arrow. But it differs in this, that what creatures receive from God is their nature, while that which natural things receive from man in addition to their nature pertains to violence. Therefore, just as the necessity of violence in the movement of the

---

[48] Cf. *The Philosophy of Being,* p. 144 ff.
[49] *Supra,* The Fifth Way, p. 45.

arrow shows the direction of the archer, so the natural necessity of creatures shows the governance of divine providence.[50]

Good Government: It appears from this that good government does not consist in ruling by violence, for this means ultimately the destruction of nature, especially a free nature. Rather, good government fundamentally consists in implanting in the governed a natural inclination to the end which is the perfection of nature. Those who are thus governed seek the end of government according to their nature and not because forced by extrinsic violence. This is essential to good government.

Deductions: From this fundamental notion of the world government, we may draw several inferences which are important and far-reaching in their consequences on our consideration and practical application of the events which affect the world.

1. All Things Are Subject to Divine Government: We must conclude that all things, all without exception, are subject to the divine government. For not only does God create the various existing natures with their natural appetites, not only does He move them to action, but likewise He gives the "to be" of every operation. Consequently, nothing does happen, nothing can happen in this world except in accordance with His divine will. This is a tremendous truth, because it is so absolute and universal. It helps us to realize that nothing takes place except for a purpose, for an end, and that this end is the good of the universe which is willed by God.[51]

2. Nothing Can Resist Divine Government: Indeed, we must add with St. Thomas, not only that nothing can happen which is not in accordance with divine providence, but nothing can resist the divine governance of the universe. This, of course, is obvious regarding the natures which are necessarily directed by their natural appetite. It is made evident regarding the free natures when we consider that although God does not force the will to act, nevertheless He, in accordance with His wisdom, freely actuates or does

---

[50] *S. Th.*, I, 103, 1, ad 3ᵐ.
[51] Cf. *S. Th.*, I, 103, 5.

not actuate in the order of existence the free acts which man would place in given circumstances. All this is in accordance with the divine plan.[52]

3. Creatures Can Be Instruments in the Work of Governance: Although we established conclusively that no creature could ever be the principal cause or even the instrument in the work of creation, nevertheless, we must add that this is not the case regarding the government of the world. The argument which was brought to bear against the possibility of creation by a creature no longer holds as to government. The reason is that government supposes an existing world of limited beings. Such existing beings, composed as they are of act and potency, at least in the order of existence, can be subject to becoming; they can be moved toward their end by the action of other creatures, for the proper operation of a creature is to cause a becoming in another. The point to be clarified is not merely that God can govern the world through creatures, but that He does. St. Thomas points out that it is the mark of a wise ruler that he delegate his power and authority to subordinate officials and through their instrumentality govern his people. Such communication of power and goodness admits of greater perfection in the government, for it is better to have a certain perfection and be able to communicate it to others than to have it but not be able to communicate it.

But since things which are governed should be led to perfection by government, so much the better will be the government as a greater perfection is communicated by the governor to the things governed. Now it is a greater perfection for a thing to be good in itself and also the cause of goodness in others, than only to be good in itself. Therefore God so governs things that He makes some of them to be causes of others in government, as in the case of a teacher who not only imparts knowledge to his pupils but also makes some of them to be the teachers of others.[53]

---

[52] Cf. *S. Th.*, I, 103, 8.
[53] *S. Th.*, I, 103, 6, c.

ARTICLE II: Conservation of Creatures in the Order of Existence

Two Principal Means of Governance of the World: There are two principal effects in the operation of divine government. These effects are, we might say, the means necessary to direct the universe to its appointed end. The first is the conservation of creatures in the order of existence; the second is the divine motion which by actuating creatures in the order of activity enables them to break forth into operation.

Conservation of Existence: Why must God conserve the "to be" of creatures? At first sight, conservation of existence seems unnecessary, useless. Once a being is created or a form educed, once a reality exists, there seems no reason why it should not continue to exist.

Necessity for This Conservation: Such a statement indicates a profound ignorance of the analysis of a limited being in an existential metaphysics. A creature is not its existence, but has a "to be" distinct from its essence. The fact that such a composite being exists becomes intelligible because of its existential relation of dependence upon an extrinsic agent which is the cause of its existence. Likewise, the fact that it continues to exist is not intelligible without a continued emanation of the entire "to be," a continued causing of existence.[54] The reason is that in the existential order, an effect must depend here and now upon its cause.[55] A limited being, then, at any time of its existence has no sufficient reason in itself for existing. It actually needs the influx of an extrinsic agent which communicates the "to be."

God Alone Conserves "To Be": The conclusion is, of course, that since God and only God can give the "to be," it follows that in an existing creature, God must continually give existence, not by a series of distinct reiterated creations but by a continuation of the initial communication of "to be." This continued communi-

---

[54] "*In tantum enim indiget creatura conservari a Deo, in quantum esse effectus dependet a causa essendi.*" (*S. Th.,* I, 104, 1, ad 2m.)

[55] "*Omnis effectus dependet a sua causa secundum quod est causa eius.*" (*S. Th.,* I, 104, 1, c.) This point was discussed at length earlier in the book (p. 18).

cation of "to be" is what we mean by conservation of creatures in existence. God, therefore, actually conserves in existence all existing creatures. This is the first effect of the governance of the universe.

> . . . A thing is said to conserve another essentially and directly, namely, in so far as what is conserved depends on the conserver so that it cannot exist without it. In this manner all creatures need the divine conservation. For the "to be" of every creature depends on God, so that not for a moment could it subsist, but would return to nothing, were it not kept in existence by the operation of the divine power.[56]

Development of Argument: This argument, because of its metaphysical implications, is developed at length by St. Thomas. He argues first from the kind of an efficient cause required to produce a complete form of the same species. To do so, that is, to produce a complete form, a cause would need to be of a higher species than the effect. For if a cause could produce an effect which is a complete form of the same species, it would follow that the cause would be able to cause itself, and that, of course, is an absurdity. The reason why such a cause would be able to cause itself is due to this: the limitation of the form of the effect is not due to the efficient cause (agent) but to the material cause, that is, to the subject (patient). Now since, in our supposition, cause and effect belong to the same species, the causing of either is identical on the part of the virtue needed in the agent. It follows, therefore, that the created agent can only be the cause of the becoming of the form.

> It is evident that if two beings belong to the same species, one cannot be essentially the cause of the other's form as such, since it would then be the cause of its own form, since both forms have the same nature; but it can be the cause of this form inasmuch as it is in matter, that is, that *this matter* receives *this form*. And this is to be the cause of *becoming*. . . .[57]

---

[56] *S. Th.*, I, 104, 1, c.
[57] *Loc. cit.*

When this argument is transferred to the causing of "to be," it is obvious that only a subsisting Existence which is its own reason for existing and is absolutely independent can cause the "to be." Only God, then, can cause a creature to exist.

Having established that creatures can only cause becoming and that existence is from God, we proceed to show the absolute need for the continued conservation of existence by God. Let us return once more to the efficient causality of a created agent. It has been established that such an agent can only cause the becoming. Beginning with a consideration of the need of a cause actually causing in order to have an actual becoming, St. Thomas rises by comparison to the absolute need of a cause continually giving "to be" in order to explain the fact of an existing creature.

> Just as the becoming [the motion] of a thing does not endure once the action of the agent causing the becoming stops, so neither can the "to be" of a thing continue should the action of the agent who is the cause of the existence of the effect cease.[58]

We are ready to conclude with St. Thomas that the continuation in existence of the universe is caused continuously by God.

> The "to be" of every creature depends on God, so that it could not subsist for a moment but would return to nothing unless the operation of divine power [virtus] would conserve it in existence.[59]

This, of course, is one of the major effects of the governance of the world. For unless the universe continued to exist, it could never reach its end which is a greater participation in the divine goodness.

Creatures, therefore, are kept in existence by God. Creatures themselves do cause the becoming which must cease at the same moment that the cause ceases to act.

Conservation of Forms: This last deduction, that creatures cause the becoming which must cease whenever the creature ceases to act, brings up a problem which has often baffled philosophers. It

---

[58] Loc. cit.
[59] Loc. cit.

is this: seemingly contrary to the principle just mentioned, it can be observed that a ball having been set in motion by the thrower continues to move, continues to become, although the thrower has ceased to cause the becoming. Again we note that water which has been heated continues to be hot and to give heat even after the fire which was the cause of the heat is no longer applied to it.

Cause of the Becoming of the Form: The answer is that the becoming caused by the thrower and the fire has terminated into a complete form.[60] This form now actuates the subject — the water or the ball — in such a manner that it must act, since a being acts in so far as it is in act. In the case of the actuated moving ball, its action will consist in continuing its motion through the air until the surrounding bodies, reacting against the moving object by resistance and friction, cause the contrary form, the form of rest, to be educed while at the same time the form of motion is corrupted and returns to the potency of the subject. In like manner, a complete form of heat having been educed as the term of the becoming which was being caused by the fire, the water remains hot in spite of the removal of the fire.

What Is the Cause of the Complete Form? All this is fairly obvious and quite in accord with the principles of an existential philosophy. The problem, however, which arises at this juncture is not easily solved. It is this. We have explained satisfactorily the cause of the becoming. What of the cause of the complete form which has been educed as the term of the becoming? If this form remains, there should be an efficient cause causing it here and now and as long as it remains, since every effect must depend upon its proper cause. What is this cause?

Conservation of Substantial Forms: Because of the erroneous physics and astronomy of his day, St. Thomas believed that the celestial bodies were the immediate causes of the complete sub-

---

[60] The thrower is the cause of the motion of the ball through the air, because the thrower by causing the becoming of the form which actuates the ball has given the form in a certain manner. *"In motibus corporalibus movens dicitur quod dat formam quae est principium motus."* (S. Th., I, 105, 3, c.)

stantial forms, as well as of the resulting "to be,"[61] whenever such a form was generated through the causing of the becoming by a corporeal being of the same species, as for example in the case of the generation of animals and plants. The reason for this assertion was that the celestial bodies were wrongly thought to be of a higher species of bodies than those of the earth. Their influx, moreover, was believed to be continuous and constant. Consequently, many powers were attributed to them, one of the most important being their causality upon generation of substantial forms.

> . . . Thus the heavenly bodies cause the generation of inferior bodies which differ from them in species. Such an agent can be the cause of the form as such. . . . Consequently, it is the cause not only of the becoming but of existing [essendi].[62]

This theory, however, is based on a false assumption as to the perfect nature of the celestial bodies. It seems, therefore, quite in accord with the principles of the Angelic Doctor to declare that not only the "to be" but all *substantial forms* as well depend *immediately* upon God.

Conservation of Accidental Forms: The problem of the production and conservation of accidental forms is not altogether similar to that of substantial forms. The reason for the difference is due to this: the substantial form of any supposit, whether living or not, is that kind of form *whose "to be" is not in another*. Its "to be," therefore, is not given or supported by another being in which and through which it exists. On the other hand, accidental forms such as the form of a house, the form of heat in the water, the form of motive power in the moving ball, depend upon another creature in order to exist, for *their "to be" is to be in another as in a subject*. Such is the case regarding the form of a house, the form of motive power in the moving ball, the form of heat in water. St. Thomas explains that while the becoming of common

---

[61] Only God, of course, can cause the "to be" absolutely. In the conservation of creatures, however, He can do so mediately and through the instrumentality of the secondary cause. *"Esse per se consequitur formam creaturae, supposito tamen influxu Dei."* (*S. Th.*, I, 104, 1, ad 1ᵐ.)

[62] *S. Th.*, I, 104, 1, c.

accidents is caused by an extrinsic agent, the complete form together with the *"to be" in another* results from the nature of the subject of these accidents. Hence, although God is the first and principal cause of "to be," the created substances must be considered as the immediate cause not only of the production of the complete form, but of its conservation as well.[63]

"The form of the house consists in composition and order. This form results from the natural virtue of certain things (i.e., from the substances which are the material of the house)."[64] "Now it is evident that the 'to be' follows the form. . . . Therefore, the 'to be' of the house depends upon the natures of these things."[65]

Deductions: Several inferences naturally follow the analysis given.

1. Although God creates immediately, He conserves the "to be" of accidental forms through the instrumentality of created substances.[66]

2. Moreover, since God freely by an act of His will conserves the "to be" of creatures, He could, absolutely speaking, annihilate all created reality by ceasing to give the divine influx necessary for existence.[67]

3. St. Thomas adds, however, that although God by absolute power could annihilate His creation, nevertheless it would seem against His wisdom to do so. Let us explain. All creation comprises spiritual and corporeal beings. Now the nature of a spirit is to be incorruptible. Were God to annihilate a spiritual being, God would be violating a nature which He Himself has brought into being in accordance with the divine exemplar. This obviously is contrary to the divine wisdom. As to corporeal creatures, al-

---

[63] Let us not forget the fundamental truth that the "to be" cannot be caused except by God. In the case of common accidents, the created substances are nothing but existential instruments, and therefore without the constant influx from God could not support these accidental forms in existence. *"Esse per se consequitur formam creaturae, supposito tamen influxu Dei."* (S. Th., I, 104, 1, ad 1^m.)

[64] S. Th., I, 104, 1, c.

[65] Loc. cit.

[66] A notable exception to this is known through revelation. It is the direct conservation of the accidents of bread and wine in the dogma of transubstantiation.

[67] S. Th., I, 104, 2, c.

though their forms are corruptible and constantly corrupt, never-theless matter, the potential element in bodies, is incorruptible, since matter is the existing subject of generation and corruption.[68] The annihilation, then, even of the world of bodies appears to be, if not a contradiction, at least opposed to the nature of these creatures. Consequently, it seems in accord with divine wisdom to say that God will never annihilate the corporeal universe.

ARTICLE III: Divine Motion in Creatures

Necessity of Divine Motion: Does God move creatures to action? If we recall the profound signification of the principle of causality, that nothing can go from potency to act except because of a being that is already in act; if, moreover, we recall the truth that in the existential order an effect depends upon its proper cause here and now; if, finally, we recall the first and, according to St. Thomas, the most evident proof of the existence of God, the proof from motion, then we must declare not only that God is the First Mover, but that here and now He must, as First Cause, give the actuation for each motion, each action, of every creature. "Thou hast wrought all our works in us, O Lord."[69] This divine motion, however, is without detriment to the created nature. For God, the Creator of nature, moves all things, not violently, that is to say, not against the nature of the creature, but according to its natural mode of operation. Hence, the divine motion on the one hand necessitates the operation of an irrational creature; on the other hand, it enables a free nature to act freely.

It is true, this overwhelming manifestation of God's goodness and power has, in a general way, been established not only in the course of metaphysics but throughout this work; nevertheless, a clearer realization of this fundamental truth will help much to understand the governance of the world.

Problem: Our present problem is not precisely whether God moves the world, and whether He moves it here and now. The

[68] *S. Th.*, I, 104, 4, c.
[69] Isa. 26:12.

truth of this matter has been sufficiently demonstrated in our exposition of the First Way, the first Thomistic proof of the existence of God. What we now wish to discuss is our understanding of this divine motion. What we want is to clarify what we mean when we declare that God moves the world, that He actuates every creature to operation, that He works in and with every worker.

We shall consider first the divine motion as regards bodies; second, how God moves the intellect and the will of a rational creature; third, that God works in and with every agent.

I. How Does God Move Bodies?[70]

We suppose the world of bodies created and in existence. God creates and conserves the "to be." In a corporeal being, motion or becoming, which is a passage from potency to act, indicates a change, a change of form, accidental or substantial. Such a becoming, therefore, will terminate in the eduction of a form and, as a result, in the corruption of its contrary. Now a being in which there is passive potency — and such is the case with bodies — can be reduced from potency to act by an active potency which has power over it. There is no doubt that God is active potency since He is absolutely omnipotent, and that He exercises this power over bodies since He creates and conserves them in existence. God, therefore, moves a body by acting efficiently upon the matter, the potential element of bodies, in order to bring about the eduction of a new form.

God, therefore, gives the initial impetus in any series of corporeal motions. The term of such motion is a complete form with its proper "to be." God is the first cause of the eduction of any existing form, substantial or accidental.

II. How Does God Move the Intellect?[71]

Can God move the intellect of man immediately? There is no difficulty regarding His mediate motion, that is, through the in-

---

[70] Cf. *S. Th.*, I, 105, 2.
[71] Cf. *S. Th.*, I, 105, 3.

strumental causality of the objects of our knowledge. For these are primarily material realities, and we have seen not only that God is the First Mover in the world of bodies but that He is the prime mover *here* and *now* in any series of motions. Our question, then, is rather this: could God, if He willed, actuate the possible intellect immediately; could He immediately educe an intelligible species without the complicated process of abstraction? Now the possible intellect is in potency and, therefore, can be actuated immediately by a being in act which has power over it and which can communicate intelligibility. God, the cause of all created intellects, is in act and He is Intelligibility Itself. God, therefore, by His action can cause immediately in the intellect a motion, a becoming, which will terminate in the intelligible species which He wills to cause.

God, then, is the first cause of the impression of any object upon the intellect. He can, however, if He wills, by an immediate divine motion, educe the intelligible species from the potency of the intellect, thereby actuating the faculty of knowledge which must, as a result of this actuation, break forth into the act of understanding and the production of the "word" (*verbum*).

Regarding this act of understanding, that is, the operation of intellectual knowledge itself, St. Thomas insists that it is *caused immediately by the intellect,* never immediately by God. We say "that the intellectual operation is indeed from the intellect in which it exists, as from its immediate cause [*sicut a causa secunda*]; it is from God as from its remote, its first cause."[72] It is Peter, not God, who understands by means of the act of understanding which is immediately caused by Peter's intellect. "*Actiones sunt suppositorum.*"

The intellect, not God, is the immediate cause of our thoughts. "God, however, moves the intellect because He gives it power [*virtutem*] to understand, power that is natural or supernatural. He moves the intellect because He impresses either mediately or

---

[72] *S. Th.,* I, 105, 3, ad 1ᵐ. This is an important truth in mystical theology.

immediately the intelligible species; and finally, He maintains and preserves both [power and species] in existence."[73]

III. How God Moves the Will

This question has been treated already in the philosophy of man.[74] There it was established that in order to place an operation, the will of man must be moved; it must be actuated in the order of exercise, that is, of efficient causality, for it is in potency to operation. It was also explained that God alone can move the will in the order of exercise, for only the maker of a nature can efficiently actuate or move that intrinsic inclination of nature which we call the natural appetite. We showed, moreover, that the divine motion does not move the will violently[75] but in accordance with the nature of the will. Hence it moves the will in accordance with its natural appetite to the absolute good, to which the will is necessarily inclined by its nature. Such motion, then, not only does not interfere with the freedom of the will, but it makes freedom possible. The reason is that the freedom of the will depends upon its necessary determination to the absolute good. For if the will is necessitated to the absolute good, it cannot be necessitated to the particular good; it is free, therefore, to choose this or the other limited good. Hence the motion of God which actuates the natural inclination of the will to the absolute good does in no manner hinder the freedom of man. Rather, it establishes it.[76]

Self-Determination of the Will: The will, being undetermined to the particular good, is not, therefore, primarily determinable in the order of efficient causality, but in the order of specification, of

---

[73] S. Th., I, 105, 3, c.

[74] Cf. The Philosophy of Man, p. 192.

[75] The word "violently" has a technical meaning here. It signifies a motion that is contrary to the natural inclination of a being.

[76] "That which is moved by another is forced if it is moved against its natural inclination. But if it is moved by another which gives to it its natural inclination, it is not forced. . . . In like manner God, while moving the will, does not force it, because He gives the will its own natural inclination." (S. Th., I, 105, 4, ad 1m.)

the object, through the intellect. This is what philosophers call
the active indetermination of the will. This active indetermination
occurs, therefore, as a result of the divine motion which actuates
the will in the order of exercise to the absolute good. For, to
repeat it once more, the will being necessitated to the absolute good
by the divine motion remains free regarding the particular good.
It must determine itself to this or that object. This it does through
the intellect which, being freely directed by the will in the order
of exercise, presents to the will in the order of specification and
by means of a practical judgment the formal determination of
the act of choice.

Could God Also Be the Object of the Will? St. Thomas explains[77]
that although God must move the will efficiently to its end, the
absolute good, nevertheless He can also move it in the order of
specification, because God Himself, the Supreme Good, is the
object of the will. If, then, God, the Supreme Good, were known
as He is in Himself, the determination to love God, the supreme
object of the will, would be necessitating. That is why the blessed
who see God as He is are necessitated to love Him. The reason
for this necessary determination of the will to its supreme object
is explained thus:

> Now the will can be moved by any good as its object, but by
> God alone is it moved *sufficiently* and *efficaciously*. For nothing
> can move a movable thing sufficiently unless the active power of
> the mover surpasses or at least equals the passive power of the
> movable thing. Now the passive power of the will extends to the
> universal good, for its object is the universal good, just as the
> object of the intellect is universal being. But every created good is
> some *particular* good, and God alone is the universal good. There-
> fore, He alone fills the capacity of the will and moves it sufficiently
> as its object.[78]

Obviously this necessary determination of the will — in the order
of specification or of the object — to love God is not to be obtained in this life.[79] It is the way of the blessed in heaven. On

---

[77] *S. Th.*, I, 105, 4.

[78] *S. Th.*, I, 105, 4, c.

[79] In theology we learn that the preparation, the beginning (*inchoatio*) of the

the contrary, the actuation of the will in the order of exercise, that is, of efficient causality moving the will necessarily to its end, the supreme good, is common to all men and necessary for every free act of the will. This actuation of the will which is necessary for every operation is from God and from God alone.

> The power of willing [virtus volendi] also is caused by God alone. For "to will" is nothing but an inclination towards the object of the will, which is the universal good. But to incline towards the universal good belongs to the first mover, to whom the ultimate end is proportioned. . . . Therefore in both ways it is proper to God to move the will, but especially in the second way, by inclining it interiorly.[80]

We conclude: God must move the will in the order of exercise to the absolute good. This motion which necessitates the will to its end, the absolute good, enables it to choose freely the particular good. The divine motion, therefore, not only does not interfere with the freedom of man; it makes freedom possible. That is what St. Thomas means when he explains that by the divine motion God wills the rational creature to exercise freedom.

IV. God Works in Every Agent

Having explained the divine motion regarding the various constitutive elements of created beings — matter, form, intellect, and will — we may state a profoundly inspiring truth. God acts in and with every supposit, and in a special manner God works in and with every person.

Doctrine of the Occasionalists: St. Thomas begins this question[81] by showing the absurdity of the position of all occasionalists. These are the thinkers who, in their effort to safeguard the omnipotence of God by attributing all action entirely to divine causality, not only succeed in bringing about a denial of God's power but make

---

vision of God as He is in Himself is initiated by the infusion of sanctifying grace and grows through the acts of the theological virtues, faith, hope, and love.

[80] S. Th., I, 105, 4, c.

[81] S. Th., I, 105, 5.

it impossible for us to arrive at a knowledge of nature.[82] This position leads necessarily to a gross skepticism, for our knowledge of natures is derived from observing their operations. St. Thomas makes rather short shrift of this doctrine.

Causal Analysis of Action: In order to understand the working of God in us, we shall give a metaphysical analysis of action, whether transient or immanent, not from the viewpoint of the action itself but from that of its causes.

There are only three types of causes which can be principles of action: final, efficient, and formal. Matter, the potential principle, can in no way be an active principle, a cause of action, for a being acts in so far as it is in act. On the other hand, the other three causes are acts[83] and, consequently, they are really principles of action. They are all necessary for placing any definite action, but their causal influx into an effect is accomplished in a different manner and according to a definite order.

The *final cause* is the first of all the causes. It is the first principle of action, for it moves the *agent* to operation. It is in the order of intention, that is, of intellect and will, for it is the *effect as desired.* The *agent,* the efficient cause, is determined by the end to a definite action. It is therefore determined to apply a *form* to the work to be accomplished as, for example, in the use of a hammer in driving a nail into the wall.

Now God operates in each of these three causal elements. Regarding the end, it is obvious that in so far as the end manifests the good, it must in some manner participate in the Supreme Good, that is, God. In like manner, we must say that in a series of existentially subordinated efficient causes, the secondary agent acts in virtue of the first which moves it here and now. Hence, in the order of efficient causality, every agent acts because of the virtue and power of God.[84] In that way God's influx is necessary for every action of the creature, for even the will of man, as we have explained, must be moved efficiently by God in order to be

---

[82] Cf. *The Philosophy of Being,* p. 132 ff.

[83] The final cause is an actuation, a determination, in the intentional order.

[84] *"Et secundum hoc omnia agunt in virtute ipsius Dei."* (*S. Th.,* I, 105, 5, c.)

able to place a free act. That is why St. Thomas can state that God is the cause of all the actions of His creatures.[85]

In the third place, we should consider that not only is God the supreme end which is directly or indirectly desired, not only does He efficiently move the various created substances by mediately or immediately actuating their operative potencies so that they must act by applying the forms and virtues (powers) of things to operation, but that He also causes the complete forms and keeps them in existence.

Consequently, God is not only the cause of the actions of creatures because He gives them their nature, because He actuates their potencies which are the immediate principles of action; but because He conserves the form and its resulting "to be" which He has communicated to them. Now the form, and most of all the "to be," are the most intimate elements of reality in an existing being. Hence, because He is "To Be," God works most intimately in all beings; because He is Subsisting Existence, He is the most profound cause of all their actions.[86] "*Omnia opera nostra operatus es in nobis, Domine.*"[87]

S U M M A R Y — Question VIII

THE GOVERNANCE OF THE UNIVERSE

Prologue

1. **Governance and Wisdom:** Wisdom consists in the proper adaptation of the means to an end. Hence, wisdom necessarily requires not only knowledge of the end and the ordering of the

---

[85] "*Et Ipse (Deus) est causa omnium actionum agentium.*" (*Loc. cit.*)

[86] "*Ipse Deus est proprie causa ipsius esse universalis in rebus omnibus, inter omnia est magis intimum rebus. . . . Et Ipse (Deus) est causa omnium actionum agentium.*" (*Loc. cit.*)

[87] Isa. 26:12.

proper means to their end, but the execution of that order. This we call *governance*.

2. **Governance and Love:** The governance of the universe is the term of the cycle of divine love, for the term of that governance is God Himself.

ARTICLE I: God Governs the World.

1. **Argument:** From the finality of nature we argue to a final cause which is identical with the first efficient cause of nature. Hence, God governs the world principally by means of an inclination of nature which He implants in all creatures.

2. **Good government** consists not in ruling by violence which is against nature, but in implanting in the governed a natural inclination to the end which is the perfection of nature. Those who are thus governed seek their end according to their nature, not because forced by extrinsic violence. This is essential to good government, which implies, not the destruction, but the perfecting of the governed.

3. **Creatures can be instruments of governance,** since governance supposes the world of creatures which can become. This is a mark of greater perfection in the government to be able to communicate power and goodness to subjects in the work of governance.

ARTICLE II: Conservation of the World in Existence.

1. **Necessity of conservation:** In the existential order, an effect must depend upon its cause here and now.

2. **God alone can conserve existence,** since God alone is the cause of "to be."

3. **Conservation of Forms.**

   a) **Substantial forms** depend immediately upon God and not upon celestial bodies, since all bodies are fundamentally the same type of being, in so far as they are limited bodies, that is, not fully actuated.

b) **Accidental forms** are supported by the substance which may be considered the cause of the complete form. Hence, the substance may also be considered to be the instrumental cause regarding the conservation of the existence of the accidental "to be" which is "to be in another," namely, the substance.

ARTICLE III: Divine Motion in Creatures.

1. Necessity of divine motion: Whatever is moved must be moved primarily by the First Mover.

2. How God moves creatures.
   a) **Bodies:** God moves bodies either directly or through the instrumentality of other creatures. In a body, God causes motion which terminates in the eduction of a new form.
   b) **Intellect:** God moves the intellect by causing the intelligible species, either *mediately,* that is, through the medium of object, phantasm, agent intellect, or *immediately* by a direct action upon the possible intellect.
   c) **Will:** The will is in potency. The divine motion, which is in the order of exercise, actuates the will so that it wills necessarily its end, *the absolute good.* The actuated will, because it wills *necessarily* the absolute good, is as a consequence *free* to choose the particular good. Hence, the freedom of the will follows as a consequence of the divine motion moving the will necessarily to the absolute good.

3. God works in every agent: There are three causal factors in every operation of the creature: efficient, final, and formal. Each one of these is dependent either mediately or immediately upon God for its actuation here and now. Hence, God works not only *with* but *in* every agent.

EPILOGUE

GOD, THEN, IS THE PRINCIPLE AND END OF ALL BEINGS.
HE IS THE PRINCIPLE OF THEIR EXISTENCE, OF THEIR
NATURE, AND OF THEIR OPERATIONS. HE IS THE END OF
ALL THINGS AND, IN A SPECIAL MANNER, OF HIS RATIONAL
CREATURE, MAN. IN THIS WORLD OF SENSIBLE BEINGS, MAN
ALONE IS MADE DIRECTLY FOR GOD, AND ONLY IN THE
KNOWLEDGE AND LOVE OF GOD CAN HE FIND HAPPINESS.

INDEX